ROMANCES AND NARRATIVES BY DANIEL DEFOE

Edited by GEORGE A. AITKEN

IN SIXTEEN VOLUMES

VOL. IV

DUNCAN CAMPBELL

AMS PRESS
NEW YORK

"A young blooming beauty come.
& slily pick up the boy."

THE HISTORY
of the Life and
Adventures of Mr.
DUNCAN CAMPBELL
By DANIEL DEFOE

Edited by GEORGE A. AITKEN
with
Illustrations by J. B. YEATS

LONDON ✱ ✱ ✱ ✱ Published by
J. M. DENT & Co. Aldine House
69 Great Eastern Street, E.C.
MDCCCXCV

Library of Congress Cataloging in Publication Data

Defoe, Daniel, 1661?-1731.
  The history of the life and adventures of Mr. Duncan
Campbell.

  Original ed. issued as v. 4 of the author's Romances
and narratives.
    1. Campbell, Duncan, 1680?-1730.   I. Title.
BF1815.C2D4   1974   133.3'2'0924 [B]   74-13463
ISBN 0-404-07914-8

Reprinted by arrangement with J.M. Dent & Sons, Ltd.

Reprinted from the edition of 1895, London
First AMS edition published, 1974
Manufactured in the United States of America

International Standard Book Number:
Complete Set: 0-404-07910-5
Volume 4: 0-404-07914-8

AMS PRESS, Inc.
New York, N.Y. 10003

CONTENTS.

CHAPTER I.

CHAPTER II.

CHAPTER III.

Chapter IV.

Chapter V.

Chapter VI.

Chapter VII.

Chapter VIII.

LIST OF ILLUSTRATIONS.

INTRODUCTION.

ON April 30, 1720, just a year after " Robinson Crusoe," Curll published Defoe's " History of the Life and Adventures of Mr Duncan Campbell, a gentleman who, though deaf and dumb, writes down any stranger's name at first sight, with their future contingencies of fortune : Now living in Exeter Court, over against the Savoy in the Strand." Copies printed on fine paper were sold at half-a-guinea. In August there was a second edition, some copies of which include a pamphlet that had been printed in June, " Mr Campbell's Pacquet, for the Entertainment of Gentlemen and Ladies." The subject was one of much popular interest, and Defoe had stated in the " Life " that a pocket volume of Campbell's select correspondence would be shortly published. It was not, however, until 1724 that there appeared a volume called " A Spy upon the Conjurer ; or, a Collection of surprising Stories, with names, places, and particular circumstances, relating to Mr Duncan Campbell. . . . Written to my Lord —— by a Lady." There can be no doubt that this book is by the novelist Eliza Haywood, whose name, indeed, was printed on the title-page of the second edition. Certainly Defoe had no concern in this curious collection of letters and

anecdotes.   Next year the same authoress published
a supplement, "The Dumb Projector, being a surprising Account of a Trip to Holland made by Mr
Duncan Campbell."   In 1726 there was another
piece, "The Friendly Demon," which appears to be
by Defoe; and in 1728 Defoe's "Life of Duncan
Campbell" was re-issued with an entirely new title-
page: "The Supernatural Philosopher . . . by William
Bond, of Bury St Edmonds, Suffolk."   Finally, after
the death both of Campbell and Defoe, came "Secret
Memoirs of the late Mr Duncan Campbell, the famous
deaf and dumb gentleman.   Written by Himself, who
ordered they should be published after his decease,"
1732.   This volume included a reprint of the "Friendly
Demon."

Duncan Campbell, about whom so much was written,
was born in 1680, in Lapland, where his father, a
Scotchman, was living.   The boy was deaf and dumb,
but he was credited with the gift of second-sight, and
in 1694 he moved to London, where he became a
favourite of society.   As Defoe's book is our principal
source of information, it is enough to say here, that
Campbell's latter years were marked by much illness,
which, together with the love for novelty, caused him
to be to a great extent forgotten long before he died.
Defoe's work was, no doubt, of great assistance to
him, and we are told in the *Daily Post* for May 4,
1720, that "last Monday Mr Campbell, the deaf and
dumb gentleman, introduced by Colonel Carr, kissed
the king's hand, and presented to his Majesty 'The
History of his Life and Adventures,' which was by
his Majesty most graciously received."   The king's
predecessor, Queen Anne, had patronised Campbell,
until, as he says, two ladies of the Court slandered
him.   By 1726 Campbell was advertising his "Pulvis
Miraculosus" and Egyptian loadstones, to be obtained

at "Dr" Campbell's house in Buckingham Court. He died in 1730.

In an early number of the *Tatler* (No. 14), Steele wrote, "All his visitants come to him full of expectations, and pay his own rate for the interpretations they put upon his shrugs and nods." Addison alludes to Campbell twice in the *Spectator*, always satirically. In No. 323 Clarinda notes in her diary: "Went in our mobs to the dumb man, according to appointment. Told me that my lover's name began with a G. *Mem.* The conjurer was within a letter of Mr Froth's name." In No. 560 it was suggested that Campbell's dumbness was assumed: "Every one has heard of the famous conjurer, who, according to the opinion of the vulgar, has studied himself dumb; for which reason, it is believed, he delivers out all his oracles in writing. Be that as it will, the blind Tiresias was not more famous in Greece than this dumb artist has been, for some years last past, in the Cities of London and Westminster." In No. 474 (one of Steele's papers), Dulcibella Thankley, in a letter quoted by Defoe, describes a visit to Campbell's house, and the wonders that he accomplished.

We need not enter into the question whether Duncan Campbell was, in whole or in part, an impostor. There is no reason to doubt that he was really deaf and dumb, though some people were sceptical, and many tricks were tried to make him betray himself. In the Dedication signed by Campbell, Defoe notices that the book had been looked forward to by people of airy tempers, and condemned by "those of a more formal class." But persons who thought the work would promote only superstition and intrigues would, he added, find their expectations disappointed. "Instead of making them a bill of fare out of patchwork romances of polluting scandal, the good old gentleman who wrote the Adventures of my Life has made it his business to treat them with a great variety of entertaining passages which always terminate in morals that tend to the edification of all readers." Campbell strongly condemned gypsies and common fortune-tellers, or conjurers dealing in black arts. Too many ladies—here Defoe was reflecting upon Pope's "Rape of the Lock"—gave themselves up to the reading of "the cabalistical systems of sylphs and gnomes and mandrakes, which are very wicked and delusive imaginations."

In the Introduction, Defoe dwelt upon the value of Lives of persons distinguished for merits of one kind or another, and hoped to include among his own readers both the "airy nice peruser of novels and romances" and the "grave philosopher, that is daily thumbing over the musty and tattered pieces of more solid antiquity." With this object, "pleasant adventures" are duly blended with an account of the reasons why, and the manner in which Nature performed by Campbell such mysterious acts. A great part of the volume, then, consists of discourses on the teaching of deaf and dumb persons; on the second-sight; on magic; on the existence of spirits, and the like. The book is none the less interesting on this account, but it is very discursive, and the story of Campbell's life is often suspended entirely to enable Defoe to enter into speculative arguments or to relate stories of apparitions and witches.

In works which followed the "Life of Duncan Campbell," Defoe often returned to the consideration of questions of the supernatural world. The latter portion of the "Serious Reflections" was called, as we have seen, "A Vision of the Angelic World," and there he discusses the subject of secret hints of the course of action to be taken at a time of doubt, a question already referred to in "Robinson Crusoe" and elsewhere. Defoe held, with Socrates, that he was accompanied by a good spirit or demon, whose secret dictates he never failed to obey. This matter is discussed at great length in the "Essay on the History and Reality of Apparitions," 1727, where Defoe argued that "almost all real apparitions are of friendly and assisting angels, and come of a kind and beneficent errand to us, and that therefore we need not be so terrified at them as we are." The spirits which hold converse with us for our good cannot, he says, be either the "proper angels" which reside in heaven, or the agents of the devil. The apparitions seen by men, are, he suggests, "an appointed, deputed sort of stationary spirits in the invisible world," spirits which have never been embodied. A spirit called up by magic and conjurations to give us information must be the devil in the guise of a good spirit; a magician can have no power over an independent free spirit. Apparitions cannot be really the departed souls of the persons they are said to represent; it is the guardian angel who assumes the shape of our departed friend.

Such is the main argument of a very curious volume, which contains much that relates to dreams and other matters which need not be considered here. From time to time Defoe remarks satirically that the taste of the time made it difficult for him to dwell upon serious matters: "We must talk politely, not religiously; we may show the scholar, but must not show a word of the Christian." To make the book amusing, therefore, Defoe inserted a large number of stories of apparitions and mysterious visitations.

The "History of the Devil, as well ancient as modern" (1726), is a curious compilation, half satirical, half serious, which belongs to the same series of works; and it was soon followed by "A System of Magic, or a

History of the Black Art," in which Defoe says, " In
the first ages there were wise men ; in the middle age,
madmen ; in these latter ages, cunning men ; in the
earliest time they were honest ; in the middle time,
rogues ; in those last times, fools." This book, like
the " History of Apparitions," contains much about
Defoe's favourite subject of good spirits, and is enlivened
by various tales of self-styled magicians. Defoe's religion involved a very real belief in the devil, though
he ridiculed the crude notions of the devil and of hell
which were then current. " Those who have prevailed
with themselves to believe there is no devil," he wrote,
" soon come to it, that there is no God."

Defoe had studied carefully all the best-known
authorities on witchcraft and apparitions. In " Duncan
Campbell " he often refers to Beaumont's " Treatise
of Spirits, Apparitions, Witchcraft, and other Magical
Practices," 1705 ; and Scott thought that that book
was by Defoe. But John Beaumont was a real person
—belonging to Stone Easton, Somerset—with whom
Defoe was acquainted, as he tells us in several places.
Other authors mentioned include Cotton Mather,
Baxter, Aubrey, and Martin, who wrote of second-
sight in his " Description of the Western Islands of
Scotland." We know that Defoe had in his library
Webster's " Displaying of supposed Witchcraft ; "
Glanvil's " Sadducismus Triumphatus," in which the
reality of witches and apparitions was asserted, in reply
to Webster ; and a French " Traité de l'Apparition
des Esprits," of 1602. He had, too, several pieces
like " The Surrey Imposter," 1697, the " Prophetical
Warnings of Elias Marion," 1707, and " An Admirable History of the possession and conversion of a
penitent Woman, seduced by a Magician," 1613.

A curious history attaches to the " Account of a
most surprising Apparition ; sent from Launceston in

Cornwall. Attested by the Rev. Mr Ruddle, minister there." This narrative formed the concluding portion of "Mr Campbell's Pacquet," which, as I have said, was added to copies of the second edition of "Duncan Campbell;" the remainder of the pamphlet was occupied by verses by "Capt. Stanhope" and others, some of them being far from complimentary to Pope.

The "Remarkable Passage of an Apparition" has no connection with "Duncan Campbell," but there is no doubt that it was contributed to the "Pacquet" by Defoe. To adduce it as a specimen of his powers of invention is, however, a great mistake, a mistake almost as striking as that which has been made by generations of critics in connection with the better-known "Apparition of Mrs Veal." Yet this is just what has been done.

The story of Mrs Dingley was told in Gilbert's "Survey of Cornwall," 1817, i. 115-19, almost in Defoe's words, but without the Postscript, or the last paragraph of the narrative; and it was communicated to Gilbert by the Rev. F. V. T. Arundell, who found a MS. in what he thought to be Dr Ruddle's own writing. The story was retold in Hitchins' "History of Cornwall," 1824, ii. 548-51, but here the woman's name is given—rightly, it is said—as Dorothy Durant; and the youth who saw the apparition is described as "young Mr Bligh."

In 1837 Mrs Bray, borrowing from Gilbert, made use of the tale in her novel of "Trelawney of Trelawne," and when she afterwards found the version told by Defoe she said that if she had not known the circumstances, she "should have fancied it a fiction of Defoe himself, like the story of Mrs Veal, prefixed to Drelincourt on Death." Mrs Bray was right as regards the "Remarkable Passage of an Apparition," though some people had suggested that Gilbert and the others had been imposed upon; but she did not dream that "Mrs Veal" was as little a work of fiction as the "Remarkable Passage."

The Rev. John Ruddle, or rather Ruddell, who told the story of Dorothy Dingley, was incumbent of Launceston from 1668 to 1698, and he died in the following year, at the age of sixty-two. In 1665, therefore, when he kept the school at Launceston, and saw the apparition, he was a young clergyman of twenty-eight. In 1870 the oft-told story reappeared, under the title of "The Botathen Ghost," in "Footprints of Former Men," by the Rev. R. S. Hawker, of Morwenstow. Mr Hawker said that the legend was well known in Cornwall, and that Parson Ruddell's own "Diurnall" had fallen into his hands. Up to a certain point the quotations given from this diurnal are in close agreement with Defoe's narrative, but the language is more archaic and pedantic. Thus Mr Hawker's version begins: "A pestilential disease did break forth in our town in the beginning of the year A.D. 1665; yea, and it likewise invaded my school, insomuch that therewithal certain of the chief scholars sickened and died."

Now, I think it will occur to students of seventeenth century literature who compare these words with Defoe's, that the archaic expressions are exaggerated. In fact, in the absence of independent evidence, I strongly suspect that Mr Hawker simply dressed up Defoe's version in a manner which he thought to be characteristic of the time, and invented the "Diurnall"—after Defoe's own manner—to give an air of reality to the story. In offering this surmise I may be wronging Mr Hawker; but in any case, in view of that gentleman's well-known eccentricities, and his personal belief in apparitions and the like, it would be very rash to attach any importance to the fresh details published in " The Botathen Ghost." We are there told that Mr Bligh's home, an old manor-house, was at Botathen; and that the ghost, which was that of Dorothy Dinglet, who had died three years before, had a pale and troubled face, and was clothed in a long loose garment of frieze. She had one hand always stretched out, and the other pressed against her side; her hair appeared to melt away while you looked at it, and she seemed to swim along the top of the grass. Mr Hawker dates the tale January, instead of the summer of 1665, and gives a long account of the manner in which Ruddell obtained the authority of his bishop before exorcising the ghost.

There in no need to tell the story—as set forth by Defoe—of the serious effect produced upon a boy called Bligh (Defoe does not mention the name) by the apparition of Dorothy Dingley, and of the steps taken by Mr Ruddell to lay the ghost. The whole narrative will be found on pages 231–242 of this volume, and it is an excellent specimen of Defoe's art of telling a narrative in a convincing manner. But Defoe did not invent the story, as he has been credited with doing; he simply retold very well a popular legend which had reached him either orally or in writing. The version published by Gilbert suggests, indeed, that Defoe followed very closely the language of the account in his possession.

It remains to say a word of " The Friendly Demon; or, the Generous Apparition. Being a true narrative of a miraculous cure newly performed upon that famous deaf and dumb gentleman, Dr Duncan Campbell, by a familiar spirit, that appeared to him in a white surplice, like a cathedral singing boy." The greater part of this curious pamphlet, which was published in 1726, and reprinted in the " Secret Memoirs of Duncan Campbell," 1732, is, I feel confident, by

Defoe, and the whole of it is given in this volume, if only for the sake of completeness. The letter signed by Campbell may of course be genuine; but there are reasons for thinking that, like the reply, it is by Defoe. Among the points of internal evidence may be mentioned the use in two places in the reply of the word "frighted"—Defoe constantly uses the verb "fright," and very rarely has the form "frighten"—and the description of the genius or demon of the ancients, where the account given on page 52 of "Duncan Campbell" is closely followed. A little further on is the well-known story—with variations—of the strange experiences of an Irish butler, as described by Lord Orrery and others. This tale is in Glanvil and Beaumont, and had already been copied by Defoe in "Duncan Campbell" (pages 53–56). Of course it may be argued that these resemblances tell against, rather than for, the genuineness of the "Friendly Demon," for it may be held that Defoe would not repeat in 1726 what he had already published in 1720. But this argument alone is not convincing, especially as Defoe was only repeating what others had written. The general style of the piece, especially the construction of the sentences, seems to me to place the authorship beyond question.

It is noteworthy that the writer is very cautious in what he says about the "powder" and the "loadstone" whose alleged wondrous powers of healing Campbell wished to advertise. Campbell had been driven by adversity to become a quack doctor; but Defoe, while anxious to help him, was not prepared, as Lee pointed out, to be a party to fraud by recommending his nostrums.

TO THE LADIES AND GENTLEMEN
OF GREAT BRITAIN.

I AM not unacquainted that, ever since this book was first promised by way of advertisement to the world, it was greedily coveted by a great many persons of airy tempers, for the same reason that it has been condemned by those of a more formal class, who thought it was calculated partly to introduce a great many new and diverting curiosities in the way of superstition, and partly to divulge the secret intrigues and amours of one part of the sex, to give the other part room to make favourite scandal the subject of their discourse, and so to make one-half of the fair species very merry over the blushes and the mortifications of the other half.   But when they come to read the following sheets, they will find their expectations disappointed, but I hope I may say too, very agreeably disappointed.   They will find a much more elegant entertainment than they expected.   Instead of making them a bill of fare out of patchwork romances of polluting scandal, the good old gentleman who wrote the adventures of my life has made it his business to treat them with a great variety of entertaining passages which always terminate in morals that tend to the edification of all readers, of whatsoever sex,

age, or profession. Instead of seducing young, innocent, unwary minds, into the vicious delight which
is too often taken in reading the gay and bewitching
chimeras of the cabalists, and in perusing the enticing
fables of new-invented tricks of superstition, my ancient
friend, the writer, strikes at the very root of these
superstitions, and shows them how they may be satisfied
in their several curiosities, by having recourse to time,
who by the talent of the second-sight (which he so
beautifully represents how nature is so kind frequently
to implant in the minds of men born in the same
climate with myself) can tell you those things naturally, which, when you try to learn yourselves, you
either run the hazard of being imposed upon in your
pockets by cheats, gipsies, and common fortune-tellers,
or else of being imposed upon in a still worse way,
in your most lasting welfare, by having recourse to
conjurers or enchanters that deal in black arts, and
involve all their consulters in one general partner-
ship of their execrable guilt; or lastly, of imposing
worst of all on your own selves, by getting into an itch
of practising and trying the little tricks of female superstition, which are often more officiously handed down
by the tradition of credulous nurses and old women,
from one generation to another, than the first principles of Christian doctrine, which it is their duty to
instil early into little children. But I hope when
this book comes to be pretty generally read among
you ladies (as by your generous and numerous sub-
scriptions I have good reason to expect), that it
will afford a perfect remedy and a thorough cure
to that distemper, which first took its rise from too
great a growth of curiosity, and too large a stock
of credulity, nursed prejudicially up with you in your
more tender and infant years.

Whatever young maid hereafter has an innocent but

longing desire to know who shall be her husband, and what time she shall be married, will, I hope, when she has read in the following sheets of a man that can set her right in the knowledge of those points, purely by possessing the gift of the second-sight, sooner have recourse innocently to such a man than use unlawful means to acquire it, such as running to conjurers to have his figure shown in their enchanted glasses, or using any of those traditionary superstitions by which they may dream of their husbands, or cause visionary shapes of them to appear on such and such festival nights of the year; all which practices are not ordinarily wicked and impious, but downright diabolical. I hope that the next twenty-ninth of June, which is St John the Baptist's Day, I shall not see the several pasture fields adjacent to this metropolis, especially that behind Montague House, thronged, as they were the last year, with well-dressed young ladies, crawling busily up and down upon their knees, as if they were a parcel of weeders, when all the business is to hunt superstitiously after a coal under the root of a plantain, to put under their heads that night, that they may dream who shall be their husbands. In order to shame them out of this silly but guilty practice, I do intend to have some spies out on that day, that shall discover who they are, and what they have been about; and I here give notice to the public that this ill-acted comedy (if it be acted at all this year) must begin, according to the rule of their superstition, on that day precisely at the hour of twelve. And so much for the pretty weeders; but as you (ladies) have had several magical traditions delivered to you, which, if you put in exercise and practice, will be greatly prejudicial to your honour and your virtue, let me interpose my counsels, which will conduct you innocuously to the same end

which some ladies have laboured to arrive at by these
impieties. Give me leave first to tell you that though
what you aim at may be arrived to by these means,
yet these means make that a miserable fortune which
would have been a good one ; because, in order to
know human things beforehand, you use preternatural
mediums, which destroy the goodness of the courses
which nature herself was taking for you, and annexes
to them diabolical influences, which commonly carries
along with them fatalities in this world as well as the
next. You will therefore give me your pardon likewise, ladies, if I relate some other of these practices ;
which bare relation, of itself, after what I have said
before, seems to me sufficient to explode them.

Another of the nurses' prescriptions is this. Upon
a St Agnes's Night, the twenty-first day of January,
take a row of pins and pull out every one, one after
another, saying a Pater Noster, or Our Father, sticking
a pin in your sleeve, and you will dream of her you
shall marry. Ben Jonson, in one of his masques,
makes some mention of this—

> " And on sweet St Agnes' night
> Please you with the promised sight,
> Some of husbands, some of lovers,
> Which an empty dream discovers."

Now what can be more infinitely profane than to use
the prayer of our Lord instituted in such a way ?

There is another prescription, which is as follows :
You must lie in another county, and knit the left garter
about the right-legged stocking (let the other garter
and stocking alone), and as you rehearse these following
verses, at every comma knit a knot—

> " This knot I knit,
> To know the thing I know not yet,
> That I may see
> The man that shall my husband be :
> How he goes, and what he wears,
> And what he does all days and years."

Accordingly, in your dream you will see him: if a musician, with a lute or other instrument; if a scholar, with a book, &c.   Now I appeal to you, ladies, what a ridiculous prescription is this?   But yet, as slight a thing as it is, it may be of great importance if it be brought about, because then it must be construed to be done by preternatural means, and then those words are nothing less than an application to the devil.

Mr Aubrey, of the Royal Society, says a gentle-woman that he knew confessed, in his hearing, that she used this method, and dreamed of her husband, whom she had never seen.   About two or three years after, as she was one Sunday at church, up pops a young Oxonian in the pulpit: she cries out presently to her sister, "This is the very face of the man I saw in my dream."   Sir William Somes's lady did the like.

Another way is to charm the moon thus (as the old nurses give out): at the first appearance of the moon after New Year's Day (some say any other new moon is as good), go out in the evening, and stand over the spars of a gate or stile, looking on the moon (here remark that in Yorkshire they kneel on a ground-fast stone), and say—

> " All hail to the moon, all hail to thee ;
> I prithee, good moon, reveal to me
> This night who my husband shall be."

You must presently after go to bed.   The aforesaid Mr Aubrey knew two gentlewomen that did thus when they were young maids, and they had dreams of those that married them.

But a great many of the wittiest part of your sex laugh at these common superstitions; but then they are apt to run into worse.   They give themselves up to the reading of the cabalistical systems of sylphs, and gnomes, and mandrakes, which are very wicked and delusive imaginations.

I would not have you imagine, ladies, that I impute these things as infirmities and frailties peculiar to your sex. No, men, and great men too, and scholars, and even statesmen and princes themselves, have been tainted with superstitions; and where they infect the minds of such great personages, they make the deeper impression, according to the stronger and more manly ideas they have of them. Their greater degree of strength in the intellect only subjects them to greater weaknesses. Such was even the great Paracelsus, the wonder and miracle of learning in the age wherein he lived; and such were all his followers, scholars, statesmen, divines, and princes, that are talismanists.

These talismans that Paracelsus pretends to owe to the excogitation and invention of honest art, seem to me to be of a very diabolical nature, and to owe their rise to being dedicated by the author to the heathen gods. Thus the cabalists, pretending to a vast penetration into arts and sciences (though all their thoughts are chimeras and extravagances, unless they be helped by preternatural means), say they have found out the several methods appropriated to the several planets. They have appropriated gold to the sun on the Sunday, silver to the moon on the Monday, iron to Mars on the Tuesday, quicksilver to Mercury on the Wednesday, tin to Jupiter on the Thursday, copper or brass to Venus on the Friday, and lead to Saturn on the Saturday. The methods they take in forming these talismans are too long to dwell upon here; but the properties which they pretend belong to them are, that the first talisman or seal of the sun will make a man beloved by all princes and potentates, and cause him to abound with all the riches his heart can wish. The second preserves travellers from danger, and is favourable to merchants, tradesmen, and workmen. The third carries destruction to any place where it is put; and it is said that a certain great minister of state ordered one of these to be carried into England in the times of the revolution of the government caused by Oliver Cromwell.   The fourth, they pretend, cures fevers and other diseases : and if it be put under the bolster, it makes the proprietor have true dreams, in which he sees all he desires to know.   The fifth, according to them, renders a man lucky and fortunate in all his businesses and undertakings ; it dissipates melancholy, drives away all importunate cares, and banishes panic fears from the mind.   The sixth, by being put into the liquor which any one drinks, reconciles mortal enemies, and makes them intimate friends ; it gains the love of all women, and renders the proprietor very dexterous in the art of music.   The seventh makes women be easily brought to bed without pain ; and if a horseman carries it in his left boot, himself and his horse become invulnerable.

This Paracelsus and his learned followers say is owing to the influence of the stars ; but I cannot help arguing these acts of diabolical impiety.   But as these arts are rarely known among the middling part of mankind, I shall neither open their mysteries, nor inveigh against them any further.

The persons who are most to be avoided, are your ordinary fortune-telling women and men about this town, whose houses ought to be avoided as a plague or a pestilence, either because they are cheats and impostors, or because they deal with black arts, none of them that I know having any pretensions to the gift of a second-sight.   Among many, a few of the most notorious that I can call to mind now, are as follow.

The first and chiefest of these mischievous fortune-tellers is a woman that does not live far from the Old Bailey.   And truly the justice hall in that place is the properest place for her to appear at, where, if she was tried for pretending to give charms written upon paper with odd scrawls, which she calls figures, she would be probably convicted, and very justly condemned, and doomed to have her last journey from the Old Bailey to Newgate, and from Newgate to Tyburn.   The other is a fellow that lives in Moorfields, in which place, those who go to consult him ought to live all their lifetimes at the famous palaces of the senseless men.   He is the successor of the famous Dr Trotter, whose widow he married ; and from being a tailor, and patching men's garments, he now cuts flourishes with his shears upon parchment, considers the heavens as a garment, and from the spangles thereupon he calculates nativities, and sets up for a very profound astrologer.   The third is an ignorant fellow that caws out strange predictions in Crow Alley, of whose croaking noise I shall here take no notice, he having been sufficiently mauled in the most ingenious *Spectators*.   These, and such counterfeits as these, I would desire all gentlemen and ladies to avoid.   The only two really learned men that I ever knew in the art of astrology were my good friends, Dr Williams and Mr Gadbury ; and I thought it necessary to pay this esteem to their manes, let the world judge of them what it will.   I will here say no more, nor hinder you any longer, gentlemen and ladies, from the diversion which my good old friend, who is now departed this life, has prepared for you in his book, which a young gentleman of my acquaintance revised, and only subscribe myself, yours, &c.,

DUNCAN CAMPBELL.

AUTHOR'S INTRODUCTION.

OF all the writings delivered in an historical manner to the world, none certainly were ever held in greater esteem than those which give us the lives of distinguished private men at full length; and, as I may say, to the life. Such curious fragments of biography are the rarities which great men seek after with eager industry, and when found, prize them as the chief jewels and ornaments that enrich their libraries; and deservedly, for they are the beauties of the greatest men's lives handed down by way of example or instruction to posterity, and commonly handed down likewise by the greatest men. Since, therefore, persons distinguished for merit in one kind or other are the constant subjects of such discourses, and the most elegant writers of each age have been usually the only authors who choose upon such subjects to employ their pens, and since persons of the highest rank and dignity, and genii of the most refined and delicate relish, are frequently curious enough to be the readers of them, and to esteem them the most valuable pieces in a whole collection of learned works, it is a wonder to me, that when any man's life has something in it peculiarly great and remarkable in its kind, it should not move some more skilful writer than myself to give the public

a taste of it, because it must be at least vastly entertaining, if it be not, which is next to impossible,
immensely instructive and profitable withal.

If ever the life of any man under the sun was remarkable, this Mr Duncan Campbell's, which I am
going to treat upon, is so to a very eminent degree.

It affords such variety of incidents, and is accompanied with such diversity of circumstances, that it
includes within it what must yield entire satisfaction
to the most learned, and admiration to persons of a
moderate understanding. The prince and the peasant
will have their several ends of worthy delight in reading
it ; and Mr Campbell's life is of that extent that it
concerns and collects (as I may say) within itself
every station of life in the universe. Besides, there
is a demand, in almost every page that relates any
new act of his, for the finest and closest disquisitions
that learning can make upon human nature, to account
how those acts could be done by him ; for he daily
practised, and still practises, those things naturally
which puts art to the rack to find out how nature
can so operate in him ; and his fleshly body, by these
operations, is a living practical system or body of new
philosophy, which exceeds even all those that have
hitherto been compounded by the labour and art of
many ages.

If one that had speculated deep into abstruse matters,
and made it his study not only to know how to assign
natural reasons for some strange new acts, that looked
like miracles by being peculiar to the individual genius
of some particular admired man, but carrying his inquiry
to a much greater height, had speculated likewise what
might possibly be achieved by human genius in the full
perfection of nature, and had laid it down as a thesis
by strong arguments, that such things might be compassed by a human genius (if in its true degree of

perfection) as are the hourly operations of the person's life I am writing, he would have been counted a wild, romantic enthusiast, instead of a natural philosopher. Some of the wisest would be infidels to so new and so refined a scheme of thinking, and demand experiment, or cry it was all against reason, and would not allow the least tittle to be true without it. Yet the man that had found out so great a mystery as to tell us what might be done by human genius, as it is here actually done, would have been a great man within himself; but wanting farther experimental proof, could lay no claim to the belief of others, or consequently to their esteem. But how great, then, is the man who makes it constantly his practice actually to do what would not otherwise have been thought to be of such a nature as might ever be acquired by mortal capacity, though in its full complement of all possible perfection? He is not only great within himself, he is great to the world: his experiments force our belief, and the amazing singularity of those experiments provokes both our wonder and esteem.

If any learned man should have advanced this proposition, that mere human art could give to the deaf man what should be equal to his hearing, and to the dumb man an equivalent for his want of speech, so that he should converse as freely almost as other hearing or talking persons; that he might, though born deaf, be by art taught how to read, write, and understand any language, as well as students that have their hearing, would not the world, and many even of the learned part of it, say that nothing could be more extravagantly wild, more mad and frantic? The learned Dr Wallis, geometry professor of Oxford, did first of all lay down this proposition, and was counted by many to have overshot the point of learning, and to have been the author of a whimsical thesis. And I should not have wondered if, after a man's having asserted this might be done before it was actually done, some blind devout people in those days had accused him of heresy, and of attributing to men a power of working miracles. The notion of the antipodes was by the most learned men of the age in which St Augustine lived, and by the great St Austin himself, treated in no milder a manner; yet if the ability of teaching the deaf and the dumb a language proved a truth in experience afterwards, ought not those to turn their contempt into admiration, ought not those very people to vote him into the Royal Society for laying down the proposition, who, before it proved true, in fact, would have been very forward to have sent him to Bedlam? The first instance of this accomplishment in a dumb person was proved before King Charles II. by this same Dr Wallis, who was a fellow of the Royal Society, and one of the most ingenious of that society.

But notwithstanding this, should I come afterwards and say, that there is now living a deaf and dumb man, and born so, who could by dint of his own genius teach all others deaf and dumb to read, write, and converse with the talking and hearing part of mankind, some would, I warrant, very religiously conclude, that I was about to introduce some strange new miracle-monger and impostor into the world, with a design of setting up some new sect of anti-Christianism as formidable as that of Brahmans. Should I proceed still farther and say, that this same person, so deaf and dumb, might be able also to show a presaging power, or kind of prophetical genius (if I may be allowed the expression) by telling any strange persons he never saw before in his life, their names at first sight in writing, and by telling them the past actions of their lives, and predicting to them determined truths of future contingencies, notwithstanding what divines say, that " in futuris contingentibus non datur determinata veritas," would not they conclude that I was going to usher in a new Mahomet? Since, therefore, there does exist such a man in London, who actually is deaf and dumb, and was born so; who does write and read, and converse as well as anybody; who teaches others deaf and dumb to write and read and converse with anybody; who likewise can, by a presaging gift, set down in writing the name of any stranger at first sight, tell him his past actions, and predict his future occurrences in fortune; and since he has practised this talent as a profession with great success for a long series of years upon innumerable persons in every state and vocation in life, from the peeress to the waiting-woman, and from the lady mayoress to the milliner and sempstress, will it not be wonderfully entertaining to give the world a perfect history of this so singular a man's life? And while we are relating the pleasant adventures with such prodigious variety, can anything be more agreeably instructive in a new way than to intersperse the reasons, and account for the manner how nature, having a mind to be remarkable, performs by him acts so mysterious?

I have premised this introduction, compounded of the merry and the serious, with the hopes of engaging many curious people of all sorts to be my readers, even from the airy nice peruser of novels and romances, neatly bound and finely gilt, to the grave philosopher, that is daily thumbing over the musty and tattered pieces of more solid antiquity. I have all the wonders to tell that such a merry kind of a prophet has told, to entertain the fancies of the first gay tribe, by which means I may entice them into some solid knowledge and judgment of human nature; and I have several solid disquisitions of learning to make, accounting for the manner of these mysterious operations, never touched

upon before in due form and order by the hands
of the ancient or modern sages, that I may bribe the
judgment of this last grave class so far as to endure
the intermixing entertainment with their severer
studies.

THE HISTORY

OF THE

LIFE AND SURPRISING ADVENTURES

OF

Mr DUNCAN CAMPBELL

Chapter i.

Mr Campbell's descent, family, birth, &c.

OF the goodness and antiquity of the name and family of this gentleman, nobody can ever make any question. He is a Campbell, lineally descended from the house of Argyll, and bears a distant relation to the present duke of that name in Scotland, and who is now constituted a duke of England, by the style and title of Duke of Greenwich.

It happens frequently that the birth of extraordinary persons is so long disputed by different people, each claiming him for their own, that the real place where he first took breath grows at last dubious. And thus it fares with the person who is the subject of the following sheets; as, therefore, it is my proposal to have

A

a strict regard to historical faith, so I am obliged to
tell the reader that I can with no certainty give an
account of him till after he was three years old, from
which age I knew him even to this day. I will answer
for the truths which I impart to the public during that
time, and as for his birth and the circumstances of it,
and how the first three years of his life passed, I can
only deliver them the same account I have received
from others, and leave them to their own judgments,
whether it ought to be deemed real or fabulous.

The father of our Mr Duncan Campbell (as these
relate the story) was from his infancy of a very curious
inquisitive nature, and of an enterprising genius, and if
he heard of anything surprising to be seen, the difficulty
in practice was enough to recommend to him the at-
tempting to get a sight of it at any rate or any hazard.
It is certain that during some civil broils and troubles
in Scotland, the grandfather of our Mr Campbell was
driven with his wife and family, by the fate of war, into
the isle of Shetland, where he lived many years, and
during his residence there, Mr Archibald Campbell, the
father of our Duncan Campbell, was born.

Shetland lies north-east from Orkney, between 60
and 61 degrees of latitude. The largest isle of
Shetland, by the natives called the Mainland, is sixty
miles in length, from south-west to the north-east, and
from sixteen to one mile in breadth.

The people who live in the smaller isles have
abundance of eggs and fowl, which contributes to maintain their families during the summer.

The ordinary folks are mostly very nimble and
active in climbing the rocks in quest of those eggs and
fowl. This exercise is far more diverting than hunting
and hawking among us, and would certainly, for the
pleasure of it, be followed by people of greater distinction, was it not attended with very great dangers,

sufficient to turn sport into sorrow, and which have often proved fatal to those who too eagerly pursue their game. Mr Archibald Campbell, however, delighted extremely in this way of fowling, and used to condescend to mix with the common people for company, because none of the youths of his rank and condition were venturesome enough to go along with him.

The most remarkable experiment of this sort is at the isle called the Noss of Brassah. The Noss standing at sixteen fathom distance from the side of the opposite main, the higher and lower rocks have two stakes fastened in each of them, and to these there are ropes tied; upon the ropes there is an engine hung, which they call a cradle, and in this a man makes his way over from the greater to the smaller rocks, where he makes a considerable purchase of eggs and fowl; but his return being by an ascent makes it the more dangerous, though those on the great rock have a rope tied to the cradle, by which they draw it and the man safe over for the most part. Over this rock Mr Archibald Campbell and five others were in that matter let down by cradles and ropes; but before they could be all drawn back again it grew dark, and their associates not daring to be benighted, were forced to withdraw, and Mr Campbell was the unfortunate person left behind, having wandered too far, and not minded how the day declined, being intent on his game. He passed that night, you may easily guess, without much sleep, and with great anxiety of heart. The night, too, as he lay in the open air, was, to add to his misfortunes, as boisterous and tempestuous as his own mind; but in the end the tempest proved very happy for him. The reader is to understand that the Hamburghers, Bremeners, and Hollanders, carry on a great fish trade there. Accordingly, a Holland vessel that was just coming in the sound of Brassah, was by this tempest driven into a creek of the rock, which nature had made into a harbour, and they were providentially saved from the bottom of the sea by a rock, from which, humanly speaking, they could expect nothing but destruction, and being sent to the bottom of that sea. As never could a man be taken hold of with so sudden and surprising a disaster, so nobody could meet with a more sudden and surprising relief than Mr Campbell found when he saw a ship so near. He made to the vessel, and begged the Hollanders to take him in. They asked him what he would give them, " or," said the barbarous sailors, " we will even leave you where you are." He told them his disaster, but they asked money, and nothing else would move them. As he knew them a self-interested people, he bethought himself that if he should tell them of the plenty of fowls and eggs they would get there, he might not only be taken in a passenger, but made a partner in the money arising from the stock. It succeeded accordingly : when he proposed it, the whole crew were all at work, and in four hours, pretty well stored the vessel, and then, returning on board, set sail for Holland. They offered Mr Campbell to put him in at his own island, but having a mind to see Holland, and, being a partner, to learn their way of merchandise, which he thought he might turn to his countrymen's advantage, he told them he would go the voyage out with them, and see the country of those who were his deliverers, a necessary way of speech, when one has a design to soothe barbarians, who but for interest would have left him unredeemed, and, for aught they knew, a perpetual sole inhabitant of a dreadful rock, encompassed round with precipices, some three hundred fathom high. Not so the islanders (who are wrongly called a savage set of mortals); no, they came in quest of him after so bitter a night, not doubting to find him, but fearing to find him in a lamentable condition. They hunted and ransacked every little hole and corner in the rock, but all in vain; in one place they saw a great slaughter of fowls, enough to serve forty families for a week, and then they guessed, though they had not the ill fortune to meet the eagles frequently noted to hover about those isles, that they might have devoured part of him on some precipice of the rock, and dropped the remnant into the sea. Night came upon them, and they were afraid of falling into the same disaster they went to relieve Mr Campbell from. They returned each to their proper basket, and were drawn up safe by their respective friends, who were amazed that one basket was drawn up empty which was let down for Mr Campbell, and that there was not the least intelligence to be had concerning him, but the supposititious story of his having been devoured by eagles. The story was told at home, and with the lamentation of the whole family, and all his friends, he was looked upon to be murdered or dead.

Return we now to Mr Archibald Campbell, still alive, and on board the Holland vessel, secure, as he thought within himself, that from the delivery he lately had by the gift of Providence, he was not intended to be liable to any more misfortunes and dangers of life, in the compass of so small a voyage. But his lot was placed otherwise in the book of fate than he too fondly imagined; his time of happiness was dated some pages lower down, and more rubs and difficulties were to be encountered with before his stars intended to lead him to the port of felicity. Just as he arrived within sight of Amsterdam a terrible storm arose, and, in danger of their lives for many hours, they weathered out the tempest, and a calm promising fair afresh, they made to the coast of Zealand; but a new hurricane prevented the ship from coming there also, and after having lost their masts and rigging, they were driven into Lapland. There they went ashore in order to careen and repair their ship, and take in provisions. While the ship was repairing by the Dutch, our islander made merry with the inhabitants, being the most inclined to their superstitious customs; he there became acquainted with a very beautiful woman, who fell in love with him, and after a very short space of time he married her. About the time when the ship departed, his wife, who was very rich, was big with child of a son, namely, Mr Duncan Campbell. He wrote a letter, by the master of the vessel, to his parents in Shetland, concerning the various adventures he had met with, which was delivered the June following, about the time of fishing, to his parents, and several persons had copies thereof; and, for aught I know, some retain them to this very day; sure I am, that many remember the particulars of this surprising affair, who are now living in that island.

The letter being very remarkable and singular in all its circumstances, I shall present it the reader, word for word, as it was given into my hands, together with some others which he wrote afterwards, in all which I am assured, by very credible persons and undoubted authorities, there are not the least alterations but what the version . of it from the then Scotch manner of expression into a more modern English dress made absolutely necessary.

MY DEAREST FATHER,—The same odd variety of accident which put it out of my power to be personally present with you for so long a time, put it likewise out of my power to write to you. At last fortune has so ordered it, that I can send a letter to you before I can come myself, and it is written expressly to tell you the adventures I have met with, which have detained me this tedious space of time from my dear father, and because the same captain of a ship that brings you this, might as easily have brought your son to speak for himself. I shall in the next place lay before you the necessity there is for my stay a little longer among the strange natives of the country where I now inhabit, and where I am in a manner become naturalised.

You have, no doubt of it, been informed by my companions, some of whom I hope got safe back again, if not all, that I was lost where many a brave man has perished before me, by going over the high precipices of the mountain Brassah in a basket, sliding down by a rope. I must suppose I have given you the anguish of a father for a son, who you thought had lost his life by such a foolhardy attempt, and I implore your pardon with all the power of filial contrition, penitence, and duty. You have always showed me such singular marks of paternal affection that I know your receipt of this letter will fill your heart with joy, and cause you to sign me an absolution and free pardon for all the errors I have committed, and think the sufferings I have undergone for my rashness and indiscretion a sufficient atonement for my crime of making you, by my undutifulness, a partner of my sorrows. To free you the more from this uneasiness, I know I need only tell you that every grief of mine is gone excepting one, which is, that I must still lose the pleasure of seeing you a little longer. There was never surely a more bitter night than that which must by me be for ever remembered, when I was lost in the mountain of Brassah, where I must, for aught I know, have lived for ever, a wild single inhabitant, but that the storm which made the night so uneasy to me, rendered the first approach of daylight beyond measure delightful. The first providential glimpse of the morning gave me

a view of a ship driven by the tempest into a creek of
the rock that was by nature formed like a harbour; a
miraculous security of deliverance as I thought, both
for the ship's crew and myself. I made all the haste
I could, you may be sure, to them, and I found them
to be Dutchmen that were come for fish; but in lieu
of fish I instructed them to load it with eggs and fowl,
which we compassed very happily in a short space of
time, and I was to be a sharer with the captain in the
lading, and bargained to go for Holland to see the sale
and nature of the traffic; but when we were at sea,
after much bad weather, we made towards Zealand,
but we were driven upon the coast of Finland by a
new storm, and thence to Lapland, where I now am,
and from whence I send you this letter.

I could not come into a place so properly named for
my reception. As I had been undutiful to you, and
fortune seemed to make me an exile or a banished man,
by way of punishment for the vices of my youth; so
Lapland (which is a word originally derived from the
Finland word, *lappi*, that is, exiles, and from the
Swedish word, *lap*, signifying banished, from which
two kingdoms most of our inhabitants were banished
hither for not embracing the Christian religion) was
certainly the properest country in the world to receive me.

When first I entered this country I thought I was
got into quite another world. The men are all of
them pigmies to our tall, brawny Highlanders; they
are, generally speaking, not above three cubits high,
insomuch that though the whole country of Lapland is
immensely large, and I have heard it reckoned by the
inhabitants to be above a hundred German leagues in
length, and fourscore and ten in breadth, yet I was the
tallest man there, and looked upon as a giant. The
district in which I live now is called Uma Lapmark.

You must understand, sir, that when I landed at North Cape, in Kimi Lapmark, another district of Lapland, there was at that time a most beautiful lady come to see a sick relation of her father's, who was prefect or governor of Uma Lapmark, which is a post of great distinction; this lady, by being frequently in the company of French merchants, who traffic now and then in that province of Uma Lapmark, understood French, and having heard of a man six feet and a half high, desired to see me, and when I came she happened mightily to like my person; and she talked French, which when I answered she made great signs of joy that she could communicate her sentiments to me, and she told me who she was, how rich, and that not one in the company besides could understand a syllable we said, and so I might speak my mind freely to her. She told me the customs of the country, that it was divided into cantons, like our shires, and those cantons into rekars, or certain grounds allotted to families that are just like our clans. As she was beyond measure beautiful, she was extremely good-humoured (a thing rarely to be met among Lapland women), of a better stature than her countrywomen, and very rich and of good birth. I thought it would be a prodigious turn of fortune for a man in my circumstances, if I could make any progress in her heart, which she seemed a little to open to me, in such a manner, for the beginning, as if such a successful event, if managed with prudence, might not be despaired of. Souls that are generous are apt to love, and compassion is the best introducer of love into a generous bosom, and that was the best stock I had to go upon in my courtship. I told her of all my calamities, my dangers, and my escapes; the goodness of my birth, as being allied to one of the greatest nobles in our island; and still she would ask me to tell it her over again, though every

time I told it, just at such passages, she was forced to
drop the tears from her eyes. In fine, I grew more
in love with her, out of a sense of gratitude now, than
by the power of her charms before. The matter in a
few days went so far, that she owned to me I had her
heart. As to marriage, I did not then know the
custom of the nation; I thought that if it proved only
dangerous to me, I loved her so well that I intended
to marry her, though the law was to pronounce me
dead for it; but I did not know whether it might not
be perilous for her too to engage in such a state with
me, and I resolved in that case rather to be singly
unhappy than to involve her in distress and make her
the fair companion of my woes. I would not tell her
so for fear she should, out of love, hide from me those
dangers, and therefore, using a kind sort of dissimula-
tion, I conjured her to tell me the laws and customs of
marriages in that country to a tittle, and that nothing
should hinder us from happiness. She told me exactly
as I find since. " Our marriage," said she, " will be
very hard to compass, provided we follow the strict
rule of the country; for our women here are bound
not to see the man who makes their addresses to them
in some time. His way of courtship is to come to the
parents, and his nearest friends and relations must make
her father presents, and supplicate him like a king to
grant him his daughter. The courtship often lasts two
or three years, and sometimes has not its effect at last;
but if it has, the woman is dragged by her father and
brother to church, as unwilling to go to be married,
which is looked upon as a greater part of modesty in
her according to the greater disinclination she shows.
My father and brother," said she, " will both be against
it; you have no relations in this country to move your
suit; I cannot be so hypocritical as to be dragged
unwillingly to him I own I desire for my lawful

husband, and therefore, as I have an inclination to you, and I dare own I have, I will not follow those methods which I disapprove.   I have talked with several Swedes and several polite Frenchmen about their manner of espousals, and I am told that when souls are naturally united by affection, the couple so mutually and reciprocally loving, though they had rather have their parents' leave if likely to be got, yet, unwilling to be disappointed, only go to the next minister's and marry for better for worse.   This way I approve of, for where two persons naturally love each other, the rest is nothing but a modest restraint to their wishes, and since it is only custom, my own reason teaches me there is no error committed, nor any harm done in breaking through it, upon so commendable an occasion. I have," added she, " a thousand reindeer belonging to me beyond my father's power of taking away, and a third share in a rekar or clan, that is ten leagues in compass, in the byar or canton of Uma Lapmark.   This is at my own disposal, and it is all your own if you please to accept of it with me. Our women are very coy when they are courted, though they have never so much an inclination to their suitor ; but good reason and the commerce I have had with persons of politer nations than ours is, teach me that this proceeds entirely from vanity and affectation, and the greatest proof of a woman's modesty, chastity, and sincerity certainly consists (contrary to the general corrupted opinion) in yielding up herself into the arms of the man she loves.   For she that can dally with a heart she prizes, can give away her heart (when she is once baulked) to any man, even though she dislikes him." You must judge, my dear father, I must be touched with a woman that was exceeding beautiful beyond any of her nation, and who had thoughts as beautiful as her person.   I therefore was all in rapture, and longed for the matrimony, but still loved her enough to propose the question I resolved to her, viz., if it would not be in her nation accounted a clandestine marriage, and prove of great damage to her.

To this she answered with all the wisdom which could be expected from a woman who had given such eminent tokens of her judgment on other points, amidst a nation so barbarous in its manners, and so corrupt in its principles, as Lapland is. "I am," said she, "answerable to my father for nothing by our laws, having no portion of him, but only what was presented me by my relations at my birth, according to custom, in lands and reindeer. My father is but deputy-governor; it is a Swede who is the Governor of Uma, and if I pay to him at every mart and fair the due tribute, which must either consist of fifty reindeer or one hundred and fifty rixdollars, he will have the priest that marries us present at the court of justice, according to our custom, and keep us in possession of our rights, that we may be enabled to pay tribute to the crown of Sweden. Indeed, before the abolition of the birkarti, which were our native judges, we could not have married thus without danger to us both; but now there is none at all."

My dear father, you must easily imagine that I could not help embracing with all tenderness so dear and so lovely a woman. In fine, I am married to her. I have lived very happily hitherto, and am now grown more happy, for she is big with child; and likely, before my letter comes to your hands, to make you a grandfather of a pretty boy. You will perhaps wonder that I name the sex of the child before it comes into the world; but we have a way in Lapland of finding that out, which, though some judicious people call superstitious, I am really persuaded of by experience, and therefore I indulged my dear wife's curiosity when she signified to me she had a mind to make the usual trial whether the child she was going to be delivered of would be a boy or a girl.

You must understand, my dear father, the people here judge of the sex of the child by the moon, unto which they compare a big-bellied woman. If they see a star appear just above the moon, it is a sign it will be a boy, but, if the star be just below the moon, they conjecture her to be big with a girl. This observation and remark of Laplanders have, I know, been accounted by some, and those wise and judicious men too, to be ridiculously superstitious; but I have been led into an easy belief of this mystery by a mistress that is superior to wisdom itself, constant, and therefore probably infallible, experience. I therefore indulged my wife in this her request, and went with her to the ceremony. The star appeared above the moon, which prognosticates a boy, which I wish may, and I scarce doubt will, prove true; and when she is brought to bed I will send you word of it. It is remarkable, likewise, that a star was seen just before the moon, which we also count a very good omen; for it is a custom likewise here in Lapland to consult the moon as an oracle about the health and vigour of the child. If a star be seen just before the moon we count it a sign of a lusty and well-grown child, without blemish; if a star comes just after, we reckon it a token that the child will have some defect or deformity, or die soon after it is born.

Having thus told you the manners of the country I live in at present, as much at large as the space of a letter will permit, and related to you my own happy circumstances, and the kindly promises of the heavens that are ushering in the birth of my child, I would not have you think that I addict myself to the superstitions of the country, which are very many and groundless, and arising partly from the remainder of Pagan worship, which is still cultivated among some of the more obstinate inhabitants. I have, on the contrary, since I married her, endeavoured to repay my wife's temporal blessings to me with those that are endless, instructed her in all the points of religion, and made her perfectly a Christian ; and she, by her devotion and prayers for me, makes me such amends for it that I hope in us two St Paul's saying will be verified, viz., that the woman shall be sanctified in her husband, and the husband shall be sanctified in his wife.

However, I must take notice in this place, with all due deference to Christianity, that though I am obliged to applaud the prudence and piety of Charles the Ninth of Sweden, who, constituting Swedish governors over this country, abrogated their practice of superstitions and art-magic upon pain of death, yet that king carried the point too far, and intermingled with these arts the pretensions to the gift of a second sight, which you know how frequent it is with us in Scotland, and which, I assure you, my wife (though she durst not publicly own it for fear of incurring the penalty of those Swedish laws) does, as it were, inherit (for all her ancestors before her have had it from time immemorial) to a greater degree than ever I knew any of our countrywomen or countrymen.

One day this last week she distracted me between the extremes of joy and sorrow. She told me I should see you shortly, and that my coming son would grow to be one of the most remarkable men in England and Scotland for his power of foresight ; but that I should speedily lose her, and meet with difficulties in my own country in the same manner as my father (meaning you, sir) had done before me, and on the same account, viz., of civil broils and intestine wars in Scotland.

These unfortunate parts of her relation I would not conceal from you, because the veracity of her notions should appear, if they are true, though you may be sure I much wish they all may prove false to the very last, excepting that wherein she tells me my son will be greatly remarkable, and that I shall shortly see my dear father, which I daily long for, and will endeavour to do, as soon as possible. Pray remember me to all friends; being, honoured sir, your most dutiful and loving son, ARCHIBALD CAMPBELL.

The Second Letter.

I am now the happiest man alive; the prosperous part of my wife's predictions, which I mentioned to you in my last, is come in some measure to pass. The child she has brought me is a boy, and as fine a one as ever I beheld, if fondness for my own makes me not blind; and sure it cannot be fondness, because other plain circumstances joined at his birth to prove it more than an ordinary remarkable one. He was born with a caul upon his head, which we count one of the luckiest signs that can be in nature; he had likewise three teeth ready cut through the gums, and we reckon that an undeniable testimony and promise given to the world by Nature that she intends such a person for her extraordinary favourite, and that he is born for great things, which I daily beg of Heaven may come to pass.

Since I have known for some months what it is to be a father, it adds a considerable weight to those affections which I had for my wife. I thought that my tenderness for her was at the height of perfection before; which shows how little we know of those parts of nature that we have yet never tried, and of which we have not yet been allotted our share to act upon the stage of life. I find that I did love her then as well as a husband could love a wife, that is, a wife without a child; but the love to a wife that has a child is a feeling wonderful and inexpressibly different. A child is the seal and pledge of love. Meditating upon this has likewise doubled my affection for you. I loved you before as a son, and because as such I felt your tenderness, but my love is much increased now, because I know the tenderness which you felt for me as a father. With these pleasing images of thought I often keep you nearer company at this vast distance than when I lived irregularly under your eye. These reflections render a solitary life dear to me; and though I have no manner of acquaintance with her relations, who hate me, as I am told, nor indeed with almost any of the inhabitants but my own domestics and those I am forced to deal with, yet I have as much, methinks, as I wish for, unless I could come over to Shetland, and live with you, which I the more ardently desire, because I think I and my wife could be true comforts to you in your advanced years, now I know what living truly is. I am daily persuading my wife to go with me, but she denies me with kind expressions, and says she owes too much to the place (however less pleasant in itself than other climates) where she had the happiness of first joining hands with me in wedlock, ever to part from it. But I must explain how I ask, and how she refuses. I resolved never directly and downrightly to ask her, because I know she can refuse me nothing, and that would be bearing hard upon the goodness of her will; but my way of persuading her consists in endeavouring to make her in love with the place by agreeable descriptions of it, and likewise of the humane temper of the people, so that I shortly shall induce her to signify to me that it is her own will to come with me, and then I shall seem rather to consent to her will than to have moved it over to my own. These hopes I have of seeing my dear father shortly, and I know such news would make this letter which I therefore send more acceptable to him, to whom I will be a most dutiful and affectionate son till death.

Archibald Campbell.

P.S.—If I cannot bring my wife to change this country for another, I have brought her to that pitch of devotion that whenever Providence, which notwithstanding her predictions, I hope will be long yet, shall call her to change this world for another, it will be happy with her there. She joins with me in begging your blessing to me, herself, and our little Duncan, whom we christened so out of a respect to the name you bear.

The Third Letter.

My dear Father,—I am lost in grief: I had just brought my wife (her that was my wife, for I have none now, I have lost all joy) in the mind of coming over to be a comfort to you. But now grief will let me say no more than that I am coming to beg comfort from you, and by this I prepare you to receive, when he comes, a son in tears and mourning.

Archibald Campbell.

P.S.—I have a babe, not much above two years old, must bear the hardships of travelling over the ice, and all through Muscovy, for no ships can stir here for many months; and I cannot bear to live in this inhospitable place, where she died that only could make it easy to me, one moment beyond the first opportunity I have of leaving it. She is in heaven; that should make me easy, but I cannot, I am not so good a Christian as she was—I am lost and ruined.

Chapter ij.

After the death of Mr Duncan Campbell's mother in
Lapland, his father Archibald returned with his
son to Scotland. His second marriage, and how
his son was taught to write and read.

MR ARCHIBALD CAMPBELL, having buried his Lapland lady, returned to Scotland, and brought over with him his son, Mr Duncan Campbell. By that time he had been a year in his own country he married a second wife, a lady whom I had known very well for some years, and then I first saw the boy; but as they went into the western islands, I saw them not again in three years. She being, quite contrary to the cruel way much in use among stepmothers, very fond of the boy, was accustomed to say she did and would always think him her own son. The child came to be about four years of age (as she has related to me the story since), and not able to speak one word, nor to hear any noise; the father of him used to be mightily oppressed with grief, and complain heavily to his new wife, who was no less perplexed that a boy so pretty, the son of so particular a woman, whom he had made his wife, by strange accidents and adventures, and a child coming into the world with so many amazing circumstances attending his birth, should lose those precious senses by which alone the social commerce of mankind is upheld and maintained, and that he should be deprived of all advantages of education which could raise him to the character of being the great man that so many concurring incidents at his nativity promised and betokened he would be.

One day a learned divine, who was of the university of Glasgow, but had visited Oxford, and been acquainted with the chief men of science there, happening to be in conversation with the mother-in-law of this child, she related to him her son's misfortunes, with so many marks of sorrow, that she moved the good old gentleman's compassion, and excited in him a desire to give her what relief and consolation he could, in this unhappy case. His particular inclination to do her good offices made him recollect that at the time he was at Oxford he had been in company with one Dr Wallis, a man famous for learning, who had told him that he had taught a man (born deaf and dumb) to write and to read, and even to utter some words articulately with his mouth; and that he told him he was then going to commit to print the method he made use of in so instructing that person, that others in the like unfortunate condition might receive the same benefits and advantages from other masters which his deaf and dumb pupil had received from him. A dumb man recovering his speech, or a blind man gaining his sight, or a deaf one getting his hearing, could not be more overjoyed than Mrs Campbell was at these unexpected tidings, and she wept for gladness when he told it. The good gentleman animated and encouraged her with the kindest promises; and to keep alive her hopes assured her he would send to one of the chief booksellers in London, to inquire after the book, who would certainly procure it him, if it was to be got; and that afterwards he would peruse it diligently, make himself master of Dr Wallis's method, and though he had many great works upon his hands at that time, he would steal from his other studies leisure enough to complete so charitable an object as teaching the dumb and deaf to read and to write, and give her son, who was by nature deprived of them, the advantages of speech, as far as art would permit that natural defect to be supplied by her powerful interposition.

When the mother came home, the child, who could

hear no knocking, and therefore it must be by a strange and inexplicable instinct in nature, was the first that ran to the door, and falling in a great fit of laughter (a thing it was not much used to before, having on the contrary rather a melancholy cast of complexion), it clung round its mother's knees, incessantly embracing and kissing them, as if just at that time it had an insight into what the mother had been doing for it, and into its own approaching relief from its misery.

When the mother came with the child in her hand to the father to tell him the welcome news, the child burst afresh into a great fit of laughter, which continued for an unusual space of time; and the scene of such reciprocal affection and joy between a wife and her own husband, on so signal an occasion, is a thing easier to be felt by parents of a good disposition, imagining themselves under the same circumstance, with regard to a child they loved with fondness, than to be expressed or described by the pen of any writer.   But it is certain, whenever they spoke of this affair, as anybody who knows the impatience of parents for the welfare of an only child may guess they must be often discoursing it over, and wishing the time was come, the boy, who used seldom so much as to smile at other times, and who could never hear the greatest noise that could be made, would constantly look wishfully in their faces and laugh immoderately, which is a plain indication that there was then a wonderful instinct in nature, as I said before, which made him foretaste his good fortune; and, if I may be allowed the expression, the dawnings, as it were, of the second-sight were then pregnant within him.

To confirm this, the happy hour of his deliverance being come, and the doctor having procured Mr Wallis's book, came with great joy, and desired to see his pupil.   Scarce were the words out of his mouth,

when the child happened to come into the room, and
running towards the doctor, fell on his knees, kissed
his hand eagerly, and laughed as before, which to me
is a demonstration that he had an insight into the good
which the doctor intended him.

It is certain that several learned men, who have
written concerning the second-sight, have demonstrated
by incontestable proofs and undeniable arguments, that
children, nay, even horses and cows, see the second-
sight, as well as men and women advanced in years.
But of this I shall discourse at large in its proper place,
having allotted a whole future chapter for that same
subject of second-sightedness.

In about half a year, the doctor taught his little
dumb pupil, first to know his letters, then to name
anything whatsoever, to leave off some savage motions
which he had taken of his own accord before, to
signify his mind by, and to impart his thoughts by his
fingers and his pen, in a manner as intelligible, and almost
as swift through the eyes, as that is of conveying our
ideas to one another by our voices, through the conduits
and port-holes of the ears.   But in little more than two
years, he could write and read as well as anybody.
Because a great many people cannot conceive this, and
others pretend it is not to be done in nature, I will a
little discourse upon Dr Wallis's foundation, and show,
in a manner obvious to the most ignorant, how this
hitherto mysterious help may be easily administered
to the deaf and the dumb, which shall be the subject
of the ensuing chapter.

But I cannot conclude this without telling the handsome saying with which this child, when not quite six
years old, as soon as he thought he could express himself well, paid his first acknowledgment to his master,
and which promised how great his future genius was
to be, when so witty a child ripened into man.   The

words he wrote to him were these, only altered into
English from the Scotch :—

" Sir,—It is no little work you have accomplished.
My thanks are too poor amends ; the world, sir, shall
give you thanks ; for as I could not have expressed
myself without your teaching me, so those that can
talk, though they have eyes, cannot see the things
which I can see, and shall tell them ; so that in
doing me this, you have done a general service to
mankind."

Chapter iij.

*The method of teaching deaf and dumb persons to write,
read, and understand a language.*

IT is, I must confess, in some measure amazing to
me, that men of any moderate share of learning
should not naturally conceive of themselves a plain
reason for this art, and know how to account for the
practicability of it, the moment they hear the proposition advanced ; the reasons for it are so obvious to the
very first consideration we can make about it.   It will
be likewise as amazing to me, that the most ignorant
should not conceive it, after so plain a reason is given
them for it as I am now going to set down.

To begin.   How are children at first taught a
language that can hear ?   Are they not taught by
sounds ?   And what are those sounds but tokens and
signs to the ear, importing and signifying such and
such a thing ?   If, then, there can be signs made to the
eye, agreed by the party teaching the child, that they
signify such and such a thing, will not the eye of the
child convey them to the mind, as well as the ear ?
They are, indeed, different marks to different senses,

but both the one and the other do equally signify the same things or notions, according to the will of the teacher, and consequently must have an equal effect with the person who is to be instructed ; for though the manners of signifying are different, the things signified are the same.

For example : If, after having invented an alphabet upon the fingers, a master always keeps company with a deaf child, and teaches it to call for whatsoever it wants, by such motions of the fingers which, if put down by letters, according to each invented motion of each finger, would form in writing a word of a thing, which it wanted ; might not he by these regular motions teach its eye the same notions of things as sounds do to the ears of children that hear ? The manner of teaching the alphabet by fingers is plainly set down in the following table.*

When the deaf child has learned by these motions a good stock of words, as children that hear first learn by sounds, we may methinks call not improperly the fingers of such a dumb infant its mouth, and the eye of such a deaf child its ear. When he has learned thus far, he must be taught to write the alphabet, according as it was adapted to the motions of his fingers. As for instance, the five vowels, *a, e, i, o, u,* by pointing to the top of the five fingers ; and the other letters, *b, c, d,* &c., by such other place or posture of a finger, as in the above-mentioned table is set forth or otherwise, as shall be agreed upon. When this is done, the marks B, R, E, A, D (and so of all other words), corresponding with such fingers, conveys through his eyes unto his head the same notion, viz., the things signified, as the sound we give those same letters, making the word " Bread," do into our heads through the ears.

* The table illustrating the positions of the fingers has not been reproduced in this edition.

This once done, he may be easily taught to understand the parts of speech, as the verb, the noun, pronoun, &c., and so by rules of grammar and syntax to compound ideas, and connect his words into a language. The method of which, since it is plainly set forth in Dr Wallis's letter to Mr Beverley, I shall set it down by way of extract, that people in the same circumstances with the person we treat of, and of the like genius, may not have their talents lost for want of the like assistance.

When once a deaf person has learned so far as to understand the common discourse of others, and to express his mind tolerably well in writing, I see no room to doubt, but that (provided nature has endowed him with a proper strength of genius, as other men that hear) he may become capable, upon further improvement, of such further knowledge as is attainable by reading. For I must here join with the learned Dr Wallis, in asserting (as the present case before us) that no reason can be assigned why such a deaf person may not attain the understanding of a language as perfectly as those that hear ; and with the same learned author I take upon me to lay down this proposition as certain, that allowing the deaf person the like time and exercise as to other men is requisite in order to attain the perfection of a language, and the elegance of it, he may understand as well, and write as good language as other men, and abating only what doth depend upon sound, as tones, cadences, and such punctilios, no whit inferior to what he may attain to, if he had his hearing as others have.

An Extract from Dr Wallis, concerning the Method of teaching the Deaf and Dumb to read.

It is most natural, as children learn the names of things, to furnish him, by degrees, with a nomenclature,

containing a competent number of names of things
common and obvious to the eye, that you may show
the thing answering to such a name, and these digested
under convenient titles, and placed under them in such
convenient order, in several columns, or other orderly
situation in the paper, as by their position best to
express to the eye their relation or respect to one
another : as contraries, or correlatives, one against the
other, subordinates or appurtenances under their principle, which may serve as a kind of local memory.

Thus, in one paper, under the title "Mankind,"
may be placed, not confusedly, but in decent order,
man, woman, child (boy, girl).

In another paper, under the title "Body," may be
written, in like convenient order, head (hair, skin, ear),
face, forehead, eye (eyelid, eyebrow), cheek, nose
(nostril), mouth (lip, chin), neck, throat, back, breast,
side (right side, left side), belly, shoulders, arm (elbow,
wrist, hand), back (palm), finger (thumb, knuckle,
nail), thigh, knee, leg (shin, calf, ankle), foot (heel,
sole), toe.

And when he hath learned the import of words in
each paper, let him write them in like manner in distinct
leaves or pages of a book prepared for that purpose, to
confirm his memory, and to have recourse to it upon
occasion.

In a third paper you may give him the "Inward
Parts," as skull (brain), throat (windpipe, gullet),
stomach, guts, heart, lungs, liver, spleen, kidney, bladder
(urine), vein (blood), bone (marrow), flesh, fat, &c.

In another paper, under the title "Beast," may be
placed horse (stone-horse, gelding, mare, colt), bull
(ox), cow, calf. Sheep, ram (wether), ewe (lamb),
hog, boar, sow, pig, dog (mastiff, hound, greyhound,
spaniel), bitch (whelp, puppy), hare, rabbit, cat, mouse,
rat, &c.

Under the title " Bird " or " Fowl " put cock, capon, hen, chick, goose (gander), gosling, duck (drake), swan, crow, kite, lark, &c.

Under the title " Fish " put pike, eel, plaice, salmon, lobster, crab, oyster, craw-fish, &c.

You may then put " Plants " or " Vegetables " under several heads, or subdivisions of the same head ; as tree (root, body, bark, bough, leaf, fruit), oak, ash, apple-tree, pear-tree, vine, &c.   " Fruit," apple, pear, plum, cherry, grape, nut, orange, lemon, flower, rose, tulip, gilliflower, herb (weed), grass, corn, wheat, barley, rye, pea, bean.

And the like of " Inanimates," as heaven, sun, moon, star, element, earth, water, air, fire ; and under the title " Earth," clay, sand, gravel, stone, metal, gold, silver, brass, copper, iron (steel), lead, tin, pewter, glass.   Under the title " Water " put sea, pond, river, stream.   Under that of " Air " put light, dark, mist, fog, cloud, wind, rain, hail, snow, thunder, lightning, rainbow.   Under that of " Fire," coal, flame, smoke, soot, ashes.

Under the title " Clothes " put woollen (cloth, stuff), linen (Holland, lawn, lockarum), silk (satin, velvet), hat, cap, band, doublet, breeches, coat, cloak, stocking, shoe, boot, shirt, petticoat, gown, &c.

Under the title " House " put wall, roof, door, window, casement, room.

Under " Room " put shop, hall, parlour, dining-room, chamber, study, closet, kitchen, cellar, stable, &c.

And under each of these, as distinct heads, the furniture or utensils belonging thereunto, with divisions and subdivisions, as there is occasion, which I forbear to mention, that I be not too prolix.

And in like manner, from time to time, may be added more collections, or clauses of names or words, conveniently digested under distinct heads, and suitable distributions; to be written in distinct leaves or pages of his book, in such order as may seem convenient.

When he is furnished with a competent number of names, though not so many as I have mentioned, it will be seasonable to teach him, under the titles singular and plural, the formation of plurals from singulars, by adding *s* or *es*; as hand, hands; face, faces; fish, fishes, &c., with some few irregulars, as man, men; woman, women; foot, feet; tooth, teeth; mouse, mice; louse, lice; ox, oxen, &c.

Which, except the irregulars, will serve for possessives, to be after taught him, which are formed by their primitives by like addition of *s* or *es*, except some few irregulars, as my, mine; thy, thine; our, ours; your, yours; his; her, hers; their, theirs, &c.

And in all those and other like cases it will be proper first to show him the particulars and then the general title.

Then teach him in another page or paper the particulars, a, an, the, this, that, these, those.

And the pronouns, I, me, my, mine; thou, thee, thy, thine; we, us, our, ours; ye, you, your, yours; he, him, his; she, her, hers; it, its; they, them, their, theirs; who, whom, whose.

Then, under the titles " Substantive, adjective," teach him to connect these, as my hand, your head; his foot, his feet; her arm, arms; our hats; their shoes, John's coat, William's band, &c.

And in order to furnish him with more adjectives, under the title " Colours," you may place black, white, grey, green, blue, yellow, red, &c. ; and having showed the particulars, let him know that these are called colours.

The like for taste and smell, as sweet, bitter, sour, stink ; and for hearing ; sound, noise, word.

Then for touch or feeling ; hot, warm, cold, cool,

wet, moist, dry, hard, soft, tough, brittle, heavy, light, &c.

From whence you may furnish him with more examples of adjectives with substantives; as white bread, brown bread, green grass, soft cheese, hard cheese, black hat, my black hat, &c.

And then inverting the order, substantive, adjective, with the verb copulative between; as, silver is white, gold is yellow, lead is heavy, wood is light, snow is white, ink is black, flesh is soft, bone is hard, I am sick, I am not well, &c., which will begin to give him some notion of syntax.

In like manner, when substantive and substantive are so connected; as, gold is a metal, a rose is a flower, they are men, they are women, horses are beasts, geese are fowls, larks are birds, &c.

Then, as those before relate to quality, you may give him some other words relating to quantity; as long, short, broad, narrow, thick, thin, high, tall, low, deep, shallow, great, big, small (little), much, little, many, few, full, empty, whole, part, piece, all, some, none, strong, weak, quick, slow, equal, unequal, bigger, less.

Then words of figure; as straight, crooked, plain, bowed, concave, hollow, convex, round, square, three-square, sphere, globe, bowl, cube, die, upright, sloping, leaning forward, leaning backward, like, unlike.

Of gesture; as stand, lie, sit, kneel, sleep.

Of motion; as move, stir, rest, walk, go, come, run, leap, ride, fall, rise, swim, sink, drawn, slide, creep, crawl, fly, pull, draw, thrust, throw, bring, fetch, carry.

Then words relating to time, place, number, weight, measure, money, &c., are in convenient time to be showed him distinctly; for which the teacher, according to his discretion, may take a convenient season.

As likewise the time of the day, the days of the week, the days of the month, the months of the year, and other things relating to the almanack, which he will quickly be capable to understand, if once methodically shown him.

As likewise the names and situation of places and countries which are convenient for him to know, which may be orderly written in his book, and showed him in the map of London, England, Europe, the world, &c.

But these may be done at leisure, as likewise the practice of arithmetic, and other like pieces of learning.

In the meantime, after the concord of substantive and adjective, he is to be showed, by convenient examples, that of the nominative and verb; as, for instance, I go, you see, he sits, they stand, the fire burns, the sun shines, the wind blows, the rain falls, the water runs, and the like, with the titles in the top nominative verb.

After this (under the titles nominative verb, accusative), give him examples of verbs transitive; as, I see you, you see me, the fire burns the wood, the boy makes the fire, the cook roasts the meat, the butler lays the cloth, we eat our dinner.

Or even with a double accusative; as, you teach me writing or to write, John teacheth me to dance, Thomas tells me a tale, &c.

After this, you may teach him the flexion or conjugation of the verb, or what is equivalent thereunto; for in our English tongue each verb hath but two tenses, the present and the preter; two participles, the active and the passive : all the rest is performed by auxiliaries, which auxiliaries have no more tenses than the other verbs.

Those auxiliaries are, do, did, will, would, shall, should, may, might, can, could, must, ought to, have, had, am, be, was. And if by examples you can insinuate the signification of these few words, you have taught him the whole flexion of the verb.

And here it will be convenient, once for all, to write him out a full paradigm of some one verb, suppose to see, through all those auxiliaries.

The verb itself hath but these four words to be learned, see, saw, seeing, seen, save that after thou, in the second person singular, in both tenses, we add est, and in the third person singular, in the present tense, eth or es, or instead thereof, st, th, s, and so in all verbs.

Then to the auxiliaries, do, did, will, would, shall, should, may, might, can, could, must, ought to, we join the indefinite see. And after have, had, am, be, was, the passive particle seen, and so for all other verbs.

But the auxiliary, am or be, is somewhat irregular in a double form:

Am, art, is ; plural are ; was, wast, was ; plural were.   Be, beest, be ; plural were ; were, wert, were ; plural were ;

Be, am, was, being, been ;

Which, attended with the other auxiliaries, make us the whole passive voice.

All verbs, without exceptions, in the active participle, are formed by adding ing, as see, seeing ; teach, teaching, &c.

The preter tense and the participle are formed regularly, by adding ed, but are often subject to contractions and other irregularities, sometime the same in both, sometime different, and therefore it is convenient here to give a table of verbs, especially the most usual, for those three cases, which may at once teach their signification and formation ; as boil, boiled ; roast, roasted, roasted ; bake, baked, baked, &c. ; teach, taught, taught ; bring, brought, brought ; buy, bought, bought, &c. ; see, saw, seen ; give, gave, given ; take, took, taken ; forsake, forsook, forsaken ;

write, wrote, written, &c.; with many more fit to be learned.

The verbs being thus despatched, he is then to learn the prepositions, wherein lies the whole regimen of the noun. For diversity of cases we have none, the force of which is to be insinuated by convenient examples, suited to their different significations; as for instance, *of*, a piece *of* bread, a pint *of* wine, the colour *of* a pot, the colour *of* gold, a ring *of* gold, a cup *of* silver, the mayor *of* London, the longest *of* all, &c.

And in like manner, for, off, on, upon, to, unto, till, until, from, at, in, within, out, without, into, out of, about, over, under, above, below, between, among, before, behind, after, for, by, with, through, against, concerning; and by this time he will be pretty well enabled to understand a single sentence.

In the last place, he is in like manner to be taught the conjunctions, which serve to connect not words only but sentences, as and, also, likewise, either, or, whether, neither, nor, if, then, why, wherefore, because, therefore, but, though, yet, &c., and these illustrated by convenient examples in each case, as, *Because* I am cold, *therefore* I go to the fire, *that* I may be warm, *for* it is cold weather;

If it were fair, *then* it would be good walking, but however, *though* it rain, *yet* I must go, *because* I promised; with other like instances.

And by this time his book, if well furnished with plenty of words, and those well digested under several heads, and in good order, and well recruited from time to time as new words occur, will serve him in the nature of a dictionary and grammar.

And in case the deaf person be otherwise of a good natural capacity, and the teacher of a good sagacity, by this method, proceeding gradually step by step, you may, with diligence and due application of teacher and learner, in a year's time, or thereabouts, perceive a greater progress than you would expect, and a good foundation laid for further instruction in matters of religion and other knowledge which may be taught by books.

It will be convenient all along to have pen, ink, and paper, ready at hand, to write down in a word what you signify to him by signs, and cause him to write, or show how to write, what he signifies by signs, which way of signifying their mind by signs deaf persons are often very good at; and we must endeavour to learn their language, if I may so call it, in order to teach them ours, by showing what words answer to their signs.

It will be convenient, also, as you go along, after some convenient progress made, to express, in as plain language as may be, the import of some of the tables; as, for instance,

The head is the highest part of the body, the feet the lowest part; the face is the forepart of the head, the forehead is over the eyes, the cheeks are under the eyes, the nose is between the cheeks, the mouth is under the nose and above the chin, &c.

And such plain discourse, put into writing, and particularly explained, will teach him by degrees to understand plain sentences; and like advantages a sagacious teacher may take, as occasion offers itself from time to time.

This extract is mostly taken out of the ingenious Dr Wallis, and lying hid in that little book, which is but rarely inquired after and too scarcely known, died in a manner with that great man. And as he designed it for the general use of mankind that laboured under the misfortune of losing those two valuable talents of hearing and speaking, I thought it might not be amiss (in the life of so particular a dumb person as I am writing) to give them this small but particular fragment of grammar and syntax.

It is exactly adjusted to the English tongue; because such are the persons with whom the Doctor had to deal, and such the persons whose benefit alone I consult in this treatise.

One of the chief persons who was taught by Dr Wallis was Mr Alexander Popham, brother-in-law (if I am not mistaken) to the present Earl of Oxford; and he was a very great proficient in this way; and though he was born deaf and dumb, understood the language so well as to give, under his hand, many rare indications of a masterly genius.

The uncle of his present Sardinian Majesty, as I have been credibly informed, had the want of the same organs, and yet was a perfect statesman, and wrote in five or six different languages elegantly well.

Bishop Burnet, in his book of travels, tells us a wonderful story, almost incredible; but tells it as a passage that deserves our belief. It is concerning a young lady at Genoa, who was not only deaf and dumb, but blind, too, it seems, into the bargain; and this lady, he assures us as a truth, could, by putting her hand on her sister's mouth, know everything she said.

But to return back to England. We have many rare instances of our own countrymen, the principal of whom I shall mention, as their names occur to my memory. Sir John Gawdy, Sir Thomas Knotcliff, Sir [Edward] Gostwick, Sir Henry Lydall, and Mr Richard Lyns of Oxford, were all of this number, and yet eminent men in their several capacities, for understanding many authors, and expressing themselves in writing with wonderful facility.

In Hatton Garden, there now lives a miracle of wit and good nature, I mean the daughter of Mr Loggin, who, though born deaf and dumb (and she has a brother who has the same impediments), yet writes her mind down upon any subject with such acuteness as would amaze learned men themselves, and put many students that have passed for wits to a blush, to see themselves so far surpassed by a woman amidst that deficiency of the common organs. If anybody speaks a word distinctly, this lady will, by observing narrowly the motion of the speaker's lips, pronounce the word afterwards very intelligibly.

As there are a great many families in England and Ireland that have several, and some even have five or six dumb persons belonging to them, and as a great many more believe it impossible for persons born deaf and dumb to write and read, and have thence taken occasion to say and assert that Mr Campbell could certainly speak, I could never think it a digression in the history of this man's life to set down the grammar by which he himself was taught, and which he has taught others (two of which scholars of his are boys of this town), partly to confute the slander made against him, and partly for the help of others dumb and deaf, whose parents may by these examples be encouraged to get them taught.

$\sim$

Chapter iv.

Young Duncan Campbell returns with his mother to Edinburgh. The Earl of Argyll's overthrow. The ruin of Mr Archibald Campbell, and his death. Young Duncan's practice in prediction at Edinburgh, while yet a boy.

OUR young boy, now between six and seven years of age, half a Highlander and half a Laplander, delighted in wearing a little bonnet and plaid, thinking it looked very manly in his countrymen; and his father, as soon as he was out of his hanging sleeves, and left off his boy's vest, indulged him with that kind of dress, which is truly antique and heroic. In this early part of his nonage he was brought to Edinburgh by his mother-in-law, where I myself grew afresh acquainted with her, his father being then but lately dead, just after the civil commotion, and off and on, I have known him ever since, and conversed with him very frequently during that space of time, which is now about three or four and thirty years; so that whatever I say concerning him in the future pages I shall relate to the reader from my own certain knowledge, which, as I resolved to continue anonymous, may not have so much weight and authority as if I had prefixed my name to the account. Be that as it will, there are hundreds of living witnesses that will justify each action I relate, and his own future actions while he lives will procure belief and credit to the precedent ones, which I am going to record; so that if many do remain infidels to my relations, and will not allow them exact (the fate of many as credible and more important historians than myself), I can, however, venture to flatter myself that greater will be the number of those who will have a faith in my writings than of those who will reject my accounts as incredible.

Having just spoke of the decease of Mr Archibald Campbell, the father of our young Duncan Campbell, it will not be amiss here to observe how true the predictions of his Lapland mother were, which arose from second sight, according to the notices given by the child's father, to his grandfather, in his letter from Lapland, even before it was born, which shows that the infant held this second-sighted power, or occult faculty of divination, even by inheritance.

In the year 1685, the Duke of Monmouth and the Earl of Argyll sailed out of the ports of Holland without any obstruction, the Earl of Argyll in May, with three ships for Scotland, and Monmouth in June with the same number for England.

The earl setting out first was also the first at landing. Argyll having attempted to land in the north of Scotland, and being disappointed by the vigilance of the Bishop of the Orcades, landed in the west, and encamped at Dunstaffnage Castle, in the province of Lorne, which had belonged to him. He omitted nothing that might draw over to him all the malcontents in the kingdom, whom he thought more numerous than they afterwards appeared to be. He dispersed about his declarations, wherein, after protesting that he had taken up arms only in defence of religion and the laws, against an unjust usurper (so he styled James the Second), he invited all good Protestants, and such Scotch as would assert the liberty to join him against a prince, he said, who was got into the throne to ruin the Reformation, and to bring in Popery and arbitrary power. Next he sent letters to those he thought his friends, among whom was Mr Archibald Campbell, who, according to the vast deference paid by the Scots to their chief, joined him, though in his heart of quite a different principle, to call them to his assistance. He detached two of his sons to make inroads in the neighbourhood, and compel some by threats, others by mighty promises, to join him. All his contrivances could not raise him above three thousand men, with whom he encamped in the Isle of Bute, where he was soon, in a manner, besieged by the Earl of Dumbarton with the king's forces, and several other bodies, commanded by the Duke of Gordon, the Marquis of Athole, the Earl of Arran, and other great men, who came from all parts to quench the fire before it grew to a head.

The Earl of Argyll being obliged to quit a post he

could not make good, went over into a part of the
country of his own name, where having hastily fortified
a castle called Ellangreig, he put into it the arms and
ammunition taken out of his ships, which lay at anchor
under the cannon of a fort he erected near that place.
There his rout began, for going out from the castle
with his forces to make an incursion, one of his parties
was defeated by the Marquis of Athole, who slew four
hundred of his men, and Captain Hamilton, who
attacked his ships with some of the king's and took
them without any resistance.

The Earl of Dumbarton advancing towards him, at
the same time, by long marches, while he endeavoured
to secure himself by rivers, surprised him passing the
Clyde, in the village of Killern, as he was marching
towards Lennox. Dumbarton coming upon them at
night, would have stayed till the next day to attack the
rebels, but they gave him not so much time, for they
passed the river in the night, in such confusion, that
being overcome with fear, they dispersed as soon as
over. Argyll could scarcely rally so many as would
make him a small guard, which was soon scattered
again, Dumbarton having passed the river, and divided
his forces to pursue those that fled. Argyll had
taken guides to conduct him to Galloway, but they
mistaking their way, and leading him into a bog, most
of those that still followed him quitted their horses,
every man shifting for himself.

Argyll himself was making back alone towards the
Clyde, when two resolute servants, belonging to an
officer in the king's army, meeting him, though they
knew him not, bid him surrender. He fired at and
missed them; but they took better aim, and wounded
him with a pistol ball. Then the earl, drawing his
two pistols out of the holsters, quitted his horse, that
was quite tired, and took the river. A country fellow,

who came with those two that had first assaulted him, pursued him with a pistol in his hand. The earl would have fired one of his, but the flint failing, he was dangerously wounded in the head by the peasant. He discovered himself, as he fell senseless, crying out, " Unfortunate Argyll." This nobleman, how far soever he may be thought misled in principle, was certainly in his person a very brave and a very gallant hero. They made haste to draw him out and bring him to himself; after which, being delivered up to the officers, the erring, unfortunate great man was conducted to Edinburgh and there beheaded.

Many gentlemen that followed the fortunes of this great man, though not in his death, they shared in all the other calamities attending his overthrow. They most of them fled into the remotest isles and the obscurest corners of all Scotland; contented with the saving of their lives, they grew exiles and banished men of their own making, and abdicated their estates before they were known to be forfeited, because, for fear of being informed against by the common fellows they commanded, they durst not appear to lay their claims. Of this number was Mr Archibald Campbell, and this new disaster wounded him deeply into the very heart, after so many late misadventures, and sent him untimely to the grave. He perfectly pined away and wasted; he was six months dying inch by inch, and the difference between his last breath and his way of breathing during all that time, was only that he expired with a greater sigh than he ordinarily fetched every time when he drew his breath.

Everything the Lapland lady had predicted so long before being thus come to pass, we may the less admire at the wonders performed by her son, when we consider this faculty of divination to be so derived to him from her, and grown, as it were, hereditary.

Our young prophet, who had taught most of his little companions to converse with him by finger, was the head at every little pastime and game they played at. Marbles (which he used to call children's playing at bowls) yielded him mighty diversion; and he was so dexterous an artist at shooting that little alabaster globe from between the end of his forefinger and the knuckle of his thumb, that he seldom missed hitting plumb (as the boys call it) the marble he aimed at, though at the distance of two or three yards. The boys always when they played coveted to have him on their side, and by hearing that he foretold other things, used to consult him when they made their little matches (which were things of great importance in their thoughts), who should get the victory. He used commonly to leave these trifles undecided; but if ever he gave his opinion in these trivial affairs, the persons fared well by their consultation, for his judgment about them was like a petty oracle, and the end always answered his prediction. But I would have my reader imagine, that though our Duncan Campbell was himself but a boy, he was not consulted only by boys; his penetration and insight into things of a high nature got air, and being attested by credible witnesses, won him the esteem of persons of mature years and discretion.

If a beautiful young virgin languished for a husband, or a widow's mind was in labour to have a second venture of infants by another spouse; if a housekeeper had lost anything belonging to her master, still little Duncan Campbell was at hand. He was the oracle to be applied to; and the little chalked circle, where he was diverting himself with his playfellows, near the cross at Edinburgh, was frequented with as much solicitation, and as much credit, as the Tripos of Apollo was at Delphos in ancient times.

It was highly entertaining to see a young blooming

beauty come and slyly pick up the boy from his company, carry him home with as much eagerness as she would her gallant, because she knew she could get the name of her gallant out of him before he went, and bribe him with a sugar-plum to write down the name of a young Scotch peer in a green ribbon that her mouth watered after.

How often, after he has been wallowing in the dust, have I myself seen nice squeamish widows help him up in their gilded chariots, and give him a pleasant ride with them, that he might tell them they should not long lie alone!   Little Duncan Campbell had as much business upon his hands as the parsons of all the parishes in Edinburgh.   He commonly was consulted, and named the couples before the minister joined them; thus he grew a rare customer to the toy-shop, from whence he most usually received fees and rewards for his advices.   If Lady Betty Such-a-one was foretold that she should certainly have Beau Such-a-one in marriage, then little Duncan was sure to have a hobbyhorse from the toy-shop, as a reward for the promised fop.   If such a widow, that was ugly but very rich, was to be pushed hard for as she pretended (though in reality easily won), little Duncan, upon ensuring her such a captain, or such a lieutenant-colonel, was sure to be presented from the same child's warehouse with a very handsome drum and a silvered trumpet.

If a sempstress had an itching desire for a parson, she would, upon the first assurance of him, give this little Apollo a pasteboard temple or church, finely painted, and a ring of bells into the bargain, from the same toy-office.

If a housekeeper lost any plate, the thief was certain to be catched, provided she took little master into the store-room, and asked him the question, after she had given him his bellyful of sweetmeats.

Neither were the women only his consulters: the grave merchants, who were anxious for many ventures at sea, applied to the boy for his opinion of their security; and they looked upon his opinion to be as safe as the insurance office for ships. If he but told them, though the ship was just set sail, and a tempest rose just after on the ocean, that it would have a successful voyage, gain the port designed, and return home safe laden with the exchange of traffic and merchandise, they dismissed all their fears, banished all their cares, set their hearts at ease, and safe in his opinion enjoyed a calm of mind amidst a storm of weather.

I myself knew one Count Cog, an eminent gamester, who was a person so far from being of a credulous disposition, that he was an unbeliever in several points of religion, and the next door to an infidel. Yet as much as he was a stranger to faith, he was mastered and overpowered so far in his incredulity by the strange events which he had seen come frequently to pass, from the predictions of this child, that he had commonly daily access to this boy, to learn his more adverse and more prosperous hours of gaming. At first, indeed, he would try, when the child foretold him his ill fortune, whether it would prove true; and, relying upon the mere hazard and turn of the dice, he had always (as he observed) a run of ill luck on those forbidden days, as he never failed of good if he chose the fortunate hours directed by the boy. One time, above all the rest, just before he was departing from Edinburgh, and when the season of gaming was almost over, most persons of wealth and distinction withdrawing for pleasure to their seats in the country, he came to young Duncan Campbell to consult, and was extremely solicitous to know how happily or unluckily he should end that term (as we may call it) of the gamester's weighty business, viz., play, there being a long vacation likely to ensue, when the gaming-table would be empty, and the box and dice lie idle and cease to rattle. The boy encouraged him so well with his predictions on this occasion, that Count Cog went to the toy-shop, brought him from thence a very fine ivory teetotum (as children call it), a pretty set of painted and gilded ninepins and a bowl, and a large bag of marbles and alloys. And what do you think the gamester got by this little present and the prediction of the boy? Why, without telling the least tittle of falsehood, within the space of the last week's play, the gains of Count Cog really amounted to no less than twenty thousand pounds sterling, neat money.

Having mentioned these persons of so many different professions by borrowed names, and perhaps in a manner seemingly ludicrous, I would not have my reader from hence take occasion of looking upon my account as fabulous. If I was not to make use of borrowed names, but to tell the real characters and names of the persons, I should do injury to those old friends of his who first gave credit to our young seer, while I am endeavouring to gain him the credit and esteem of new ones, in whose way it has not yet happened to consult him. For many persons are very willing to ask such questions as the foregoing ones, but few or none willing to have the public told they ask them, though they succeeded in their wish, and were amply satisfied in their curiosity. I have represented them, perhaps, in a ludicrous manner, because, though they are mysterious actions, they are still the actions of a boy; and as the rewards he received for his advices did really and truly consist of such toys as I have mentioned, so could they not be treated of in a more serious manner, without the author's incurring a magisterial air of pedantry, and showing a mind, as it were, of being mighty grave and sententious about trifles. There are, however, some things of greater weight and importance done by him in a more advanced stage of life, which will be delivered to the public with that exactitude and gravity which becomes them ; and in some of those relations the names of some persons that are concerned shall be printed, because it will not at all be injurious to them, or because I have their leave, and they are still living to testify what I shall relate.

In the meantime, as the greatest part of his nonage was spent in predicting almost innumerable things, which are all, however, reduced to the general heads above-mentioned, I will not tire the reader with any particulars ; but instead of doing that, before I come to show his power of divination in the more active parts of his life, and when, after removing from Edinburgh to London, he at last made it his public profession, I shall account how such divinations may be made, and divert the reader with many rare examples (taken from several faithful and undoubted historians) of persons who have done the like before him, some in one way, and some in another ; though in these he seems to be peculiar, and to be (if I may be allowed the expression) a species by himself, alone in the talent of prediction ; that he has collected within his own individual capacity all the methods which others severally used, and with which they were differently and singly gifted in their several ways of foreseeing and foretelling.

This art of prediction is not attainable any otherwise than by these three ways : First, it is done by the company of familiar spirits and genii, which are of two sorts, some good and some bad, who tell the gifted person the things of which he informs other people. Secondly, it is performed by the second-sight, which is very various, and differs in most of the possessors, it being but a very little in some, very extensive and constant in others ; beginning with some in their infancy, and leaving them before they come to years; happening to others in a middle age; to others again in an old age that never had it before, and lasting only for a term of years, and now and then for a very short period of time; and in some intermitting, like fits, as it were, of vision, that leave them for a time, and then return to be as strong in them as ever; and it being in a manner hereditary to some families, whose children have it from their infancy, without intermission, to a great old age, and even to the time of their death, which they often foretold, before it came to pass, to a day, nay even to an hour. Thirdly, it is attained by the diligent study of the lawful part of the art of magic.

Before I give the reader an account (as I shall do in three distinct discourses), first, concerning the intercourse which familiar spirits, viz., the good and bad genii, have had and continue to have, to a great degree, with some select parts of mankind; secondly, concerning the wonderful and almost miraculous power of a second-sight, with which many, beyond all controversy, have been extraordinarily but visibly gifted; and thirdly, concerning the pitch of perfection to which the magic science has been carried and promoted by some adepts in that mysterious art, I will premise a few particulars about the genii which attended our little Duncan Campbell, and about the second-sight which he had when yet a child, and when we may much more easily believe that the wonders he performed and wrote of must have been rather brought about by the intervention of such genii and the meditation of such a sight than that he could have invented such fables concerning them, and compassed such predictions as seemed to want their assistance by the mere dint of a child's capacity.

One day, I remember, when he was about nine years of age, going early to the house where he and his mother lived, and it being before his mother was stirring,

I went into little Duncan Campbell's room, to divert myself with him. I found him sitting up in his bed, with his eyes broad open, but as motionless as if he had been asleep, or even (if it had not been for a lively beautiful colour which the pretty fair silver-haired boy always had in his cheeks) as if he had been quite dead ; he did not seem so much as to breathe ; the eyelids of him were so fixed and immovable, that the eye-lashes did not so much as once shake, which the least motion imaginable must agitate ; not to say that he was like a person in an ecstasy, he was at least in what we commonly call a brown study to the highest degree, and for the largest space of time I ever knew. I, who had been frequently informed by people who have been present at the operations of second-sighted persons, that, at the sight of a vision, the eyelids of the person are erected, and the eyes continue staring till the object vanishes, I, I say, sat myself softly down on his bedside, and with a quiet amazement observed him, avoiding diligently any motion that might give him the least disturbance, or cause in him any avocation or distraction of mind from the business he was so intent upon. I remarked that he held his head sideways, with his mouth wide open and in a listening posture, and that after so lively a manner, as, at first general thought, made me forget his deafness, and plainly imagine he heard something, till the second thought of reflection brought into my mind the misfortune that shut up all passage for any sound through his ears. After a stead-fast gaze, which lasted about seven minutes, he smiled, and stretched his arms, as one recovering from a fit of indolence, and rubbed his eyes ; then turning towards me, he made the sign of a salute, and hinted to me, upon his fingers, his desire for pen, ink, and paper, which I reached him from a little desk that stood at his bed's foot.

Placing the paper upon his knees, he wrote me the following lines, which, together with my answers, I preserve by me, for their rarity, to this very day, and which I have transcribed word for word, as they form a little series of dialogue.

Duncan Campbell—" I am sorry I cannot stay with you, but I shall see my pretty youth and my lamb by-and-by in the fields, near a little coppice, or grove, where I go often to play with them ; and I would not lose their company for the whole world ; for they and I are mighty familiar together, and the boy tells me everything, that gets me my reputation among the ladies and nobility, and you must keep it secret."

My question—" I will be sure to keep it secret. But how do you know you are to meet them there to-day ? Did the little boy appoint you ? "

Duncan Campbell—" Yes, he did, and signified that he had several things to predict to me concerning people that he foreknew would come to me the week following to ask me questions."

My question—" But what was you staring at when I came in ? "

Duncan Campbell—" Why, at that little boy, that goes along with the lamb I speak of, and it was then he made me the appointment."

My question—" How does he do it ? Does he write ? "

Duncan Campbell—" No, he writes sometimes ; but oftener he speaks with his fingers, and mighty swift ; no man can do it so quick, or write half so soon ; he has a little bell in his hand, like that which my mother makes me a sign to shake when she wants the servants ; with that he tickles my brain most strangely, and gives me an incredible delight in feeling in the inside of my head ; he usually wakes me with it in the morning, when he comes to make me an appointment. I fancy 'tis what you call hearing, which makes me mighty desirous I could hear in your way ; 'tis sweeter to the feeling, methinks, than anything is to the taste ; it is just as if my head was tickled to death, as my nurse used to tickle my sides ; but it is a different feeling, for it makes things like little strings tremble in my temples, and behind my ears. Now I remember, I will tell you what 'tis like, that makes me believe it is like your hearing, and that strange thing, which you that can speak call sound, or noise ; because, when I was at church with my mother, who told me the bells could be heard ringing a mile off, as I was kneeling on the bench, and leaning over the top of the pew, and gnawing the board, every time the man pulled the rope, I thought all my head beat, as if it would come to pieces ; but yet it pleased me, methought, rather than pained me, and I would be always gnawing the board when the man pulled the rope, and I told my mother the reason. The feeling of that was something like the little bell, but only that made my head throb, as if it would break, and this tickles me, and makes, as it were, little strings on the back of my ears dance and tremble like anything ; is not that like your way of hearing? If it be, it is a sweet thing to hear ; it is more pleasant than to see the finest colours in the world ; it is something like being tickled in the nose with a feather till one sneezes ; or like the feeling after one strikes the leg when it has been numb, or asleep, only with this difference, that those two ways give a pain and the other a pleasure. I remember, too, when I had a great cold, for about two months, I had a feeling something like it, but that was blunt, dull, confused, and troublesome. Is not this like what you call hearing?"

My question—" It is the finest kind of hearing, my dear ; it is what we call music. But what sort of a boy is that that meets you? and what sort of a lamb?"

Duncan Campbell—"Oh! though they are like other boys and lambs which you see, they are a thousand times prettier and finer. You never saw such a boy nor such a lamb in your lifetime."

My question—"How big is he? As big as you are? And what sort of a boy is he?"

Duncan Campbell—"He is a little pretty boy, about as tall as my knee; his face is as white as snow, and so are his little hands; his cheeks are as red as a cherry, and so are his lips; and, when he breathes, it makes the air more perfumed than my mother's sweet bags that she puts among the linen; he has got a crown of roses, cowslips, and other flowers, upon his head, such as the maids gather in May; his hair is like fine silver threads, and shine like the beams of the sun; he wears a loose veil down to his feet, that is as blue as the sky in a clear day, and embroidered with spangles that look like the brightest stars in the night; he carries a silver bell in one hand, and a book and pencil in the other; and he and the little lamb will dance and leap about me in a ring as high as my head. The lamb has got a little silver collar, with nine little bells upon it; and every little piece of wool upon its back, that is as white as milk, is tied up all round it in puffs like a little miss's hair, with ribbons of all colours; and round its head, too, are little roses and violets stuck very thick in the wool that grows upon its forehead, and behind and between its ears, in the shape of a diadem. They first meet me dancing thus; and after they have danced some time, the little boy writes down wonderful things in his book, which I write down in mine; then they dance again, till he rings his bell, and then they are gone all of a sudden, I know not where; but I feel the tickling in the inside of my head, caused by the bell, less and less, till I don't feel it at all ; and then I go home, read over my lesson in my book, and when I have it by heart, I burn the written leaves, according as the little boy bids me, or he would let me have no more. But I hear the little bell again ; the little boy is angry with me, he pulled me twice by the ear, and I would not displease him for anything ; so I must get up and go immediately to the joy and delight of my life."

I told him he might, if he would promise me to tell me further another time ; he said he would if I would keep it secret. I told him I would, and so we parted ; though just before he went, he said he smelt some venison, and he was sure they would shortly have some for dinner ; and nothing was so sure as that my man had my orders to bring a side of venison to me the next day to Mrs Campbell's, for I had been hunting, and came thither from the death of a deer that morning, and intended, as usual, to make a stay there for two or three days.

There are, I know, many men of severe principles, and who are more strict, grave, and formal in their manner of thinking than they are wise, who will be apt to judge of these relations as things merely fabulous and chimerical, and, not contented with being disbelievers themselves, will labour to insinuate into others this pernicious notion, that it is a sign of infirmity and weakness of the head to yield them credit. But though I could easily argue these Sir Gravities down— though a sentence or two would do their business, put them beyond the power of replying, and strike them dumb—yet do I not think it worth my while ; their greatest and most wonted objection to these Eudemons and Kakodemons being, that it arises all from the work of fancy, in persons of a melancholic blood. If we consider the nature of this child's dialogue with me,

will it not be more whimsically strange and miraculous
to say that a child of nine years old had only a fancy
of such things as these, of which it had never heard
anybody give an account, and that it could, by the
mere strength of imagination, predict such things as
really after came to pass, than it is (when it does so
strangely predict things) to believe the child does it in
the manner itself owns it does, which is by the intervention of a good demon, or happy genius.   Departing,
therefore, from these singular wise men's opinions, who
will believe nothing excellent can happen to others
which it has not been their lot to enjoy a share of, I
shall take my farewell hastily of them, without losing
my own time or theirs, in the words of the ingenious
and learned Monsieur Le Clerc :—" Acerbos homines
non moror, indignos quippe, qui hæc studia tractent,
aut quorum judicii ulla ratio habeatur."

I shall rather see how these things have lain open to
the eyes of, and been explained by the ancient sages ;
I will relate who among them were happy in their
genii, and who among the moderns, whose examples
may be authorities for our belief; I will set down,
as clearly as I can, what perception men have had of
genii, or spirits, by the sense of seeing ; what by the
sense of hearing, what by the sense of feeling, touching,
or tasting ; and, in fine, what perception others have
had of these genii by all the senses, what by dreams
and what by magic, a thing rarely to be met with at
once in any single man, and which seems particular
to the child, who was the subject of our last little
historical account.   When I have brought examples,
and the opinions of wise philosophers, and the evidence
of undeniable witnesses, which one would think sufficient to evince persons of the commerce men have
with spirits, if they were not past all sense of conviction, I shall, not so much to corroborate what I

say as to shame some wiseacres, who would by their frail reason scan all things, and pretend to solve the mysteries ascribed to spirits as facts merely natural, and who would banish from the thoughts of men all belief of spirits whatsoever,—I shall, I say, in order to put to shame these wiseacres, if they have any shame left, produce the opinions of the fathers, as divines, show the doctrines of spirits in general to be consistent with Christianity, that they are delivered in the Scripture and by Christian tradition; in which, if they will not acquiesce, I shall leave them to the labyrinth of their own wild opinions, which in the end will so perplex their judgments of things, that they will be never able to extricate themselves; and these different heads will be the subject of the chapter ensuing, and will, or I am greatly mistaken, form both an instructive, edifying, and entertaining discourse, for a reader really and truly intelligent, and that has a good taste and relish for sublime things.

***

Chapter v.

An argument proving the perception which men have, and have had, by all the senses, as seeing, hearing, &c., of demons, genii, or familiar spirits.

IT is said in the ninth book of the Morals of Aristotle, it is better to come at the probable knowledge of some things above us in the heavens, than to be capable of giving many demonstrations relating to things here below. This is no doubt an admirable proposition, and speaks the lofty aims of that sublime mind from whence it proceeded. Among all the disquisitions in this kind, none seem to me more excellent than those which treat concerning the genii that attend

upon men, and guide them in the actions of life.   A
genius or demon of the good kind, is a sort of mediate
being, between human and divine, which gives the mind
of man a pleasant conjunction with the angelic and
celestial faculties, and brings down to earth a faint
participation of the joys of heaven.   That there have
been such fortunate attendants upon wise men we
have many rare instances ; they have been ascribed
to Socrates, Aristotle, Plotinus, Porphyrius, Jamblicus,
Chicus, Scaliger, and Cardan.   The most celebrated
of all these ancients was Socrates ; and as for his
having a genius, or demon, we have the testimonies
of Plato, Xenophon, and Antisthenes, his contem-
poraries, confirmed by Laertius, Plutarch, Maximus,
Tyrius, Dion, Chrysostomus, Cicero, Apuleius, Ficinus,
and others, many of the moderns, besides Tertullian,
Origen, Clemens, Alexandrinus, Austin, and others ;
and Socrates himself, in " Plato's Theage," says, " By
some divine lot I have a certain demon, which has
followed me from my childhood as an oracle," and in
the same place intimates that the way he gained his instruction was by hearing the demon's voice.   Nothing
is certainly so easy as for men to be able to contradict
things, though never so well attested with such an air
of truth, as to make the truth of the history doubted by
others as well as themselves, where no demonstrative
proof can be brought to convince them.   This has
been the easy task of those who object against the
demon of Socrates ; but when no demonstrative proof
is to be had on either side, does not wisdom incline us
to lead to the most probable ?   Let us then consider
whether the evidences are not more credible, and witnesses of such a thing are not persons of more authority
than these men are, who vouchsafe to give no reason
but their own incredulity for maintaining the contrary,
and whether those therefore, by the right rule of

judging, ought not much sooner than these, to gain over our assent to their assertions.

We will, however, laying aside the histories of those ancient times, the sense whereof, by various readings and interpretations being put upon the words, is rendered obscure and almost unintelligible, descend to more modern relations, the facts whereof shall be placed beyond doubt, by reason of the evidences we will bring to attest them, and shall consequently prove the perception men have of spirits, or genii, by every sense.

Section I.

We will first begin as to the perception of spirits by the sight.

Mr Glanvil, in his collections of relations for proving apparitions, spirits, &c., tells us of an Irishman that had like to have been carried away by spirits, and of the ghost of a man who had been seven years dead, that brought a medicine to his bedside.

The relation is thus:

A gentleman in Ireland, near to the Earl of Orrery's, sending his butler one afternoon to buy cards; as he passed a field, to his wonder, he espied a company of people sitting round a table, with a deal of good cheer before them, in the midst of the field; and he going up towards them they all arose and saluted him, and desired him to sit down with them; but one of them whispered these words into his ear:—"Do nothing this company invites you to." Hereupon he refused to sit down at the table, and immediately table and all that belonged to it were gone, and the company were now dancing and playing upon musical instruments; and the butler being desired to join himself with them, but he refusing this also, they all fall to work, and he not being to be prevailed with, to accompany them in working,

any more than in feasting or dancing, they all dis-
appeared, and the butler is now alone ; but instead of
going forwards, home he returns, as fast as he could
drive, in a great consternation, and was no sooner
entered his master's door but he fell down, and lay
some time senseless ; but coming again to himself, he
related to his master what had passed.

The night following there comes one of his company
to his bedside and tells him, that if he offered to stir
out of doors the next day he would be carried away.
Hereupon he kept within ; but towards the evening,
having occasion to make water, he adventured to put
one foot over the threshold, several standing by, which
he had no sooner done, but they espied a rope cast
about his middle ; and the poor man was hurried away
with great swiftness, they following him as fast as they
could, but could not overtake him.   At length they
espied a horseman coming towards him, and made signs
to him to stop the man whom he saw coming near him,
and both ends of the rope, but nobody drawing ; when
they met, he laid hold of one end of the rope, and
immediately had a smart blow given him over his arm
with the other end ; but by this means the man was
stopped, and the horseman brought him back with
him.

The Earl of Orrery, hearing of these strange passages,
sent to the master to desire him to send this man to his
house, which he accordingly did ; and the morning
following, or quickly after, he told the earl that his
spectre had been with him again, and assured him that
that day he should most certainly be carried away, and
that no endeavours should avail to the saving of him.
Upon this he was kept in a large room, with a considerable number of persons to guard him, among whom
was the famous stroker, Mr Greatrix, who was a
neighbour.   There were, besides other persons of

quality, two bishops in the house at the same time, who were consulted concerning the making use of a medicine the spectre, or ghost, prescribed, of which mention will be made anon, but they determined on the negative.

Till part of the afternoon was spent, all was quiet; but at length he was perceived to rise from the ground, whereupon Mr Greatrix, and another lusty man, clapt their arms over his shoulders, one of them before him, the other behind him, and weighed him down with all their strength; but he was forcibly taken up from them, and they were too weak to keep their hold, and for a considerable time he was carried into the air, to and fro over their heads, several of the company still running under him to prevent his receiving hurt, if he should fall; at length he fell, and was caught before he came to the ground, and he had by that means no hurt.

All being quiet till bed-time, my lord ordered two of his servants to lie with him, and the next morning he told his lordship that his spectre was again with him, and brought a wooden dish, with grey liquor in it, and bid him drink it off. At the first sight of the spectre, he said that he endeavoured to awake his bed-fellows, but it told him that that endeavour should be in vain, and that he had no cause to fear him, he being his friend, and that he had at first given him the good advice in the field, which had he not followed, he had been before now perfectly in the power of the company he saw there; he added, that he concluded it was impossible but that he should have been carried away the day before, there being so strong a combination against him; but now he could assure him, there would be more attempts of that nature; but he being troubled with two sorts of sad fits, he had brought that liquor to cure him of them, and bid him drink it.

He peremptorily refusing, the spectre was angry, and upbraided him with great disingenuity, but told him, however, he had a kindness for him, and that if he would take plantain juice, he should be well of one sort of fits, but he should carry the other to his grave. The poor man having by this somewhat recovered himself, asked the spectre whether by the juice of plantain he meant that of the leaves or roots; it replied, the roots.

Then it asked him whether he did not know him. He answered, No. It replied, I am such a one. The man answered, he had been long dead. "I have been dead," said the spectre, or ghost, "seven years, and you know that I lived a loose life; and ever since I have been hurried up and down in a restless condition with the company you saw, and shall be to the day of judgment." Then he proceeded to tell him, that had he acknowledged God in his ways, he had not suffered such severe things by their means; and further said, "You never prayed to God that day, before you met with this company in the fields."

This relation was sent to Dr Henry More by Mr E. Fowler, who said Mr Greatrix told it several persons. The Lord Orrery also owned the truth of it; and Mr Greatrix told it to Dr Henry More himself, who particularly inquired of Mr Greatrix about the man's being carried up into the air, above men's heads in the room, and he did expressly affirm that he was an eye-witness thereof.

A vision which happened to the ingenious and learned Dr Donne may not improperly be here inserted. Mr Isaac Walton, writing the life of the said doctor, tells us, that the doctor and his wife were living with Sir Robert Drury, who gave them a free entertainment at his house in Drury Lane. It happened that the Lord Haye was by King James sent in an

embassy to the French king, Henry IV., whom Sir
Robert resolved to accompany, and engaged Dr Donne
to go with them, whose wife was then with child at
Sir Robert's house. Two days after their arrival at
Paris, Dr Donne was left alone in that room in which
Sir Robert and he and some other friends had dined
together. To this place Sir Robert returned within
half-an-hour, and as he left so he found Dr Donne,
alone, but in such an ecstasy, and so altered in his looks,
as amazed Sir Robert to behold him, insomuch that
he earnestly desired Dr Donne to declare what had
befallen him in the short time of his absence, to which
Dr Donne was not able to make a present answer;
but after a long and perplexed pause, did at last say,
" I have seen a dreadful vision since I saw you; I
have seen my dear wife pass twice by me through this
room, with her hair hanging about her shoulders, and a
dead child in her arms; this I have seen since I saw
you." To which Sir Robert replied, " Sure, sir,
you have slept since I saw you, and this is the result of
some melancholy dream, which I desire you to forget,
for you are now awake." To which Dr Donne's
reply was, " I cannot be surer that I am now alive
than that I have not slept since I saw you, and am as
sure, at her second appearing, she stopped and looked
at me in the face, and vanished." Rest and sleep had
not altered Dr Donne's opinion on the next day; for
he then affirmed this vision with a more deliberate and
so confirmed a confidence, that he inclined Sir Robert
to a faint belief that the vision was true, who immediately
sent a servant to Drury House, with a charge to hasten
back and bring him word whether Mrs Donne were
alive; and if alive, what condition she was in as to her
health. The twelfth day, the messenger returned with
this account; that he found and left Mrs Donne very
sad and sick in bed, and that after a long and dangerous

labour, she had been delivered of a dead child; and upon examination, the abortion proved to be the same day, and about the very hour, that Dr Donne affirmed he saw her pass by in his chamber. Mr Walton adds this as a relation which will beget some wonder, and well it may; for most of our world are at present possessed with an opinion that visions and miracles are ceased; and though it is most certain that two lutes being both strung and tuned to an equal pitch, and then one played upon, the other, that is not touched, being laid upon the table at a fit distance, will, like an echo to a trumpet, warble a faint audible harmony, in answer to the same tune, yet many will not believe that there is any such thing as a sympathy with souls, &c.

Section II.

I shall next relate some little histories, to show what perception men have had of spirits by the sense of hearing; for, as Wierus says, spirits appear sometimes invisibly, so that only a sound, voice, or noise is perceived by men, viz., a stroke, knocking, whistling, sneezing, groaning, lamenting, or clapping of the hands, to make men attent to inquire or answer.

In Luther's " Colloquia Mensalia," &c., set forth in Latin at Frankfort, anno 1557, it being a different collection from that of Aurifaber, which is translated from High Dutch into English, we have the following relation :—

" It happened in Prussia, that as a certain boy was born, there presently came to him a genius, or what you please to call it (for I leave it to men's judgments), who had so faithful a care of the infant, that there was no need either of mother or servant; and, as he grew up, he had a like care of him. He went to school with him, but so that he could never be seen, either by him-

self, or any others, in all his life. Afterwards, he
travelled into Italy; he accompanied him, and whensoever any evil was like to happen to him, either on the
road or in the inn, he was perceived to foretell it by
some touch or stroke; he drew off his boots as a servant; if he turned his journey another way, he continued
with him, having the same care of him in foretelling
evil.   At length he was made a canon, and as, on a
time, he was sitting and feasting with his friends, in
much jollity, a vehement stroke was struck on a sudden
on the table, so that they were all terrified.   Presently the canon said to his friends, ' Be not afraid;
some great evil hangs over my head.'   The next day
he fell into a great fever, and the fit continued on him
for three whole days, till he died miserably."

Captain Henry Bell, in his narrative prefixed to
Luther's "Table," printed in English, anno 1652,
having acquainted us how the German copy printed of
it had been discovered underground, where it had lain
fifty-two years, that edition having been suppressed by
an edict of the Emperor Rudolphus II., so that it was
death to keep a copy thereof; and having told us that
Casparus Van Spar, a German gentleman, with whom
he was familiarly acquainted while he negotiated affairs
in Germany for King James I., was the person who
discovered it, anno 1626, and transmitted it to England to him, and earnestly desired him to translate
the said book into English, says, he accordingly set
upon the translation of it many times, but was always
hindered from proceeding in it by some intervening
business.   About six weeks after he had received the
copy, being in bed with his wife one night, between
twelve and one o'clock, she being asleep, but himself
awake, there appeared to him an ancient man, standing
at his bedside arrayed all in white, having a long and
broad white beard hanging down to his girdle, who,

taking him by his right ear, said thus to him, " Sirrah !
will you not take time to translate that book, which is
sent to you out of Germany ? I will shortly provide
for you both place and time to do it." And then he
vanished. Hereupon, being much affrighted, he fell
into an extreme sweat, so that his wife, awaking and
finding him all over wet, she asked him what he ailed ?
He told her what he had seen and heard ; but he never
regarded visions or dreams, and so the same fell out of
his mind. But a fortnight after, being on a Sunday,
at his lodgings in King Street, Westminster, at dinner
with his wife, two messengers were sent from the whole
council board, with a warrant to carry him to the Gate-
house, Westminster, there to be kept till further order
from the lords of the council ; upon which warrant he
was kept there ten whole years, close prisoner, where he
spent five years of it in translating the said book, having
good cause to be mindful of the old man's saying,
" I will shortly provide for you both place and time to
translate it."

Though the perception of spirits chiefly affects the
hearing and seeing faculties, yet are not the other
senses without some participation of these genial
objects, whether good or evil ; for, as St Austin
says, the evil work of the devil creeps through all
the passages of the senses ; he presents himself in
figures, applies himself to colours, adheres to sounds,
introduces odours, infuses himself in savours, and fills
all the passages of intelligence ; sometimes cruelly
tormenting with grief and fear, sometimes sportingly
diverting man, or taunting with mocks. And on
the other hand, as the learned Walter Hilton, a great
master of contemplative life, in his "Scale of Perfection," sets forth, that appearances or representations
to the corporeal senses may be both good and evil.

But before I conclude upon this head, to give still

more weight and authority to the perception we have had of these genii, both by the senses of hearing and seeing, I will relate two very remarkable fragments of history of this kind, told us by persons who demand our credit, and done within the memory of our grandfathers and fathers.

The first is concerning that Duke of Buckingham who was stabbed by Felton, August the 23rd, 1628.

Mr Lilly, the astrologer, in his book entitled " Monarchy and no Monarchy in England," printed in quarto, 1651, having mentioned the Duke of Buckingham, writes as follows :—" Since I am upon the death of the Duke of Buckingham, I shall relate a true story of his being admonished often of the death he should die in this manner :

" An aged gentleman, one Parker, as I now remember, having formerly belonged unto the duke, or of great acquaintance with the duke's father, and now retired, had a demon appeared several times to him in the shape of Sir George Villiers, the duke's father. This demon walked many times in Parker's bedchamber, without any action or terror, noise, hurt, or speech ; but, at last, one night broke out in these words : ' Mr Parker, I know you loved me formerly, and my son George at this time very well. I would have you go from me (you know me very well to be his father, old Sir George Villiers of Leicestershire), and acquaint him with these and these particulars, &c., and that he above all refrain the counsel and company of such and such (whom he then nominated), or else he will come to destruction, and that suddenly.' Parker, though a very discreet man, partly imagined himself in a dream all this time : and being unwilling to proceed upon no better grounds, forbore addressing himself to the duke ; for he conceived, if he should acquaint the duke with the words of his father, and the manner of his appearance to him (such apparitions being not usual), he should be laughed at, and thought to dote, in regard he was aged.   Some few nights passed without further trouble to the old man; but, not very many nights after, old Sir George Villiers appeared again, walked quick and furiously in the room, seemed angry with Parker, and at last said, 'Mr Parker, I thought you had been my friend so much, and loved my son George so well, that you would have acquainted him with what I desired, but I know you have not done it; by all the friendship that ever was betwixt you and me, and the great respect you bear my son, I desire you to deliver what I formerly commanded you to my son.'   The old man, seeing himself thus solicited, promised the demon he would, but first argued it thus, that the duke was not easy to be spoken withal, and that he would account him a vain man to come with such a message from the dead; nor did he conceive the duke would give any credit to him: to which the demon thus answered: 'If he will not believe you have this discourse from me, tell him of such a secret (and named it) which he knows none in the world ever knew but myself and him.'   Mr Parker being now well satisfied that he was not asleep, and that the apparition was not a vain delusion, took a fit opportunity, and seriously acquainted the duke with his father's words, and the manner of his apparition. The duke laughed heartily at the relation, which put old Parker to a stand, but at last he assumed courage, and told the duke that he acquainted his father's ghost with what he found now to be true, viz., scorn and derision: 'But, my lord,' says he, 'your father bid me acquaint you by this token, and he said it was such as none in the world but your two selves did yet know.'   Hereat the duke was amazed and much astonished, but took no warning or notice thereof, keeping the same company still, advising with such counsellors, and performing such actions as his father by Parker countermanded. Shortly after, old Sir George Villiers, in a very quiet but sorrowful posture, appears again to Parker, and said, 'Mr Parker, I know you delivered my words to George my son; I thank you for so doing, but he slighted them, and now I only request this more at your hands, that once again you repair to my son, and tell him that if he will not amend and follow the counsel I have given him, this knife or dagger (and with that he pulled a knife or dagger from under his gown) shall end him; and do you, Mr Parker, set your house in order, for you shall die at such a time.' Mr Parker once more engaged, though very unwillingly, to acquaint the duke with the last message, and so did; but the duke told him to trouble him no further with such messages and dreams, and told him he perceived he was now an old man and doted; and within a month after, meeting Mr Parker on Lambeth Bridge, said, 'Now, Mr Parker, what say you of your dream?' who only returned, 'Sir, I wish it may never have success,' &c.; but, within six weeks after, he was stabbed with a knife, according to his father's admonition beforehand, and Mr Parker died soon after he had seen the dream or vision performed."

This relation is inserted also in the great Lord Clarendon's History, and in Sir Richard Baker's Chronicle. The Lord Clarendon, in his history, vol. i. l. 1, having given some relations, says that, amongst others, there was one (meaning this of Parker) which was upon a better foundation of credit than usually such discourses are founded upon; and he tells us that Parker was an officer in the king's wardrobe in Windsor Castle, of a good reputation for honesty and discretion, and then about the age of fifty years or more. This man had in his youth been bred in a school in the parish where Sir George Villiers, the father of the duke, lived, and had been much cherished and obliged in that season of his age by the said Sir George, whom afterwards he never saw.   About six months before the miserable end of the Duke of Buckingham the apparition was seen; after the third appearance he made a journey to London, where the court then was; he was very well known to Sir Ralph Freeman, one of the masters of the requests, who had married a lady that was nearly allied to the duke, and was himself well received by him.   He informed the duke with the reputation and honesty of the man, and Sir Ralph Freeman carried the man the next morning, by five of the clock, to Lambeth, according to the duke's appointment, and there presented him to the duke, who received him courteously at his landing, and walked in conference near an hour with him, and Sir Ralph's and the duke's servants at such a distance that they heard not a word; but Sir Ralph always fixed his eyes on the duke, who sometimes spoke with great commotion and disorder; and the man told Sir Ralph in their return over the water, that when he mentioned those particulars that were to gain him credit, the duke's colour changed, and he swore he could come to that knowledge only by the devil; for that those particulars were known only to himself and to one person more, who he was sure would never speak of them.   So far the Lord Clarendon.

I will now subjoin an authentic relation which Mr Beaumont tells us at the end of his book of genii or familiar spirits, printed in the year 1705, he had just before received from the mouth of the then Bishop of Gloucester himself.   It is as follows, word for word:—

 " Sir Charles Lee, by his first lady, had only one

daughter, of which she died in childbirth; and when she died, her sister, the Lady Everard, desired to have the education of the child; and she was by her very well educated till she was marriageable, and a match was concluded for her with Sir William Perkins, but was then prevented in an extraordinary manner. Upon a Thursday night, she, thinking she saw a light in her chamber after she was in bed, knocked for her maid, who presently came to her, and she asked why she left a candle burning in her chamber? The maid said she left none, and there was none but what she brought with her at that time. Then she said it was the fire; but that the maid told her was quite out, and said she believed it was only a dream; whereupon she said it might be so, and composed herself again to sleep; but about two of the clock she was awakened again, and saw the apparition of a little woman between her curtain and her pillow, who told her she was her mother, and that she was happy, and that by twelve of the clock that day she should be with her; whereupon she knocked again for her maid, called for her clothes, and when she was dressed, went into her closet, and came not out again till nine, and then brought out with her a letter sealed to her father; brought it to her aunt, the Lady Everard; told her what had happened, and desired that, as soon as she was dead, it might be sent to him. But the lady thought she was suddenly fallen mad, and thereupon sent presently away to Chelmsford for a physician and surgeon, who both came immediately, but the physician could discern no indication of what the lady imagined, or of any indisposition of her body; notwithstanding the lady would needs have her let blood, which was done accordingly; and when the young woman had patiently let them do what they would with her, she desired that the chaplain might be called to read prayers, and when prayers were ended she took her guitar and psalm-book and sat down upon a chair without arms, and played and sung so melodiously and admirably, that her music-master, who was then there, admired at it; and near the stroke of twelve she rose and sat herself down in a great chair with arms, and presently fetching a strong breathing or two, immediately expired, and was so suddenly cold as was much wondered at by the physician and surgeon. She died at Waltham, in Essex, three miles from Chelmsford, and the letter was sent to Sir Charles at his house in Warwickshire; but he was so afflicted with the death of his daughter, that he came not till she was buried; but when he came, he caused her to be taken up, and to be buried by her mother at Edmonton, as she desired in her letter." This was about the year one thousand six hundred and sixty-two or sixty-three; and this relation the Right Reverend the Lord Bishop of Gloucester had from Sir Charles Lee himself; and Mr. Beaumont printed it in his book above-mentioned, from the bishop's own mouth.

The relations which I have given above are not like the trifling accounts too often given of these things, and therefore causing grave ones to be ridiculed in common with them. They are of that nature that, whoever attempts to ridicule them, will, instead of turning them into jest, become the object of ridicule himself.

The first story, which has in it such amazing circumstances, and such uncommon and dreadful incidents concerning the butler in Ireland, is (as the reader sees) attested by no less a personage than an Earl of Orrery, two bishops, and many other noblemen and gentlemen, being present and eye-witnesses of what the earl said. What greater testimony would the most incredulous have? They say such things are told for interest; what interest could an earl and many noblemen have in promoting such an imposture? The incredulous say likewise, great and learned men delight sometimes in putting frauds upon the world, and after laugh at their credulity; would a number of noble laymen choose two prelates to carry on such a fraud? And would two pious bishops probably combine with several, and some servants there present, in spreading such a deceit? It is past believing, and it demands the strictest of moral faith that can be given, to the most unquestioned history that the pen of man ever wrote.

The second story is founded, first, upon the experience of one of the most ingenious men of that age, Dr Donne, and then upon the proof made by his friend, Sir Robert Drury, who could at first scarce believe it; and shall we doubt the credit of men whose company (for their credit be it spoken) a British ambassador was proud of gaining?

The third story is told by Luther himself, who began the great work of the Reformation.

The fourth is told by one that was a king's public minister, and told from his own trial of the matter, where he could have no interest in the telling it.

The fifth is related by those great historians the Lord Clarendon and Sir Richard Baker, as a truth relied upon by themselves, and fit to be credited by their readers.

The sixth and last was related to Mr Beaumont by the Lord Bishop of Gloucester, who received the account from Sir Charles Lee himself, to whose granddaughter the matter happened.

Men who will not believe such things as these, so well attested to us, and given us by such authorities, because they did not see them themselves, nor anything of the like nature, ought not only to deny the demon of Socrates, but that there was such a man as Socrates himself; they should not dispute the genii of Cæsar, Cicero, Brutus, Mark Antony, but avow that there were never any such men existing upon earth, and overthrow all credible history whatsoever. Meanwhile all men, but those who run such lengths in their fantastical incredulity, will, from the facts abovementioned, rest satisfied that there are such things as evil and good genii, and that men have sometimes a commerce with them by all their senses, particularly those of seeing and hearing, and will not therefore be startled at the strange fragments of histories which I am going to relate of our young Duncan Campbell, and look upon some wonderful adventures which he performed by the intervention of his familiar demon or genius, as falsehoods, only because they are uncommon and surprising ; more especially since they were not done in a corner, but by an open way of profession of a predictor of things, in the face of the metropolis of London, where he settled young, as will appear in the progress of his life. However, some people, notwithstanding all this, may allege that though a man may have a genius appear to him so as to convey into his mind, through his senses, the knowledge of things that are to come to pass, yet this happens but on very eminent and extraordinary occasions. The murder, for example, of a prime minister, and the favourite of a monarch, in such a manner as it was performed on the great Buckingham by Felton, was a thing so uncommon that it might perhaps deserve, by the permission of heaven, an uncommon prediction. The others likewise are instances eminent in their way, particularly that of the Lady Everard's niece ; for that young lady being then marriageable, and a treaty for that end being on foot with Sir William Perkins, the divine Providence foreseeing that such a state might call away her thoughts, hitherto bent on Him and spiritual affairs, and fix them on the trifles of this world, might perhaps permit her to be called by a holy mother to a state of happiness she before her enjoyed, lest her daughter's mind should change, and she go into the ways of a sinner. But if these super-eminent, these scarce and rare examples, may be admitted of man's holding a conversation with the spiritualised beings of another world, it will, however, be far below the dignity of human reasons, methinks, to make such large concessions to people who pretend to converse that wonderful way, as to allow them the credit of being able to do it upon every slight occasion, and every indifferent occurrence of human life.

I cannot help acknowledging that a man of wisdom may, at first thought, make such an objection; but reflection will presently retract it, and the same good sense that taught him to make an objection so well upon the first thought, will teach him, upon second thoughts, to acquiesce in the answer.

Infants may have, no doubt, the benefit of such an attending genius, as well as people more advanced in years; as may be seen in one of the instances, which is a very famous one, relating to the boy born in Prussia, who was attended by one constantly from the time of his birth to his death. Besides, it is a mistake in the understanding to imagine that death, which is the determination and end of life, is of more consequence to be known than the manner of regulating that life; for in reality, according to the right way of considering, death, or the determination of a man's life, derives its importance from the steps which he took in the due regulation of it; and therefore every the least step proper to be taken for the due regulation of life, is of more consequence to be known than the death of a person, though this at first sight carries the face of significance, and the other nothing better than the look of a trifle. Marriage, for example, is a step in life of the utmost importance, whether we consider that estate with regard to this or the next world. Death is but the finishing of one person, but marriage may be the introducing of many into the world with happiness; it is therefore a thing of more importance to be known beforehand, and consequently more worthy of the communication of a genius to the man with whom he conversed. Possidonius tells us that a certain Rhodian dying, nominated six of his equals, and said who should die first, who next, and so on, and the event answered the prediction; why then (though some people are apt to make a jest of it) may not a man, by the intervention of his good genius, tell a woman that is to have six husbands who she shall have first, who next, and so on, and the event answer the prediction? If men of learning may acquire such knowledge as to attain to extraordinary things by their ordinary faculties, why may not ordinary things be taught others in this extraordinary way? For will anybody say that it is easier for a man to accommodate himself to the knowledge of a demon or genius than for a demon or genius to accommodate himself to the knowledge of a man? Certain it is, indeed, that if this good genius (that induces a man with a prophetic kind of science) be anything resembling a good angel, the primary end of his being permitted to direct mankind, must consist in things relating more to their welfare hereafter; yet I know not why they may not sometimes inspire or openly direct them in human knowledge and in things relating to human life, so they are of a good tendency, more especially since a good inspiration may be a counterbalance to the bad knowledge which some have been inspired with by evil spirits. I would not be thought to go too far in a point of this nature, and have therefore (though perhaps I could say much more if I followed entirely my own private opinion, and would venture to introduce it here, in order to communicate it to others, and make it a public one) said no more on this head than what divines generally teach.

But the most unexceptionable mistress that teaches these things to be in Nature is experience. If we had very many people gifted this way, the extraordinary thing would have become ordinary, and therefore I cannot help wondering that it should be so ordinary a thing for wise men themselves to wonder too much at things because they are extraordinary, and suspect them as frauds because they are uncommon.

There has scarce been any period of time in which some person of this prophetic class has not existed, and has not been consulted by the greatest of men, and their predictions found at the long run to come true. Ignorant men always rise to their belief of them by experience, and the most learned men submit their great opinions to experience; but your men of middling talents, who make up their want of reason with bustling obstinacy and noisy contradiction, have been and still continue to be their own opposers; and without discovering the reason for what they say, they content themselves with having the laugh on their sides, and barely affirming without proving that it is a kind of ideal juggle, and intellectual legerdemain, by which these modern predictors impose things upon the eye and reason, as the corporeal eye is imposed upon by sleight of hand; but it is a strange thing that men of such quick reason cannot give us a sample of the frauds. Thus I remember to have read, I cannot tell where, a story of some courtiers, who, when a great artist of legerdemain was to act before the king, pretended to be so quick-sighted, that nothing he did should escape their discovery, were left by his nimble fingers in the dark, and forced at last, with blushes, to own they had no better eyes than other people. In a word, if people will be led by suspicions and remote possibilities of fraud and contrivance of such men, all historical truth shall be ended, when it consists not with a man's private humour or prejudice to admit it. Now, therefore, to prove by experience and undeniable testimonies, that these kind of genii will submit to little offices in order to bring men to greater good, I will give the reader three or four curious passages that will set the reasonable reader at ease and prepare him for reading the passages of Mr. Campbell's life with pleasure, and as a fine history of wonderful facts, that though they seem to surpass belief yet ought to have his credit.

What in nature can be more trivial than for a spirit to employ himself in knocking on a morning at the wainscot by the bed's head of a man who got drunk over night, according to the way that such things are ordinarily explained? And yet I shall give you such a relation of this, that not even the most devout and precise Presbyterian will offer to call in question, for Mr Baxter, in his historical discourse of apparitions, writes thus :—

"There is now in London an understanding, sober, pious man, oft one of my hearers, who has an elder brother, a gentleman of considerable rank, who, having formerly seemed pious, of late years does often fall into the sin of drunkenness. He often lodges long together here in his brother's house; and whensoever he is drunk and has slept himself sober, something knocks at his bed's head, as if one knocked on a wainscot; when they remove his bed it follows him; besides other loud noises, on other parts where he is, that all the house hears, they have often watched him, and kept his hands lest he should do it himself. His brother has often told it me, and brought his wife, a discreet woman, to attest it; who avers, moreover, that as she watched him, she has seen his shoes under the bed taken up, and nothing visible to touch them. They brought the man himself to me, and when we asked him how he dare sin again after such a warning, he had no excuse; but being persons of quality, for some special reason of worldly interest I must not name him.

"Two things are remarkable in this instance," says Mr Baxter; "first, what a powerful thing temptation and fleshly concupiscence is, and what an hardened heart sin brings men to; if one rose from the dead to warn such sinners, it would not of itself persuade them."

"Secondly," says Mr Baxter, "it poses me to think what kind of spirit this is, that has such a care of this man's soul, which makes me hope he will recover. Do good spirits dwell so near us, or are they sent on such messages? or is it his guardian angel? or is it the soul of some dead friend that suffers, and yet retaining love to him, as Dives to his brethren, would have him saved? God yet keeps such things from us in the dark."

So far we have the authority of the renowned and famous Mr Baxter, who makes this knocking of the spirit at the bed's head (though what we commonly call frivolous) an important errand.

Another relation of this kind was sent to Mr John Beaumont (whom I myself personally know), and which he has inserted in his account of genii, or familiar spirits, in a letter by an ingenious and learned clergyman of Wiltshire, who had given him the relation likewise before by word of mouth. It is as follows :—

"Near eighty years since, in the parish of Wilcot (which is by the Devizes), in the vicar's house, there was heard for a considerable time the sound of a bell constantly tolling every night; the occasion was this. A debauched person who lived in the parish came one night very late and demanded the keys of the church of the vicar, that he might ring a peal, which the vicar refused to let him have, alleging the unseasonableness of the time, and that he should, by granting his desires, give a disturbance to Sir George Wroughton and his family, whose house adjoined to the churchyard. Upon this refusal the fellow went away in a rage, threatening to be revenged of the vicar, and going some time after to the Devizes, met with one Cantle or Cantlow, a person noted in those days for a wizard, and he tells him how the vicar had served him, and begs his help to be even with him. The reply Cantlow made him was this: ' Does he not love ringing ? He shall have enough of it.' And from that time a bell began to toll in his house, and continued so to do till Cantlow's death, who confessed at Fisherton Gaol in Sarum (where he was confined by King James during his life), that he caused that sound, and that it should be heard in that place during life. The thing was so notorious that persons came from all parts to hear it, and King James sent a gentleman from London on purpose to give him satisfaction concerning the truth of the report.'' Mr Beaumont had likewise this story, as he tells, from the mouth of Sir George Wroughton's own son, with this remarkable circumstance, that if any in the house put their heads out of the window they could not hear the sound, but heard it immediately again as soon as they stood in the room.

The reader here sees that good and bad genii exercise themselves upon very little functions, knocking at beds'-heads and ringing of bells. For proof of this we have the testimonies of two divines, of a man of quality and probity, and the same satisfaction that a learned king had, who sent to inquire into the matter ; and after this there can be, I think, no room for doubt.

But to carry the point still nearer home, inasmuch as I know some will leave no stone unturned to make the extraordinary actions which the person whose life I write has performed appear impostures, and inasmuch as for this end they may say that though many people may have been gifted in this extraordinary manner, yet not so as to make a profession of it, and therefore from thence they take their suspicions, I shall in this place, to remove every nicest scruple they can have touching this affair, give the reader one instance of this kind likewise before I proceed with my history.

There lived not many years since a very aged gentlewoman, in London, in Water Lane, by Fleet Street, whose name was Pight, who was endowed with a prophetic spirit. And the ingenious Mr Beaumont, whom I personally knew, and who had a familiar genius himself, gives the world this account of her. "She was very well known," says he, "to many persons of my acquaintance now living in London. Among others, a gentleman, whose candour I can no way suspect, has told me that he often resorted to her, as to an oracle; and that as soon as he came into her presence, she would usually tell him that she knew what he was coming for, for that she had seen his spirit for some time before. And without his saying anything to her, she would commonly tell him what the business was which he came to consult her about, and what the event of it would be, which he always found to fall out as she said; and many other persons now living can testify the like experience of her as to themselves."

Before I conclude this chapter, I am willing to give the public one further little history of the like kind with the foregoing ones, with this only difference, that if it be valued according to the worth the world has always attributed to the very ingenious person whom it concerns, it will be far the most famous of them all, and therefore fittest to finish this chapter, and to crown this part of the work, in which we are showing that persons have had a perception of genii or spirits, not visible at the same time to others.

The famous Torquatus Tasso, prince of the Italian poets, and scarce inferior to the immortal Virgil himself, and who seems to enjoy the intermingled gifts of the most accurate judgment of this Latin poet, and the more fertile and copious invention and fancy of the Greek one, Homer, strongly asserted his own experience in this kind. His life was written and published in French, anno 1692, by D. C. D. D. V., who, in his preface, tells us, that in what he writ, he has followed chiefly the history given us in Italian by John Baptista Manso, a Neapolitan gentleman, who had been a very intimate friend to Tasso. In his life, among other things, he acquaints us that Tasso was naturally of that melancholic temperament which has always made the greatest men, and that this temperament being aggravated by many hardships he had undergone, it made him sometimes beside himself, and that those melancholy vapours being despatched, he came again to himself, like those that return from fits of the falling sickness, his spirit being as free as before. That near his latter end he retired from the city of Naples to his friend Manso, at Bisaccia, a small town in the kingdom of Naples, where Manso had a considerable estate, and passed an autumn there in the diversions of the season.

And here the French author gives us an account of Tasso's sensible perception of a genius as follows:— As after these amusements he usually retired to his chamber to entertain himself there with his friend Manso, the latter had the opportunity to inquire into one of the most singular effects of Tasso's melancholy (of this heroic melancholy, as I may call it), which raised and brightened his spirit, so far it was from depressing or rendering it obscure, and which among the ancients would have reasonably caused them to have ascribed a familiar demon to him, as to Socrates. They were often in a warm debate concerning this spirit, with which Tasso pretended to have so free a communication. "I am too much your friend," said Manso to him one day, "not to let you know what the world thinks of you concerning this thing, and what I think of it myself. Is it possible that, being enlightened as you are, you should be fallen into so great a weakness as to think you have a familiar spirit? and will you give your enemies that advantage to be able to prove, by your own acknowledgment, what they have already published to the world? You know they say you did not publish your 'Dialogue of the Messenger' as a fiction; but you would have men believe that the spirit which you make to speak there was a real and true spirit; hence men have drawn this injurious consequence, that your studies have embroiled your imagination, so that there is made in it a confused mixture of the fictions of the poets, the inventions of the philosophers, and the doctrine of religion."

"I am not ignorant," answered Tasso, " of all that is spread abroad in the world on the account of my 'Dialogue.' I have taken care divers times to disabuse my friends, both by letter and word of mouth. I prevented even the malignity of my enemies, as you know, at the time I published my 'Dialogue.' Men could not be ignorant that I composed it for the young Prince of Mantua, to whom I would explain, after an agreeable manner, the principal mysteries of the Platonic philosophy. It was at Mantua itself, after my second flight from Ferrara, that I formed the idea of it, and I committed it to paper a little after my unfortunate return. I addressed it to this prince, and all men might have read in the epistle dedicatory the protestation I there make that this 'Dialogue' being written according to the doctrine of the Platonics, which is not always conformable to revealed truths, men must not confound what I expose there as a philosopher with what I believe as a Christian. This distinction is by so much the more reasonable, that at that time nothing extraordinary had happened to me, and I spake not of any apparition. This can be attested by all those with whom I lodged, or whom I frequented in this voyage, and therefore there is no reason for confounding the fiction of my 'Dialogue' with what has happened to me since."—"I am persuaded of all you say to me," replied Manso, "but truly I cannot be of what you believe at present concerning yourself. Will you imagine that you are in commerce with a spirit? And I ask you of what order is that spirit? Shall we place him in the number of the rebels, whom their pride precipitated into the abyss? or of the intelligences, who continued firm in faith and submission to their Creator? For there is no mean to take in the true religion, and we must not fall into the extravagances of the gnomes and sylphs of the Cabalists.

"Now, the spirit in question cannot be a demon. You own that, instead of inspiring you with anything contrary to piety and religion, he often fortifies in you the maxims of Christianity; he strengthens your faith by profound reasonings, and has the same respect with you for sacred names and things. Neither can you say that it is an angel, for though you have always led a regular life, and far from all dissoluteness, though for some years past you have applied yourself, after a particular manner, to the duties of a true Christian, you will agree with me that these sorts of favours are not common, that a man must have attained to a high degree of sanctity, and not be far from the pureness of celestial spirits, to merit a familiar converse and bear a harmony with them. Believe me, there is nothing in all these discourses which you imagine you have with this spirit. You know better than any man those symptoms which the black humours wherewith you are tormented causes in you. Your vapours are the source of your visions, and yourself would not judge otherwise of another person to whom a like thing should happen, and you will come to this in your own respect also, if you will make a mature reflection, and apply yourself to blot out, by an effort of reason, these imaginations which the violence of your evil effect causes in you."—"You may have reason," replied Tasso, "to think so of the things that pass in me ; but as to myself, who have a sensible perception of them, I am forced to reason after another manner. If it were true that the spirit did not show himself to me but in the violent assault of my vapours ; if he offered to my imagination but wandering and confused species, without connection or due sequel ; if he used to me frivolous reasonings which ended in nothing ; or if, having begun some solid reasoning, he broke it off on a sudden and left me in darkness, I should believe with you that all things that pass are but mere dreams and phantoms ; but it is quite otherwise : this spirit is a spirit of truth and reason, and of a truth so distinct, of a reason so sublime, that he raises me often to knowledges that are above all my reasonings, though they appear to me no less clear ; that he teaches me things which, in my most profound meditations, never came into my spirit, and which I never heard of any man, nor read in any book. This spirit, therefore, is somewhat of real ; of whatsoever order he be I hear and see him, nevertheless for its being impossible for me to comprehend and define him." Manso did not yield to these facts which Tasso would have passed for proofs. He pressed him with new questions, which were not without answers. "Since you will not believe me on my word," said Tasso to him another day, after having well disputed, "I must convince you by your own eyes that these things are not pure imaginations." And the next day, conversing together in the same chamber, Manso perceived that on a sudden he fixed his eyes towards the window, and that he stood as it were immovable; he called to him and jogged him many times, but instead of answering him—"See there the spirit," says Tasso at last, "that has been pleased to come and visit me, and to entertain himself with me; look on him, and you will acknowledge the truth of what I say."

Manso, somewhat surprised, cast his eyes towards the place he showed him, and perceived nothing but the rays of the sun passing through the glass, nor did he see anything in all the chamber, though he cast his eyes round it with curiosity, and he desired him to show him the spirit, which he looked for in vain, while he heard Tasso speak with much vehemency. He declares in a letter which he wrote concerning this to the Admiral of Naples, that he really heard no other voice but Tasso's own; but they were sometimes questions made by him to the pretended spirit, sometimes answers that he made to the pretended questions of the spirit, and which were couched in such admirable terms, so efficacious concerning subjects so elevated and so extraordinary, that he was ravished with admiration, and dared not to interrupt him. He hearkened therefore attentively, and being quite beside himself at this mysterious conversation, which ended at last by a recess of the spirit, as he found by the last words of Tasso; after which Tasso, turning himself to him, "Well," said he, "are your doubts at last dissipated?" —"On the contrary," answered Manso, "I am more embroiled than ever. I have truly heard wonderful things, but you have not showed me what you promised me."—"You have seen and heard," resumed Tasso, "perhaps more than——" He stopped here, and Manso, who could not recover himself of his surprise, and had his head filled with the ideas of this extraordinary entertainment, found himself not in a condition to press him farther. Meanwhile he engaged himself not to speak a word to any man of these things he had heard, with a design to make them public, though he should have liberty granted him. They had many other conversations concerning this matter, after which Manso owned he was brought to that pass that he knew not what to think or say, only that if it were a weakness in his friend to believe these visions, he much feared it would prove contagious to him, and that he should become at last as credulous as himself.

Dr Beaumont, who is still living, and with whom I have had formerly some acquaintance myself, has set down among the others this relation at large concerning Tasso, and gives this reason for it :—"Because," says the doctor, "I think it contains a sufficient answer to what many learned friends have said to myself on the like occasion."

Perhaps it may not be ungrateful to the reader if I subjoin here the short eulogium written on Tasso by the famous Thuanus, which is as follows :—

"Torquatus Tasso died about the forty-fifth year of his age, a man of a wonderful and prodigious wit, who was seized with an incurable fury in his youth, when he lived at the court of Ferrara, and nevertheless, in lucid intervals, he wrote many things both in verse and prose with so much judgment, elegance, and extreme correctness of style, that he turned at length that pity which many men had conceived for him, into an amazement; while by that fury which in others makes their

F

minds outrageous, or dulls them after it was over, his understanding became as it were more purified, more ready in inventing things, more acute in aptly disposing them after they were invented, and more copious in adorning them with choice words and weight of sentences; and that which a man of the soundest sense would scarce excogitate at his leisure, with the greatest labour and care imaginable, he, after a violent agitation of the mind set beside itself, naturally performed with a wonderful felicity, so that he did not seem struck with an alienation of mind, but with a divine fury. He that knows not these things, which all men know that have been in Italy, and concerning which himself sometimes complains, though modestly, in his writings, let him read his divine works, and he must necessarily conclude either that I speak of another man than Tasso, or that these things were written by another man than Tasso."

After having given my readers so many memorable accounts concerning the perception men have had in all ages, and still continue to have, of genii or familiar spirits, by all the senses, as seeing, hearing, &c., which accounts have been attested by men of the greatest learning and quality, if any of them still remain dissatisfied I am contented, and desire them for their punishment to lay down the book before they arrive at the more pleasant parts of it, which are yet to come, and not to read one tittle farther. These unbelieving gentlemen shall then be at liberty, according as their different spirits dictate, to ridicule me in the same manner as many more learned and greater men than I have been satirised before my time by persons of a like infidel temper, who would fain pass incredulity upon the world as wisdom; and they may, with all the freedom in nature, bestow upon me those merry appellations which I very well know such extraordinary free-

thinkers imagine to belong of right to any author that
either believes himself, or would possess the world with
an opinion and belief that there is such a thing as the
holding commerce and conversation, in this habitable
world, with genii and familiar spirits. I shall only
first tell them all I have to say to terminate the dispute
between them and me.

Those who, to give themselves the air and appearance
of men of solid wisdom and gravity, load other men,
who believe in spirits, with the titles of being men of
folly, levity, or melancholy, are desired to learn, that
the same folly (as they are pleased to term it) of
opinion is to be found in the greatest men of learning
that ever existed in the universe. Let them, in order
to be convinced of this, read Apuleius's book, " De
Deo Socrat. ; " Censorinus's book, " De Die Nat.,"
c. 3 ; Porphyrius, in his book " De Abstinentia ; "
Agrippa, in his treatise " De Occult. Phil.," l. 3,
c. 22, and also c. 21 ; Natalis Comes in his " Myth.,"
l. 4, c. 3 ; Maraviglia, in his " Pseudomantia," Dissertation 9 and 11, and Animadversion 10 ; Plato, in his
" Timæus " and " Cratylus ; " Ammianus Marcellinus's
" History," book 21 ; Hieronimus Cardanus, in his
book " De Vitâ Propriâ," c. 47 ; the great Kircher, in
his " Œdipus Ægyptiacus," vol. 3, p. 474 ; Pausanias,
in " Cliac. Poster. ; " that immortal orator, Cicero, lib.
1, " De Divinatione ; " lib. 2, " De Naturâ Deorum ; "
the " Histoire Prodigieuse," written by Père Arnault ;
and a book entitled " Lux e Tenebris," which is a
collection of modern visions and prophecies in Germany,
by several persons ; translated into Latin by Jo. Amos.
Comenius, printed at Amsterdam, 1655. And if they
will be at the pains of having due recourse to these
quotations, they will find, that all these men, whose
learning is unquestionable, and most of whom have
been in firm and undisputed possession of fame for

many centuries, have all unanimously agreed in this opinion (how foolish soever they may think it), that there ever was and ever would be a communication held between some select men and genii or familiar spirits. I must therefore desire their pardon if I rejoice to see them remain wise by themselves, and that I continue to be esteemed by them a fool among so much good company.

Others, out of a mere contempt of religion, or cowardly, for fear of being thought pusillanimous by men, turn bravoes to Heaven, and laugh at every notion of spirits as imbibed from the nurse or imposed upon us by priests, and may top these lines upon us with an elegant and a convincing magisterial sneer, though the divine Socrates was of our opinion, and even experienced it to be true, having a genius himself.

> The priests but finish what the nurse began
> And thus the child imposes on the man.

These bring into my mind a saying of Sir Roger l'Estrange on Seneca, which I must apply to Socrates: I join in opinion with a Christian heathen, while they remain heathen Christians.

The third sort, out of a pretended veneration to religion and divinity, may call me superstitious and chimerical. To them I answer, I will continue chimerical and superstitious with St Austin, who gives the same opinion in his "Civitate Dei" with Ludovicus Vives; let them be solider and more religious divines than St Austin in disowning it. Thus I bid these austere critics heartily farewell; but let my better-natured readers go on and find a new example of this conversation, being held with the genii by our Duncan Campbell.

Chapter vi.

A narrative of Mr Campbell's coming to London and taking upon him the profession of a predictor ; together with an account of many strange things that came to pass just as he foretold.

TO proceed on regularly with the life of young Duncan Campbell, I must let the reader know that he continued thus conversing with his little genius, as is set forth above in the dialogue he had with me, and predicting many things of the like nature, as I have described, till the year 1694, when he was just fourteen years of age, and then he left Scotland.

But before I come to speak of the manner of his departure from thence, his half-native country, inasmuch as his father was of that country, and he had his education there (what education he could have, being deaf and dumb) ; I must let the reader know that in the year 1692, my very good friend Mrs Campbell, his mother-in-law, died, and left him there at Edinburgh, an orphan of twelve years of age. He was, I may venture to say, the most beautiful boy of that age I ever knew ; and the sensible reader, who considers a child of good birth, with the misfortunes of being deaf and dumb, left fatherless and motherless in the wide world, at twelve years old, without any competency for his maintenance and support, without any relations, in a manner, that knew him or assisted him, all the little fortune his father had having been lost in the civil commotions in Scotland, as I have related above, need not hear me describe the compassion I and many more had for him, because such a reader must certainly feel in his own bosom the same lively acts of pity and commiseration, at the hearing of such a mishap, as I

had at the seeing it, or at least as I have now revived
afresh within me at the relating it.

However, it came so to pass, that a person of the
name of Campbell, and who was a distant relation of
the boy, though he himself was but in indifferent circumstances, was resolved to see him provided for one
way or another, in a manner somewhat suitable to his
condition, and till that time to take the best care of
him himself that he was able.

Several ladies of quality, who had known his perfections, coveted to make the boy one of their domestics,
as a page, or a playfellow to their children ; for though
he could not speak, he had such a vivacity in all his
actions, such a sprightliness of behaviour, and such a
merriment accompanying all his gestures, that he afforded
more entertainment than the prettiest and wittiest little
prattlers at those years are wont to do.   Mr Campbell
had certainly accepted of some of these fortunate offers
for his little cousin, which were many of them likely
to prove very advantageous, if it had not been put in
his head by some friends, particularly myself, that if he
had a mind to dispose of the boy in that manner, the
best way he could take would be to present him to the
late Earl of Argyll, who for his name's sake, and
his father's sake, as well as the qualifications and
endowments of the boy, would more naturally (according to all probability) take a greater pleasure and
delight in him, and consequently provide better for
him, and with a more lasting care, than any other
person of quality that had a sudden liking to him,
which might change, and took him as a stranger out of
a bare curiosity.   Mr Campbell was by these reasons
overruled in the disposal of his little dumb prophetical cousin, as he called him, and resolved that
an offer should be made of him to the present illustrious Duke of Argyll's most noble father.   But it so

unfortunately happened, that the earl making very much a longer stay at London than was expected, Mr Campbell, the uncle, sent our young Duncan Campbell, his nephew, handsomely accoutred, and with a handsome sum of money in his pocket, by sea, with Captain Meek, of Kirkcaldy, to London, with letters of recommendation to the earl's favour, and just a few days before young Duncan arrived in London the earl was set out on his journey to his seat in Scotland.

I had now left him for near three years, not having seen him since about a year after his mother's death; and then coming to London, I had, by mere accident, an appointment to meet some Scotch gentlemen at the Buffalo, in Charing Cross. There happened at that time to be a great concourse of Scotch nobility there at an entertainment, and one of the ladies and gentlemen passing by and seeing one of my friends, desired him to come in, and told him both he and his companions should be very welcome to partake of the diversion. The lady told him they had got a lovely youth, a Scotch miracle, among them, that would give us exquisite delight, and write down to us all the occurrences of our future lives, and tell us our names upon our first appearance. The moment I heard of it, Duncan Campbell came into my head; but as it is a thing not rare to be met with in Scotland for second-sighted persons to tell such things, and as the Earl of Argyll was in the north, I thought little Duncan had been under his protection and with him, and did not dream of meeting with him there, and accordingly told my friend, before I went in, that I believed I knew a lad in Scotland would exceed this in foresight, let him be as dexterous in his art as he would.

As soon as I entered the room I was surprised to find myself encompassed and surrounded by a circle of the most beautiful females that ever my eyes beheld.

In the centre of this angelic tribe was seated a heavenly youth, with the most winning comeliness of aspect that ever pleased the sight of any beholder of either sex; his face was divinely fair, and tinged only with such a sprightly blush, as a painter would use to colour the picture of health with, and the complexion was varnished over by a blooming, like that of flourishing fruit, which had not yet felt the first nippings of an unkind and an uncivil air; with this beauty was joined such a smiling draught of all the features, as is the result of pleasantry and good humour. His eyes were large, full of lustre, majestic, well-set, and the soul shone so in them, as told the spectators plainly how great was the inward vivacity of his genius. The hair of his head was thick, and reclined far below his shoulders; it was of a fine silver colour, and hung down in ringlets like the curling tendrils of a copious vine. He was by the women entertained, according to the claim which so many perfections, joining in a youth just ripening into manhood, might lay to the benevolent dispositions of the tender sex. One was holding the basin of water, another washing a hand, a third, with a towel, drying his face, which another fair had greedily snatched the pleasure of washing before, while a fourth was disposing into order his silver hairs with an ivory comb, in a hand as white, and which a monarch might have been proud to have had so employed in adjusting the crown upon his head; a fifth was setting into order his cravat; a sixth stole a kiss, and blushed at the innocent pleasure, and mistook her own thoughts as if she kissed the angel and not the man; and they all rather seemed to adore than to love him, as if they had taken him not for a person that enjoyed the frequent gift of the second-sight, but as if he had been some little prophet peculiarly inspired; and while they all thus admired and wondered, they all consulted him as an oracle. The surprise of seeing a young man so happy amidst the general concurring favours of the fair, made me for awhile lost in a kind of delightful amazement, and the consideration of what bliss he was possessed, made me scarce believe my own eyes when they told me it was Duncan Campbell, who I had left an unhappy orphan at Edinburgh. But so it was, though he was much altered in stature, being now shot up pretty fast in his growth since I had seen him, and having gained a kind of a fixed comportment, such as we may daily observe in those who are taking leave of their minority and stepping into a stage of maturer life.

The first remarkable thing I knew him do in London, being in this splendid company, where there were so many undoubted witnesses of quality too that had ocular proof of his predictions at that public tavern. I choose to record it here in the first place according to its due order. It was in the year 1698.

Among this angelical class of beauties were Dr W[e]lw[oo]d's lady and daughter. Upon earth there was not sure a more beautiful creature than the daughter was; she was the leading light of all the sparkling tribe; and Otway's character suits her exactly, for she was among ten thousand eminently fair. One would imagine prosperous and lucky fortune was written upon her face, and that nothing unhappy could be read in so fair a book; and it was, therefore, the unanimous consent of all, that, by way of good omen to the rest, his predictions should begin to be opened luckily that day, and that therefore he should first of all be consulted about her.

Accordingly the mother, to be satisfied of his talent before she proceeded to any other questions, asked him in writing if he knew the young lady, her name, and who she was. After a little ruminating and pondering upon

the matter, and taking an exact view of the beauty, he
wrote down her name, told Mrs W[e]lw[oo]d she was
her daughter, and that her father was a doctor.   Convinced, by his so readily telling the name and quality
of persons he had never seen in his lifetime, that fame
had not given a false character of his capacity, she proceeded in her questions as to her future fortune.   He
gazed afresh at her very eagerly for some time, and his
countenance during that time of viewing her seemed to
be ruffled with abundance of disturbance and perplexity.
We all imagined that the youth was a little touched at
the heart himself with what he saw, and that instead
of telling hers, he had met in her bright eyes, with his
own destiny, the destiny of being for ever made a slave
and a captive to so many powerful and almost irresistible
charms.

At length, after having a long debate within himself,
which we thought proceeded from the strugglings of
love and passion, he, fetching a great sigh, which still
convinced us more, took the pen and wrote to Mrs
W[e]lw[oo]d, that he begged to be excused, and that his
pen might remain as dumb and silent as his tongue on
that affair.   By this answer we concluded, one and all,
that our former conjectures were true, and we joined
in pressing him the more earnestly to deliver his real
and sincere opinion concerning the accidents upon
which the future fortunes of her life were to turn and
depend.   He showed many mighty reluctances in the
doing it ; and I have often since considered him in the
same anguish as the late great Dr Radcliffe, who was
endeavouring by study to save a certain fair one, whom
he loved with a vehemence of temper, and who was
(as his reason told him) got far away beyond the reach
of the art of physic to recover.   At last, he wrote in
plain terms that his backwardness and unwillingness to
tell it arose from his wishes that her fortune would be

better than his certain foreknowledge of it told him it
would be, and begged that we would rest satisfied with
that general answer, since it was in so particular a case
where he himself was a well-wisher, in vain, to the
lady about whom he was consulted. The young lady
herself thinking that, if she knew any disasters that
were to befall her, she might, by knowing the nature
of them beforehand and the time when they were
likely to happen, be able, by timely prudence and fore-
cast, to avert those evils, with many beseechings urged
him to reveal the fatal secret. After many struggles
to avoid it, and as many instances made to him both by
mother and daughter for the discovery of his prescience
on that point, he complied with very great difficulty,
and, blotting the paper with tears that trickled fast
from his eyes, he gave her the lamentable scroll containing the words that follow, viz. :—" I wish it had
not fallen to my lot to tell this lady, whom everybody
that but once looks at her must admire, though they
must not have leave to love, that she is not much
longer to be possessor of that lovely face, which gains
her such a number of adorers. The small-pox will
too soon turn a ravisher, and rifle all those sweets and
charms that might be able to vanquish a king and to
subdue a conqueror of mighty battles. Her reign is
doomed, alas! to be as short as it is now great and
universal. I believe she has internal beauties of the
mind not the least inferior to those external ex-
cellences of the body, and she might perhaps, by the
power of her mind alone, be absolute queen of the
affections of men, if the small-pox threatened not too
surely to be her further enemy, and, not contented to
destroy the face, was not perversely bent to destroy the
whole woman. But I want words to express my
sorrow. I would not tell it if you did not extort the
baneful secret from my bosom. This fair creature,

whose beauty would make one wish her immortal, will, by the cruel means of the small-pox, give us too sudden a proof of her mortality.   But neither the mother nor herself ought too much to repine at this, seeing it appears to be the decree of Providence, which is always to be interpreted as meant for our good, and seeing it may be the means of translating her the sooner only to her kindred angels, whose beauty she so much resembles here on earth, and to be among the lowest class of whom is better than being the greatest beauty of the world here below, and wearing an imperial crown.   While I comfort you I cannot help the force of nature, which makes me grieve myself, and I only give you, because you compel me to it, so particular and so exact an answer to so particular and so exacting a question."

The mother, who took the paper, was prudent enough to conceal from the daughter what he said, but nature would force its way, and bubbled from her eyes; and the daughter perceiving that, pressed hard to see it, and wept at the consideration that hard fate (though she knew not particularly what way) was to befall her. Never surely was anything so beautiful in tears, and I obtained of the mother to see the writing.   At last, in general terms, to free her from suspense of mind, it was told her that some trouble should happen to her that would diminish her beauty.   She had courage enough to hear that misfortune with disdain, and crying, " If that be all, I am armed, I don't place much pride in that, which I know age must shortly after destroy, if trouble did not do it before ; " and she dried up her tears, and (if what Mr Bruyere says be true, viz., that the last thing a celebrated woman thinks of when she dies is the loss of her beauty) she showed an admirable pattern of female philosophy in bearing such a cruel prediction with such unspeakable magnanimity as exceeded even the patience of stern stoicism, considering she was a woman, to whom beauty is more dear than life.

If any evil that is impending over people's heads could be evaded by foreknowledge, or eluded by art, she had the fairest opportunity of having this prediction annulled (which would have been more to the satisfaction of the predictor than knowing it verified) than ever any woman had. Her mother was specifically told that the fatal distemper should be the small-pox. Her father was, and is still, a very eminent physician; and distempers of that kind especially are much more easily prevented by care than cured by art, and by art more easily set aside when there is a timely warning given to a physician to prepare the body against the danger of the poison, than when the distemper has once caught hold of a body at unawares, when it is unpurged of any gross humours that may accompany it. But neither the foreknowledge and caution of the mother, nor the skill and wisdom of the great physician her father, were sufficient to ward off the approaching harm that was written in the books of fate. Not many suns had finished their yearly courses before she was forced to submit to the inevitable stroke of death, after the infectious and malicious malady had first ravaged her beauty, rioted in all her sweets, and made an odious deformed spectacle of the charmer of mankind. The death of the daughter worked hard upon the mother's bowels, and dragged her speedily after her with a broken heart to the grave.

This lady, whose fortune so great and so distinguished an assembly had chosen to hear as a happy forerunner and lucky omen of all their own, which were to be asked afterwards in their turns, proving, so contrary to their expectations, already unfortunate in the prediction, and having been in tears about the matter, disheartened

all the rest of the beauties from consulting him further
that day. The person who kept the tavern, by name
Mrs Irwin, alleged that as some people were very
fortunate and others unfortunate upon the same day, so
one lady might be before told a mishap one minute, and
another lady all the prosperity in nature the very next
minute following, and therefore that what the unfortunate lady had heard was not to be taken as ominous,
or as what could malignantly influence the day, neither
ought it to be the least hindrance to any who had the
curiosity of being let into the secrets of time beforehand.
However, whether the ladies were convinced or no, if
she prevailed over their belief in that point she could
not prevail over their humour, which (though they
might not believe the former prediction ominous to
themselves) was naturally awed for fear of the like,
peradventure, for a time ; and so it was agreed, *nemine
contradicente*, as a witty lady wrote it down, that no
more petitions should for that day be presented by any
of that company to his dumb, yet oracular, majesty.
Mrs Irwin, however, would have her way ; said she
did not presume to such honour as to call herself of
that company, and that therefore she might consult him
without breaking through the votes of the assembly.
Many endeavoured to dissuade her, but as she was
passionately fond of knowing future events, and had
a mighty itch to be very inquisitive with the oracle,
about what might happen, not only to herself but her
posterity ; it was agreed that he should have the liberty
of satisfying her curiosity, since she presumed her
fortune was sure to be so good, and was so forward
and eager for the knowledge of it. But, alas, such
is too often the fantastical impulse of nature unluckily
depraved, that it carries often into wishes of knowing
what when known we would be glad to unknow again,
and then our memory will not let us be untaught.

"She brought in her three
pretty children."

Mrs Irwin was at that time in a pretty commodious way of business, everything in plenty round about her, and lived more like a person of distinction, that kept such a cellar of wine, open house, and a free table, than like one who kept a tavern. She brought in her three pretty children, that were then almost babies, the youngest having not long been out of the nurse's arms, or trusted to the use of its own legs. These children she loved as a mother should love children; they were the delight of her eyes all day, and the dream of her imagination all night. All the passions of her soul were confined to them; she was never pleased but when they were so, and always angry if they were crossed; her whole pride was centred in them, and they were clothed and were attended more like the infants of a princess than of a vintner's relict. The fortune of these was what she had near at heart, and of which she was so eager of being apprised. Her impatience was proportionate to the love she had for them, and which made her wish to foreknow all the happiness that was like to attend them. She sat cheerfully down, presented one to him, and smiling, wrote the question in general terms, viz., " Is this boy to be happy or unhappy ? " A melancholy look once more spread itself all over the face of the predictor, when he read the two inquisitive words, and he seemed mightily to regret being asked a question to which he was, by his talent of foreseeing, compelled to give so unwelcome an answer. The colour of the poor woman flushed and vanished alternately, and very quick, and she looked not quite like the picture of despair, but a disconsolate woman, with little hopes on one hand, and great doubts and dismal fears on the other. She confessed she read great evil in the troubles of his face, thanked him for his good nature, told him that they all knew, that though he could foretell, he could not alter the acts and decretals of fate, and therefore desired him to tell her the worst, for that the misfortunes, were they never so great, would be less dreadful to her than remaining in the state of fear and suspension. He at last wrote down to her that great and unexpected and even unavoidable accidents would involve the whole family in new calamities, that the son she asked him about would have the bitterest task of hardship to go through withal, while he lived, and that to finish all more unhappily, he would be basely and maliciously brought to an untimely end, by some mortal enemy or other; but that she should not trouble herself so much on that head, she would never see it, for it would happen some years after she was departed from the world. This melancholy account closed up the book of predictions for that day, and put a sad stop to all the projected mirth and curiosity. Now I must tell the reader how and when the event answered the prediction, and in a few words, it was thus: poor Mrs Irwin, by strange accidents, decayed in the world, and dying poor, her sons were forced to be put apprentices to small trades; and the son whom the above-mentioned prediction concerned was, for stealing one cheese from a man in the Haymarket, severely prosecuted at the Old Bailey, and on Wednesday, the twenty-third of December, 1713, hanged at Tyburn, with several other criminals.

The two foregoing passages are of so tragical a nature that it is time I should relieve the minds of my readers with some histories of ladies who consulted him with more success and advantage, to whom his predictions were very entertaining, when they came to pass in their favour, the relation whereof will consequently be agreeable to all readers who have within them a mixture of happy curiosity and good-nature.

Two ladies, who were the most remarkable beauties

in London, and the most courted, turned at the same time their thoughts to matrimony, and being satiated, I may say wearied, with the pleasure of having continually after them a great number and variety of adorers, resolved each, about the same time, to make a choice of their several men, to whom they thought they could give most happiness, and from whom they might receive most. Their names (for they are both persons of distinction) shall be Christallina and Urbana. Christallina was a virgin, and Urbana a young widow. Christallina engrossed the eyes, the hearts, and the sighs of the whole court, and wherever she appeared put any court lady out of her place that had one before in the heart of any youth, and was the celebrated toast among the beau monde. Urbana's beauty made as terrible a havoc in the city; all the citizens' daughters that had many admirers, and were in fair hopes of having husbands when they pleased themselves, as soon as Urbana had lost her old husband, found that they every day lost their lovers, and it was a great fear among the prettiest maids that they should remain maids still, as long as Urbana remained a widow. She was the monopoliser of city affection, and made many girls that had large stocks of suitors bankrupts in the trade of courtship, and broke some of their hearts when her charms broke off their amours. Well, but the day was near at hand when both the belles of the court and the city damsels were to be freed from the ravages which these two tyrants, triumphant in beauty, and insolent in charms, made among the harvest of love. Each had seen her proper man, to whom the enjoyment of her person was to be dedicated for life. But it being an affair of so lasting importance, each had a mind to be let into the knowledge of the consequences of such a choice, as far as possible, before they stepped into the irrevocable

G

state of matrimony. Both of them happened to take it into their heads that the best way to be entirely satisfied in their curiosity was to have recourse to the great predictor of future occurrences, Mr Duncan Campbell, whose fame was at that time spread pretty largely about the town.   Christallina and Urbana were not acquainted with each other, only by the report which fame had made of beauty.   They came to Mr Campbell's on the same day, and both with the same resolution of keeping themselves concealed, and under masks, that none of the company of consulters who happened to be there might know who they were.   It happened that on that very day, just when they came, Mr Campbell's rooms were more than ordinarily crowded with curious clients of the fair sex, so that he was obliged to desire these two ladies, who expressed so much precaution against and fear of having their persons discovered, to be contented with only one room between them, and with much ado they complied with the request, and condescended to sit together incog.   Distant compliments of gesture passed between them, the dress and comportment of each making them appear to be persons of figure and breeding, and after three or four modish curtsies, down they sat, without so much as once opening their lips, or intending so to do.   The silence between them was very formal and profound for near half-an-hour, and nothing was heard but the snapping of fans, which they both did very tunably, and with great harmony, and played, as it were, in concert.

At last one of the civil well-bred mutes happening to sneeze, the other very gracefully bowed, and before she was well aware out popped the words, " Bless you, madam."   The fair sneezer returned the bow with an " I thank you, madam."   They found they did not know one another's voices, and they began to talk very merrily together, with pretty great confidence, and they taking a mutual liking from conversation, so much familiarity grew thereupon instantly between them, that they began not only to unmask, but to unbosom themselves to one another, and confess alternately all their secrets. Christallina owned who she was, and told Urbana the beau and courtier that had her heart. Urbana as frankly declared that she was a widow, that she would not become the lady's rival, that she had pitched upon a second husband, an alderman of the city. Just by that time they had had their chat out, and wished one another the pleasure of a successful prediction, it came to Christallina's turn to visit the dumb gentleman, and receive from his pen oracular answers to all the questions she had to propose. Well, he accordingly satisfied her in every point she asked him about; but while she was about this, one of Mr Campbell's family going with Urbana to divert her a little, the widow railed at the virgin as a fool, to imagine that she should ever make a conquest of the brightest spark about the court, and then let fly some random bolts of malice to wound her reputation for chastity. Now it became the widow's turn to go and consult, and the same person of Mr Campbell's family in the meantime entertained Christallina. The maid was not behindhand with the widow; she railed against the widow, represented her as sometimes a coquette, sometimes a lady of pleasure, sometimes a jilt, and lifted up her hands in wonder and amazement that Urbana should imagine so rich a man as an alderman such-a-one should fall to her lot. Thus Urbana swore and protested that Christallina could never arrive at the honour of being the wife to the courtly Secretarius, let Mr Campbell flatter her as he would; and Christallina vowed that Campbell must be a downright wizard if he foretold that such a one as Urbana would get

Alderman Stiffrump for a husband, provided a thing so improbable should come to pass.

However, it seems Duncan had told them their own names and the names of their suitors, and told them further, how soon they were both to be married, and that, too, directly to their hearts' content, as they said rejoicingly to themselves, and made their mutual gratulations.

They went away each satisfied that she should have her own lover, but Christallina laughed at Mr Campbell for assigning the alderman to Urbana, and Urbana laughed at him for promising the courtier to the arms of Christallina.

This is a pretty good figure of the tempers of two reigning toasts with regard to one another.

First, their curiosity made them, from resolving to be concealed, discover one another wilfully, from utter strangers grow as familiar as old friends in a moment, swear one another to secrecy, and exchange the sentiments of their hearts together, and from being friends become envious of each other's enjoying a similitude of happiness; the compliments made on either side face to face were, upon the turning of the back, turned into reflections, detraction, and ridicule; each was a self-lover and admirer of her own beauty and merit, and a despiser of the other's.

However, Duncan Campbell proved at last to be in the right. Urbana was wrong in her opinion of Christallina's want of power over Secretarius, and Christallina was as much out in her opinion that Urbana would miss in her aim of obtaining Stiffrump; for they both proved in the right of what they thought with regard to their own dear single persons, and were made happy according to their expectations, just at the time foretold by Mr Campbell.

Christallina's ill wishes did not hinder Urbana from

being mistress of Alderman Stiffrump's person and stock, nor did Urbana's hinder Christallina from showing herself a shining bride at the ring in Secretarius's gilded chariot, drawn by six prancers of the proud Belgian kind, with her half-dozen of liveries, with favours in their hats, waiting her return at the gate of Hyde Park. Both loved and both envied, but both allowed of Mr Campbell's foreknowledge.

Having told you two very sorrowful passages, and one tolerably successful and entertaining, I shall now relate to you another of my own knowledge, that is mixed up with the grievous and the pleasant, and chequered, as it were, with the shade and the sunshine of fortune.

Though there are vicissitudes in every stage of life under the sun, and not one ever ran continually on with the same series of prosperity, yet those conditions which are the most liable to the signal alterations of fortune, are the conditions of merchants, for professed gamesters I reckon in a manner as men of no condition of life at all, but what comes under the statute of vagabonds.

It was, indeed, as the reader would guess, a worthy and a wealthy merchant, who was to run through these different circumstances of being. He came and visited our Mr Campbell in the year 1707 ; he found him amidst a crowd of consulters, and being very eager and solicitous to know his own fortune just at that critical juncture of time, he begged of him (if possible) to adjourn his other clients to the day following, and sacrifice that one wholly to his use, which, as it was probably more important than all the others together, so he wrote down that he would render the time spent about it more advantageous to Mr Campbell, and by way of previous encouragement, threw him down ten guineas as a retaining fee.

Mr Campbell, who held money in very little esteem,

and valued it so much too little that he has often had my reprehensions on that head, paused a little, and after looking earnestly in the gentleman's face, and reading there, as I suppose, in that little space of time in general, according to the power of the second-sight, that what concerned him was highly momentous, wrote him this answer, that he would comply with his request, adjourn his other clients to the day following, and set apart all the remnant of that, till night, for inspecting the future occurrences of which he had a mind to be made a master.

There is certainly a very keen appetite in curiosity. It cannot stay for satisfaction; it is pressing for its necessary repast, and is without all patience. Hunger and thirst are not appetites more vehement and more hard and difficult to be repressed than that of curiosity; nothing but the present now is able to allay it. A more expressive picture of this I never beheld than in the faces of some, and the murmurs and complaints of others in that little inquisitive company, when the unwelcome note was given about signifying an adjournment for only twenty-four hours.

The colour of a young woman there came and went a hundred times (if possible) in the space of two minutes; she blushed like a red rose this moment, and in the switch of an eyelash she was all over as pale as a white one. The suitor, whose name her heart had gone pit-a-pat for the space of an hour to be informed of from the pen of a seer, was now deferred a whole day longer; she was once or twice within an ace of swooning away, but he comforted her in particular by telling her (though he said it only by way of jest) that the day following would be a more lucky day to consult about husbands than the present that she came on. The answer was a kind of cordial to her hopes, and brought her a little better to herself.

Two others, I remember, sisters and old maids, that

it seems were misers, women ordinarily dressed, and in blue aprons, and yet by relation worth no less than two thousand pounds each, were in a peck of troubles about his going and leaving them unsatisfied. They came upon an inquiry after goods that were stolen, and they complained that by next morning at that time, the thief might be got far enough off, and creep into so remote a corner, that he would put it beyond the power of the devil, and the art of conjuration, to find him out, and bring him back again. The disturbance and anxiety that was to be seen in their countenances was just like that which is to be beheld in the face of a great losing gamester, when his all, his last great stake, lies upon the table, and is just sweeping off by another winning hand into his own hat.

The next was a widow, who bounced because, as she pretended, he would not tell her what was best to do with her sons, and what profession it would be most happy for them to be put to ; but in reality all the cause of the widow's fuming and fretting was, not that she wanted to provide for her sons, but for herself ; she wanted a second husband, and was not half so solicitous about being put in a way of educating those children she had already, as of knowing when she should be in a likelihood of getting more. This was certainly in her thoughts, or else she would never have flounced about in her weeds, from one end of the room to the other, and all the while of her passion smile by fits upon the merchant, and leer upon a young pretty Irish fellow that was there. The young Irishman made use of a little eye-language ; she grew appeased, went away in quite a good humour, scuttled too airily downstairs for a woman in her clothes, and the reason was certainly that she knew the matter before, which we took notice of presently after ; the Irishman went precipitately after her downstairs without taking his leave.

But neither were the two misers for their gold, the virgin for a first husband, nor the widow for a second, half so eager, as another married woman there, was for the death of her spouse. She had put the question in so expecting a manner for a lucky answer, and with so much keen desire appearing plainly in her looks, that no big-bellied woman was ever more eager for devouring fruit; no young hasty bridegroom, just married to a beauty, more impatient for night and enjoyment, than she was to know (what she thought a more happy moment), the moment of her husband's last agonising gasp. As her expectation was the greatest, so was her disappointment too, and consequently her disorder, upon his going and leaving her unresolved. She was frantic, raging, and implacable; she was in such a fury at the delay of putting off her answer to the day following, that in her fury she acted as if she would have given herself an answer, which of the two should die first, by choking herself upon the spot, with the indignation that swelled in her stomach and rose into her throat on that occasion. It may look like a romance to say it, but indeed they were forced to cut her lace, and then she threw out of the room with great passion; but yet had so much of the enraged wife left (beyond the enraged woman) as to return instantly upstairs, and signify very calmly, she would be certain to be there next day, and beseeched earnestly that she might not meet with a second disappointment.

All this hurry and bustle created a stay a little too tedious for the merchant, who began to be impatient himself, especially when word was brought up that a fresh company was come in: but Mr Campbell was denied to them; and to put a stop to any more interruptions, the merchant and the dumb gentleman agreed to slip into a coach, drive to a tavern in the city, and settle matters of futurity over a bottle of French claret.

The first thing done at the tavern was Mr Campbell's saluting him upon a piece of paper by his name, and drinking his health. The next paper held a discourse of condolence for a disaster that was passed long since, namely, a great and considerable loss that happened to his family in the dreadful conflagration of the city of London. In the third little dialogue which they had together, he told the merchant that losses and advantages were general topics, which a person, unskilled in that art, might venture to assign to any man of his profession, it being next to impossible that persons who traffic should not sometimes gain and sometimes lose.—— " But," said Mr Campbell, " I will sketch out particularly and specify to you some future misfortunes, with which you will unavoidably meet ; 'tis in your stars, it is in destiny, that you should have some trials, and therefore, when you are forewarned, take a prudent care to be forearmed with patience, and by longanimity, and meekly and resignedly enduring your lot, render it more easy, since impatience can't avert it, and will only render it more burthensome and heavy." He gave these words to the merchant, who pressed for his opinion that moment. " By your leave," resuming the pen, said the dumb gentleman in writing, " we will have this bottle out first and tap a fresh one, that you may be warmed with courage enough to receive the first speculative onset of ill fortune that I shall predict to you, with a good grace, and that may perhaps enable you to meet it, when it comes to reduce itself into action, with a manful purpose and all becoming resolution." The merchant agreed to the proposal, and put on an air of the careless and indifferent as well as he could, to signify that he had no need to raise up an artificial courage from the auxiliary forces of the grape. But nature, when hard pressed, will break through all disguises, and not only notwithstanding the air of pleasantry he gave himself, which appeared forced and constrained, but in spite of two or three sparkling and enlivening bumpers, a cloud of care would ever and anon gather and shoot heavily across his brow, though he laboured all he could to dispel it as quickly, and to keep fair weather in his countenance.

Well, they had cracked the first bottle and the second succeeded upon the table, and they called to blow a pipe together. This pipe Mr Campbell found had a very ill effect; it is certainly a pensive kind of instrument, and fills a mind anything so disposed with disturbing thoughts, black fumes, and melancholy vapours, as certainly as it doth the mouth with smoke. It plainly took away even the little sparks of vivacity which the wine had given before; so he wrote for a truce of firing those sort of noxious guns any longer, and they laid down their arms by consent, and drank off the second bottle. A third immediately supplied its place, and at the first glass of the opening of the bottle Mr Campbell began to open to him his future case in the following words:—" Sir, you have now some ventures at sea from such and such a place, to such a value. Do not be discomforted at the news which you certainly will have within three months (but 'twill be false at last), that they are, by three different tempests, made the prey of the great ocean, and enrich the bottom of the sea, the palace of Neptune. A worse storm than all these attends you at home, a wife who is and will be more the tempest of the house wherein she lives. The high and lofty winds of her vanity will blow down the pillars of your house and family; the high tide of her extravagance will roll on like a resistless torrent, and leave you at low water, and the ebb of all your fortunes. This is the highest and the most cutting disaster that is to befall you; your real shipwreck is not foreign but domestic; your bosom friend is to be your greatest foe, and even your powerful undoer for a time; mark what I say, and take courage; it shall be but for a time provided you take courage; it will, upon that condition, be only a short and wholesome taste of adversity given to you, that you may relish returning prosperity with virtue, and with a greater return of thanks to Him that dispenses it at pleasure to mankind. Remember, courage and resignation is what I advise you to; use it, as becomes you, in your adversity, and believe that as I foretold that adversity, so I can foretell a prosperity will again be the consequence of those virtues; and the more you feel the one ought not to cast you down, but raise your hopes the more, that he who foretold you that so exactly could likewise foretell you the other." The merchant was by this put into a great suspense of mind, but somewhat easier, by the second prediction being annexed so kindly to the first fatal one. They crowned the night with a flask of Burgundy, and then parting, each went to their respective homes.

The reader may perchance wonder how I, who make no mention of my being there (as in truth I was not at the tavern), should be able to relate this as of my own knowledge; but if he pleases to have patience to the end of the story, he will have entire satisfaction in that point.

About half a year after the merchant came again, told him that his prediction was too far verified, to his very dear cost, and that he was now utterly undone and beyond any visible means of a future recovery, and doubting lest the other fortunate part of the prediction was only told him by way of encouragement (for groundless doubts and fears always attend a mind implunged in melancholy), besought him very earnestly to tell him candidly and sincerely if there was no real prospect of good, and rid him at once of the uneasiness of such a suspension of thought; "but pray do," said he, with all the vehemence of repeated expostulation, "satisfy me if there are any further hopes on this side the grave?"

To this Duncan Campbell made a short but a very significant reply in writing. "May the heavens preserve you from a threatening danger of life. Take care only of yourself, great and mighty care, and if you outlive Friday next, you will yet be great and more fortunate than ever you was in all the height of your former most flourishing space of life." He coloured inordinately when Duncan Campbell said Friday, and conjured him to tell him as particularly as he could what he meant by Friday. He told him he could not particularise any further, but that great danger threatened him that day; and that without extraordinary precaution it would prove fatal to him, even to death. He shook his head, and went away in a very sorrowful plight. Friday passed, Saturday came, and on that very Saturday morning came likewise the joyful tidings that what ventures of his were given over for lost at sea were all come safe into the harbour. He came the moment he received those despatches from his agent to Mr Duncan Campbell's apartment, embraced him tenderly, and saluted him with much gladness of heart, before a great room full of ladies, where I happened to be present at the time; crying out in a loud voice, before he knew what he said, that Mr Campbell had saved his life; that Friday was his birthday, and he had intended with a pistol to shoot himself that very day. The ladies thought him mad; and he, recovered from his ecstasy, said no more, but sat down till Mr Campbell dismissed all his clients; and then we three went to the tavern together, where he told me the whole little history or narrative just as is above related.

The fame which Mr Duncan Campbell got by the

foregoing and several other predictions of the like kind, was become very large and extensive, and had spread itself into the remotest corners of this metropolis. The squares rung with it; it was whispered from one house to another through the more magnificent streets, where persons of quality and distinction reside; it catched every house in the city, like the news of stock from Exchange Alley; it run noisily through the lanes and little thoroughfares where the poor inhabit; it was the chat of the tea-table and the babble of the streets, and the whole town, from the top to the bottom, was full of it. Whenever any reputation rises to a degree like this, let it be for what art or accomplishment, or on what account soever it will, malice, envy, and detraction are sure to be the immediate pursuers of it with full mouth and to hunt it down, if possible, with full cry. Even the great Nostradamus, though favoured by kings and queens (which always without any other reason creates enemies), was not more pursued by envy and detraction for his predictions in Paris and throughout France, than our Duncan Campbell was in London, and even throughout England. Various, different, and many were the objections raised to blot his character and extenuate his fame, that, when one was confuted, another might not be wanting to supply its place, and so to maintain a course and series of back-biting according to the known maxim—"Throw dirt, and if it does not stick, throw dirt continually, and some will stick."

Neither is there any wonder; for a man, that has got applauders of all sorts and conditions, must expect condemners and detractors of all sorts and conditions likewise. If a lady of high degree, for example, should say, smiling (though really thinking absolutely what she says), for fear of being thought over-credulous, "Well, I vow some things Mr Campbell does are

surprising, after all ; they would be apt to incline one
to a belief that he is a wonder of a man, for one would
imagine the things he does impossible," why, then, a
prude, with an assumed supercilious air and a scornful
" tihee," would, in order to seem more wise than she was,
reply, " Lard, madam, it is more a wonder to me that
you can be imposed upon so.   I vow to Gad, madam,
I would as soon consult an almanac-maker, and pin my
faith upon what he pricks down ; or believe, like my
creed, in the cross which I make upon the hand of a
gipsy.   Lard, madam, I assure your la'ship he knows
no more than I do of you.   I assure you so, and
therefore believe me.   He has it all by hearsay."   If
the lady that believed it should reply, that if he had
notice of every stranger by hearsay, he must be a
greater man than she suspected, and must keep more
spies in pay than a prime minister, the prude's answer
would be with a loud laugh, and giggling out these
words, " Lard, madam, I assure you nothing can
be more easy ; and so take it for granted."   Because
she was inclined to say so, and had the act of wisdom
on her side, forsooth, that she appeared hard of belief
(which some call hard to be put upon), and the other
lady credulous (which some, though believing upon
good grounds, are called) and so thought foolish ; the
prude's answer would be thought sufficient and convincing.

Thus malice and folly, by dint of noise and impudence, and strong though empty assertions, often run
down modesty and good sense.   Among the common
people it is the same, but only done in a different manner.
For example, an ordinary person that had consulted
might say (as he walked along), " There goes the
dumb gentleman, who writes down any name of a
stranger at first sight ; " up steps a blunt fellow, that
takes stubbornness for sense, and says, " That is a

confounded lie; he is a cheat and an impostor, and you are one of his accomplices. He'll tell me my name, I suppose, if you tell it him first. He is no more dumb than I am; he can speak and hear as well as us, I have been with those that say they have heard him. I wish I and two or three more had him in our stable, and I warrant you with our cart-whips we would lick some words out of his chops, as dumb as you call him. I tell you 'tis all a lie and all a bite." If the other desires to be convinced for himself by his own experience, the rougher rogue, who perhaps has stronger sinews than the other, answers, "If you lie any further I will knock you down;" and so he is the vulgar wit, and the mouth of the rabble-rout, and thus the detraction spreads below with very good success, as it does above in another kind.

As there are two comical adventures in his life which directly suit and correspond with the foregoing reflections, this seems the most proper place to insert them in. The first consists of a kind of mob-way of usage he met with from a fellow, who got to be an officer in the army, but by the following behaviour will be found unworthy of the name and the commission.

In the year 1701 a lady of good quality came and addressed herself to him much after the following manner. She told him she had choice of lovers, but preferred one above the rest, but desired to know his name, and if she made him her choice what would be the subsequent fate of such a matrimony. Mr Duncan Campbell very readily gave her down in writing this plain and honest reply :—That of all her suitors she was most inclined to a captain, a distinguished officer and a great beau (naming his name), and one that had a great many outward engaging charms sufficient to blind the eyes of any lady that was not thoroughly acquainted with his manner of living. He therefore assured her (and thought himself bound, being conjured so to do, having received his fee, though there was danger in such plain and open predictions) that he was a villain and a rogue in his heart, a profligate gamester, and that if she took him to her bed she would only embrace her own ruin. The lady's woman, who was present, being in fee with the captain, resolving to give intelligence for fear the officer, her so good friend, should be disappointed in the siege, slily shuffled the papers into her pocket, and made a present of them to the military spark. Fired with indignation at the contents, he vowed revenge, and in order to compass it conspires with his female spy about the means. In fine, for fear of losing the lady though he quarrelled with Duncan Campbell, a method was to be found out how to secure her by the very act of revenge. At last it was resolved to discover to her that he had found out what she had been told by Mr Campbell, but the way how he had been informed was to remain a secret. He did do so, and ended his discovery with these words:—" I desire, madam, that if I prove him an impostor you would not believe a word he says." The lady agreed to so fair a proposal. Then the captain swore that he himself would never eat a piece of bread more till he had made Mr Campbell eat his words; nay, he insisted upon it that he would bring him to his tongue, and make him own by word of mouth that what he had written before was false and calumnious. To which the lady answered again, that if he performed what he said she would be convinced. This brave military man, however, not relying upon his own single valour and prowess to bring about so miraculous a thing as the making a person that was dumb to speak, he took with him for this end three lusty assistants to combine with him in the assassination. The ambuscade was settled to be at the Five Bells tavern in Wych Street in the Strand.   After the ambush was settled with so much false courage, the business of decoying Mr Campbell into it was not practicable any other way than by sending out false colours.   The lady's woman, who was by her own interest tied fast to the interest of the beau, was to play the trick of Dalilah, and betray this deaf and dumb Samson (as he will appear to be a kind of one in the sequel of the story) into the hands of these Philistines.   She smooths her face over with a complimenting lie from her mistress to Mr Campbell, and acted her part of deceit so well that he promised to follow her to the Five Bells with all haste, and so she scuttled back to prepare the captain, and to tell him how lucky she was in mischief, and how she drew him out by smiles into perdition.   The short of the story is, when they got him in among them they endeavoured to assassinate him, but they missed of their aim; yet it is certain they left him in a very terrible and bloody condition, and the captain went away in as bad a plight as the person was left in whom he assaulted so cowardly with numbers, and to such disadvantage.   I was sent for to him upon this disaster, and the story was delivered to me thus by one of the drawers of the tavern when I inquired into it :—They began to banter him, and speaking to him as if he heard, asked him if he knew his own fortune; they told him it was to be beaten to death.   This was an odd way of addressing a deaf and dumb man.   They added they would make him speak before they had done.   The boy seeing he made no reply, but only smiled, thought what passed between them was a jest with an old acquaintance, and withdrew about his business.   The door being fastened, however, before they began the honourable attack, they vouchsafed to write down their intent in the words above mentioned, which they had uttered

H

before, to make sure that he should understand their meaning, and what this odd way of correction was for. All the while, the maid who had brought him into it, was peeping through a hole, and watching the event, as appears afterwards. Mr Campbell wrote them the following answer, viz., that he hoped for fair play; that he understood bear-garden as well as they; but if a gentleman was amongst them he would expect gentlemanly usage.

The rejoinder they made to this consisted, it seems, not of words, but of action. The officer, in conjunction with another ruffian, one of the strongest of the three he had brought, commenced the assault. As good luck would have it, he warded off their first blows, it seems, with tolerable success, and a wine quart pot standing upon the table, Duncan took to his arms, and at two or three quick blows, well managed, and close laid in upon the assailants, felled them both to the ground. Here it was that the maid discovered her knowledge of it and privity to the plot to the whole house; for she no sooner sees the famous leader, the valiant captain, lie sprawling on the floor with bleeding temples, but she shrieked out with all the voice she could exert, "Murder, murder, murder!" Alarmed at this outcry, the master and all the attendants of the tavern scampered upstairs, burst into the room, and found Duncan Campbell struggling with the other two, and the quart pot still fast clenched in his hand, which they were endeavouring to wrench from him. The drawers rescued him out of their hands, and inquired into the matter. The maid in a fright confessed the whole thing. The officer and his associate rubbed their eyes as recovering from a stunning sleep, reeled as they went to rise, paid the reckoning, and slunk pitifully away, or, as the rake's term for it is,—they brushed off, and for all their odds had the worst of the lay. I, who had some authority with Mr. Campbell, by reason of my years and the strict acquaintance I had with his mother, when I came and found him in that pickle, and had the whole relation told me by the people of the house, though I could not forbear pitying him within my own mind, took upon me to reprehend him, and told him that these hardships would by Providence be daily permitted to fall upon him (for he met with them twenty times) while he continued in that irregular way of living and spending his time, that might be so precious to himself and many others, in drunkenness and debauchery; and I think the lessons I wrote down to him upon that head, though a little severe just at that juncture, were, notwithstanding, well timed, and did, as I guessed they would, make a more solid impression on him than at any other. In all these scuffles (whether it is that being deaf and dumb an affront works deeper upon a man, and so renders him far more fierce and resolute) it must be said that, though nature has been very kind in making him very strong, robust, and active withal, yet he has bore some shocks one would imagine beyond the strength of a man, having sometimes got the better of five or six ruffians in rencounters of the like kind.

The next banter he met with was in a gentler way from an unbelieving lady, and yet she came off with very ill success, and the banter turned all upon herself in the end.

A lady of distinction, whose name shall therefore be concealed in this place, came with two or three of her special friends, who took her for the most merry, innocent, spotless virgin upon earth, and whose modesty was never suspected in the least by her relations or servants that were nearest about her; after having rallied Mr. Campbell with several frivolous questions, doubting his capacity, and vexing and teasing him with gay impertinences beyond all patience, was by him told that he did not take fees in his profession to be made a jest of like a common fortune-teller, but to do real good to those who consulted him, as far as he was able by his predictions; that he was treated with more respect by persons of a higher condition, though her own was very good, and so offered her guinea back again with a bow and a smile. She had a little more generosity of spirit than not to be a little nettled at the proffer she had caused by so coarse an usage. She affected appearing grave a little, and told him she would be serious for the future, and asked him to set down her name, which she had neglected before, to ask other questions that were nothing to the purpose. He promised to write it down, but pausing a little longer than ordinary about it, she returned to her former way of uncivil merriment and ungallant raillery. She repeated to him, in three or four little scraps of paper, one after another, as fast as she could write them, the same words, viz., that he could not tell her name, nor whether she was maid, wife, or widow; and laughed as if she would split her sides, triumphing to the rest of her companions over his ignorance and her own wit, as if she had posed him and put him to an entire stand. But see what this overweening opinion of security ended in: the man of the second-sight was not to be so easily baffled. Vexed at being so disturbed, and coming out of his brown study, he reaches the paper and begins to write. Now it was the lady's turn to suffer; she had deserved hearty punishment, and it came into her hands with the note to a degree of severity (as you will perceive by the contents of it just now). She read it, and swooning away, dropped from her chair. The whole room being in a bustle, I that was in the outward chamber ran in. While Mr Campbell was sprinkling water in her face, a lady

snatched up the note to read it, at which he seemed
mightily displeased. I therefore, who understood his
signs, recovered it out of her hands by stratagem, and
ran to burn it, which I did so quick that I was not
discovered in the curiosity, which I must own I satisfied myself in by reading it first; a curiosity raised too
high by so particular an adventure, to be overcome in
so little a time of thought, as I was to keep it in my
hands; and so I came by the knowledge of it myself
without being informed by Mr Campbell. This shows
how a sudden curiosity, when there is not time given
to think and correct it, may overcome a man as well
as a woman; for I was never over curious in my life,
and though I was pleased with the oddness of the
adventure, I often blushed to myself since for the un-
manly weakness of not being able to step with a note
from one room to another, to the fireside, without
peeping into the contents of it. The contents of it
were these. "Madam, since you provoke me, your
name is ———. You are no widow, you are no wife,
and yet you are no maid; you have a child at nurse
at such a place, by such a gentleman, and you were
brought to bed in Leicestershire." The lady, convinced by this answer of his strange and mystical power,
and pleased with his civility in endeavouring to conceal
from others the secret, after so many repeated provoca-
tions, though she showed great disorder for that day,
became one of his constant attenders some time after,
and would not take any step in her affairs without his
advice, which, she often has said since, she found very
much to her advantage. She was as serious in her
dealings with him afterwards, and improved by being
so, as she was gay and turbulent with him before, and
smarted for it. In fine, she was a thorough convert,
and a votary of his; and the only jest she used afterwards to make concerning him was a civil witticism to

his wife, to whom she was wont, every now and then, smiling, to address herself after this manner—"Your husband, madam, is a devil, but he is a very handsome and a very civil one."

Not long after this came another lady with a like intent to impose upon him, and was resolved, as she owned, to have laughed him to scorn if she had succeeded in her attempt. She had very dexterously dressed herself in her woman's habit, and her woman in her own; her footman squired the new-made lady in a very gentlemanly dress, hired, for the purpose of a disguise, from Monmouth Street. The strange and unknown masqueraders entered Mr Campbell's room with much art. The fellow was by nature of a clean make and had a good look, and from following a genteel master when he was young, copied his gait a little, and had some appearance of a mien, and a tolerable good air about him. But this being the first time of his being so fine, and he a little vain in his temper, he over-acted his part: he strutted too much; he was as fond of his ruffles, his watch, his sword, his cane, and his snuff-box, as a boy of being newly breeched; and viewed them all too often to be thought the possessor of any such things long. The affectation of the chambermaid was insufferable; she had the toss of the head, the jut of the bum, the sidelong leer of the eye, the imperious look upon her lady, now degraded into her woman, that she was intolerable, and a person without the gift of the second-sight would have guessed her to have been a pragmatical upstart, though it is very probable that during that time she fancied herself really better than her mistress. The mistress acted her part of maid the best, for it is easier for genteel modesty to act a low part than for affected vanity to act a high one. She kept her distance like a servant, but would, to disguise things the better, be

every now and then pert, according to their way, and
give occasion to be chid.   But there is an air of gen-
tility inborn and inbred to some people, and even when
they aim to be awkward, a certain grace will attend
all their minutest actions and gestures, and command
love, respect, and veneration.   I must therefore own
that there was not need of a man's being a conjurer to
guess who ought to be the lady and who the maid ;
but to know absolutely who was the lady and who
was the maid did require that skill.   For how many
such real ladies have we that are made so from such
upstarts, and how many genteel waiting-women of great
descent, that are born with a grace about them, and are
bred to good manners.   Mr Campbell's art made him
positive in the case ; he took the patches from the face
of the maid and placed them on the mistress's ; he
pulled off her hood and scarf and gave it to the lady,
and taking from the lady her riding-hood, gave it the
maid in exchange ; for ladies at that time of day were
not entered into that fashion of cloaking themselves.
Then he wrote down that he should go out, and ought
to send his maid in to undress them quite, and give the
mistress her own clothes and the maid hers, and with
a smile wrote down both their names and commended
her contrivance ; but after that it was remarked by the
lady that he paid her less respect than she expected,
and more to her footman, who was in gentleman's
habit, whom he took by his side, and told a great many
fine things ; whereas he would tell the lady nothing
further.   The lady, nettled at this, wrote to him that
she had vanity enough to believe that she might be
distinguished from her maid in any dress ; but that he
had shown his want of skill in not knowing who that
gentleman was.   Mr Campbell told her her mistake
in sharp terms ; and begging her pardon, assured her he
knew several chambermaids as genteel and as well-born

as her, and many mistresses more awkward and worse born than her maid; that he did not go, therefore, by the rule of guess and judging what ought to be, but by the rule of certainty, and the knowledge of what actually was. She, however, unsatisfied with that answer, perplexed him mightily to know who the man was. He answered, he would be a great man. The lady laughed scornfully, and said she wanted to know who he was, not what he would be. He answered again, he was her footman, but that she would have a worse. She grew warm, and desired to be informed why, since he knew the fellow's condition, he respected her so little and him so much; and accused him of want of practising manners if he had not want of knowledge. He answered, "Madam, since you will be asking questions too far, this footman will advance himself to the degree of a gentleman, and have a woman of distinction to his wife; while you will degrade yourself by a marriage to be the wife of a footman. His ambition is laudable, your condescension mean, therefore I give him the preference; I have given you fair warning and wholesome advice, you may avoid your lot by prudence, but his will certainly be what I tell you."

This coming afterwards to pass exactly as was predicted, and his disappointing so many that had a mind to impose upon him, has rendered him pretty free from such wily contrivances since, though now and then they have happened, but still to the mortification and disappointment of the contrivers. But as we have not pretended to say, with regard to these things, that he has his genius always at his elbow or his back, to whisper in his ear the names of persons, and such little constant events as these; so, that we may not be deemed to give a fabulous account of his life and adventures, we think ourselves bound to give the reader an insight into the particular power and capacity which he has for bringing about these particular performances, especially that of writing down names of strangers at first sight, which I do not doubt will be done to the satisfaction of all persons who shall read the succeeding chapter concerning the gift of the second-sight.

—∽✐∾—

Chapter vij.

Concerning the Second-sight.

MR Martin lately published a book, entitled "A Description of the Western Isles of Scotland, called by the ancient geographers, Hebrides." It contains many curious particulars relating to the natural and civil history of those islands, with a map of them ; and in his preface he tells us, that perhaps it is peculiar to those isles that they have never been described till now by any man that was a native of the country, or had travelled them as himself has done ; and in the conclusion of the said preface he tells us he has given here such an account of the second-sight as the nature of the thing will bear, which has always been reckoned sufficient among the unbiassed part of mankind ; but for those that will not be satisfied they ought to oblige us with a new scheme by which we may judge of matters of fact. The chief particulars he has given us concerning the second-sight are here set down, by way of abstract or epitome, that they may not be too tedious to the reader.

1. In the second-sight the vision makes such a lively impression on the seers, that they neither see nor think of anything else but the vision as long as it continues ; and then they appear pensive or jovial according to the object which was presented to them.

2. At the sight of a vision the eyelids of the person are erected, and the eyes continue staring till the object vanish, as has often been observed by the author and others present.

3. There is one in Skye, an acquaintance of whom observed, that when he sees a vision the inner part of his eyelids turn so far upwards, that, after the object disappears, he must draw them down with his fingers, and sometimes employs others to draw them down, which he finds to be much the easier way.

4. The faculty of the second-sight does not lineally descend in a family, as some imagine, for he knows several parents that are endowed with it, but not their children, and so on the contrary. Neither is it acquired by any previous compact ; and after a strict inquiry he could never learn from any among them that this faculty was communicable any way whatsoever.

Note, that this account is differing from the account that is given by Mr Aubrey, a gentleman of the Royal Society ; and I think Mr Martin's reason here against the descent of this faculty from parents to children is not generally conclusive. For, though he may know parents endowed with it, and not children, and so *vice versâ*, yet there may be parents who are endowed with it, being qualified, as Mr Aubrey has said (viz., both being second-sighted, or even one to an extraordinary degree), whose children may have it by descent. And as to this faculty being any other way communicable, since the accounts differ, I must leave it to a further examination.

5. The seer knows neither the object, time, nor place of a vision before it appears, and the same object is often seen by different persons living at a considerable distance from one another. The true way of judging as to the time and circumstance of an object is by observation ; for several persons of judgment

without this faculty are more capable to judge of the design of a vision than a novice that is a seer. As an object appears in the day or night it will come to pass sooner or later accordingly.

6. If an object be seen early in the morning, which is not frequent, it will be accomplished in a few hours afterwards. If at noon, it will commonly be accomplished that very day; if in the evening, perhaps that night; if after candles be lighted, it will be accomplished that night. It's later always in accomplishment by weeks, months, and sometimes years, according to the time of the night the vision is seen.

7. When a shroud is perceived about one, it is a sure prognostic of death; the time is judged according to the height of it about the person; for if it be not seen above the middle, death is not to be expected for the space of a year, and perhaps some months longer; and as it is frequently seen to ascend higher towards the head, death is concluded to be at hand in a few days, if not hours, as daily experience confirms. Examples of this kind were shown the author, when the persons of whom the observations were made enjoyed perfect health.

There was one instance lately of a prediction of this kind, by a seer that was a novice, concerning the death of one of the author's acquaintance; this was communicated to a few only, and with great confidence. The author being one of the number, did not in the least regard it till the death of the person, about the time foretold, confirmed to him the certainty of the prediction. The aforesaid novice is now a skilful seer, as appears from many late instances. He lives in the parish of St Mary's, the most northern in Skye.

8. If a woman be seen standing at a man's left

hand, it is a presage that she will be his wife, whether they are married to others or unmarried at the time of the apparition. If two or three women are seen at once standing near a man's left hand, she that is next him will undoubtedly be his wife first, and so on, whether all three, or the man, be single or married at the time of the vision, of which there are several late instances of the author's acquaintance. It is an ordinary thing for them to see a man that is to come to the house shortly after, and though he be not of the seer's acquaintance, yet he not only tells his name, but gives such a lively description of his stature, complexion, habit, &c., that upon his arrival he answers the character given of him in all respects. If the person so appearing be one of the seer's acquaintance, he can tell by his countenance whether he comes in good or bad humour. The author has been seen thus, by seers of both sexes, at some hundreds of miles' distance. Some that saw him in this manner had never seen him personally, and it happened according to their visions, without any previous design of his to go to those places, his coming there being purely accidental ; and in the nineteenth page of his book, he tells us that Mr Daniel Morrison, a minister, told him, that upon his landing in the island Rona, the natives received him very affectionately, and addressed themselves to him with this salutation—" God save you, pilgrim ! You are heartily welcome here, for we have had repeated apparitions of your person amongst us ;" viz., after the manner of the second-sight.

9. 'Tis ordinary with them to see houses, gardens, and trees, in places void of all three, and this in process of time used to be accomplished ; of which he gives an instance in the Island of Skye.

10. To see a spark of fire fall upon one's arm or breast, is a forerunner of a dead child to be seen in the

arms of those persons, of which there are several fresh instances.

To see a seat empty at the time of one's sitting in it, is a presage of that person's death quickly after.

When a novice, or one that has lately obtained the second-sight, sees a vision in the night-time without doors, and comes near a fire, he presently falls into a swoon.

Some find themselves, as it were, in a crowd of people having a corpse which they carry along with them; and after such visions the seers come in sweating, and describe the people that appeared; if there are any of their acquaintance among them, they give an account of their names and also of the bearers, but they know nothing concerning the corpse.

All those that have the second-sight do not always see these visions at once, though they are together at the time; but if one who has this faculty designedly touch his fellow-seer at the instant of a vision's appearing, then the second sees it as well as the first.

11. There is the way of foretelling death by a cry that they call Taisk, which some call a Wraith in the lowland. They hear a loud cry without doors, exactly resembling the voice of some particular person, whose death is foretold by it, of which he gives a late instance, which happened in the village Rigg, in Skye Isle.

12. Things are also foretold by smelling sometimes, as follows:—Fish or flesh is frequently smelt in the fire, when at the same time neither of the two are in the house, or, in any probability, likely to be had in it for some weeks or months. This smell several persons have who are endued with the second-sight, and it is always accomplished soon after.

13. Children, horses, and cows, have the second-sight, as well as men and women advanced in years.

That children see it, it is plain from their crying aloud at the very instant that a corpse or any other vision appears to an ordinary seer; of which he gives an instance in a child when himself was present.

That horses likewise see it's very plain, from their violent and sudden starting when the rider or seer in company with them sees a vision of any kind by night or day. It is observable of a horse that he will not go forward that way till he be led about at some distance from the common road, and then he is in a sweat. He gives an instance of this in a horse in the Isle of Skye.

That cows have the second-sight appears from this; that if a woman milking a cow happens to see a vision by the second-sight, the cow runs away in a great fright at the same time, and will not be pacified for some time after.

In reference to this, Paracelsus, tom. 9, l. "De arte presagâ," writes thus, "Horses also have their auguries, who perceive by their sight and smell wandering spirits, witches, and spectres and the like things, and dogs both see and hear the same."

Here in the next place the author answers objections that have lately been made against the reality of the second-sight.

First, it's objected that these seers are visionary and melancholy people, who fancy they see things that do not appear to them or anybody else.

He answers, the people of these isles, and particularly the seers, are very temperate, and their diet is simple and moderate in quantity and quality; so that their brains are not, in all probability, disordered by undigested fumes of meat or drink. Both sexes are free from hysteric fits, convulsions, and several other distempers of that sort. There are no madmen among them, nor any instance of self-murder. It's observed among them that a man drunk never has a vision of the second-sight, and he that is a visionary would discover himself in other things as well as in that; nor are such as have the second-sight judged to be visionaries by any of their friends or acquaintance.

Secondly, it is objected that there are none among the learned able to oblige the world with a satisfactory account of these visions; therefore they are not to be believed.

He answers, if everything of which the learned are not able to give a satisfactory account shall be condemned as false and impossible, we shall find many other things, generally believed, which must be rejected as such.

Thirdly, it's objected that the seers are impostors, and the people who believe them are credulous, and easy to be imposed upon.

He answers, the seers are generally illiterate and well-meaning people, and altogether void of design; nor could he ever learn that any of them made the least gain of it; neither is it reputable among them to have that faculty; besides, the people of the isles are not so credulous as to believe an impossibility before the thing foretold be accomplished: but when it actually comes to pass, afterwards, it is not in their power to deny it without offering violence to their senses and reason. Besides, if the seers were deceivers, can it be reasonable to imagine that all the islanders who have not the second-sight should combine together and offer violence to their understandings and senses to force themselves to believe a lie from age to age? There are several persons among them whose birth and education raise them above the suspicion of concurring with an imposture, merely to gratify an illiterate and contemptible sort of persons. Nor can a reasonable man believe that children, horses, and cows could be engaged in a combination to persuade the world of the reality of a second-sight.

Every vision that is seen comes exactly to pass, according to the rules of observation, though novices and heedless persons do not always judge by those rules, concerning which he gives instances.

There are visions seen by several persons in whose days they are not accomplished; and this is one of the reasons why some things have been seen that are said never to have come to pass, and there are also several visions seen which are not understood till they are accomplished.

The second-sight is not a late discovery seen by one or two in a corner or a remote isle, but it is seen by many persons of both sexes in several isles, separated about forty or fifty leagues from one another. The inhabitants of many of these isles never had the least converse by word or writing, and this faculty of seeing visions having continued, as we are informed by tradition, ever since the plantation of these isles, without being disproved by the nicest sceptic after the strictest inquiry, seems to be a clear proof of its reality.

It's observable that it was much more common twenty or thirty years ago than at present; for one in ten does not see it now that saw it then.

The second-sight is not confined to the Western Isles alone, the author having an account that it is in several parts of Holland, but particularly in Bommel, where a woman has it, for which she is courted by some and dreaded by others. She sees a smoke about one's face, which is the forerunner of the death of a person so seen, and she actually foretold the deaths of several that lived there. She was living in that town a few winters ago.

The second-sight is likewise in the Isle of Man, as appears by this instance. Captain Leathes, the chief commander of Belfast, in his voyage, 1690, lost thirteen men by a violent storm, and upon his landing in the Isle of Man, an ancient man, clerk to a parish there, told him immediately that he had lost thirteen men there; the captain inquired how he came to the knowledge of that; he answered, that it was by thirteen lights which he had seen come into the churchyard, as Mr Sacheverell tells us in his late description of the Isle of Man. Note—that this is like the sight of the corpse-candles in Wales, which is also well attested.

Here the author adds many other instances concerning the second-sight, of which I shall set down only a few.

A man in Knockow, in the parish of St Mary's, the northernmost part of Skye, being in perfect health, and sitting with his fellow servants at night, was on a sudden taken ill, dropped from his seat backward, and then fell a-vomiting; at which the family was much concerned, he having never been subject to the like before; but he came to himself soon after, and had no sort of pain about him. One of the family, who was accustomed to see the second-sight, told them that the man's illness proceeded from a very strange cause, which was thus:—An ill-natured woman (whom he named) who lives in the next adjacent village of Bornskittag, came before him in a very angry and furious manner, her countenance full of passion and her mouth full of reproaches, and threatened him with her head and hands till he fell over, as you have seen him. This woman had a fancy for the man, but was like to be disappointed as to her marrying of him. This instance was told the author by the master of the family and others who were present when it happened.

Sir Norman Macleod and some others playing at tables, at a game called in Irish "falmermore," wherein

I

there are three of a side, and each of them throw the dice by turns, there happened to be one difficult point in the disposing of one of the table-men. This obliged the gamester to deliberate before he was to change his man, since upon the disposing of it the winning or losing of the game depended; at length the butler, who stood behind, advised the player where to place the man, with which he complied and won the game. This being thought extraordinary, and Sir Norman hearing one whisper him in the ear, asked who advised him so skilfully? He answered, it was the butler, but this seemed more strange, for it was generally thought he could not play at tables. Upon this Sir Norman asked him how long it was since he had learned to play? And the fellow owned that he had never played in his life, but that he saw the spirit Brownie (a spirit usually seen in that country) reaching his arm over the player's head, and touching the part with his finger where the table-man was to be placed. This was told the author by Sir Norman, and others who happened to be present at the time.

Daniel Bow, alias Black, an inhabitant of Born-skittag, who is one of the precisest seers in the isles, foretold the death of a young woman in Minginis within less than twenty-four hours before the time, and accordingly she died suddenly in the fields, though at the time of the prediction she was in perfect health, but the shroud appearing close about her head was the ground of his confidence that her death was at hand.

The same person foretold the death of a child in his master's arms by seeing a spark of fire fall on his left arm, and this was likewise accomplished soon after the prediction.

Some of the inhabitants of Harris, sailing round the Isle of Skye with a design to go to the opposite main-land, were strangely surprised with an apparition of two men hanging down by the ropes that secured the mast, but could not conjecture what it meant; they pursued their voyage, but the wind turning contrary they were forced into Broadford, in the Isle of Skye, where they found Sir Donald Macdonald keeping a sheriff's court, and two criminals receiving sentence of death there. The ropes and mast of that very boat were made use of to hang those criminals. This was told the author by several who had this instance related to them by the boat's crew.

Several persons living in a certain family told the author that they had frequently seen two men standing at a gentlewoman's left hand, who was their master's daughter; they told the men's names, and being her equals, it was not doubted but she would be married to one of them, and perhaps to the other after the death of the first. Some time after a third man appeared, who seemed always to stand nearest to her of the three, but the seers did not know him, though they could describe him exactly; and within some months after, this man, who was seen last, actually came to the house, and fully answered the description given of him by those who never saw him but in a vision, and he married the woman shortly after. They live in the Isle of Skye, and both themselves and others confirmed the truth of this instance when the author saw them.

Archibald Macdonald, of the parish of St Mary's, in the Isle of Skye, being reputed famous in his skill of foretelling things to come by the second-sight, happening to be in the village Knockow one night, and before supper told the family that he had just then seen the strangest thing he ever saw in his life, viz., a man with an ugly long cap always shaking his head, but that the strangest of all was a little kind of a harp which he had with four strings only, and that it had two hart's horns fixed in the front of it. All that heard this odd vision fell a-laughing at Archibald, telling him that he was dreaming, or had not his wits about him, since he pretended to see a thing which had no being, and was not so much as heard of in any part of the world. All this could not alter Archibald's opinion, who told them that they must excuse him if he laughed at them after the accomplishment of the vision. Archibald returned to his own house, and within three or four days after a man with a cap, harp, &c., came to the house, and the harp, strings, horns, and cap answered the description of them at first view, and he shook his head when he played, for he had two bells fixed to his cap. This harper was a poor man, who made himself a buffoon for his bread, and was never seen before in those parts, and at the time of the prediction he was in the Isle of Barray, which is about twenty leagues distant from that part of Skye. This relation is vouched by Mr Daniel Martin, and all his family, and such as were then present, and they live in the village where this happened.

One Daniel Nicholson, minister of St Mary's, in Skye, the parish in which Mr Archibald Macdonald lived, told the author that one Sunday, after sermon, at the Chapel Uig, he took an occasion to inquire of Archibald if he still retained that unhappy faculty of seeing the second-sight, and wished him to get rid of it, if possible; for, said he, it's no true character of a good man. Archibald was highly displeased, and answered that he hoped he was no more unhappy than his neighbours, for seeing what they could not perceive. "I had," said he, "as serious thoughts as my neighbours in time of hearing a sermon to-day, and even then I saw a corpse laid on the ground close to the pulpit; and I assure you it will be accomplished shortly, for it was in the day-time." There were none in the parish then sick, and few are buried at that little chapel, nay, sometimes, not one in a year. Yet when Mr Nicholson returned to preach in the said chapel, a fortnight or three weeks after, he found one buried in the very spot named by Archibald. This story is vouched by Mr Nicholson, the minister, and several of the parishioners still living.

Note, that it's counted by many an argument of somewhat evil attending this faculty of the second-sight, because there are instances given of some persons who have been freed of it, upon using some Christian practices. But I shall hereafter show that this opinion cannot be entirely true.

Sir Norman Macleod, who has his residence in the Isle of Bernera, which lies between the Isles of N. Uist and Harris, went to the Isle of Skye about business, without appointing any time for his return; his servants, in his absence, being all together in the large hall at night, one of them, who had the second-sight, told the rest they must remove, for there would be abundance of company in the hall that night. One of his fellow servants answered, that there was very little likelihood of that, because of the darkness of the night, and the danger of coming through the rocks that lay round the isle; but within an hour after one of Sir Norman's men came to the house, bidding them provide lights, &c., for his master had newly landed.

Sir Norman being told of this, called for the seer and examined him about it. He answered, that he had seen the spirit Brownie, in human shape, come several times and make a show of carrying an old woman, that sat by the fire, to the door, and at last seemed to carry her out by neck and heels; which made him laugh heartily, and gave occasion to the rest to conclude him mad, to laugh so much without any reason. This instance was told the author by Sir Norman himself.

Four men, from the Isle of Skye and Harris, went to Barbadoes, and stayed there some years ; who, though they had wont to see the second-sight in their native country, never saw it in Barbadoes, but upon their return to England, the first night after their landing they saw the second-sight, as the author was told by several of their acquaintance.

John Morrison, who lives in Bernera of Harris, wears the plant called *fuga dæmonum* sewed in the neck of his coat, to prevent his seeing visions, and says he never saw any since he first carried that plant about him.

A spirit, by the country people called Brownie, was frequently seen in all the most considerable families in the isles and north of Scotland, in the shape of a tall man, having very long brown hair. But within these twenty years past he has been seen but rarely.

There were spirits also that appeared in the shape of women, horses, swine, cats, and some like fiery balls, which would follow men in the fields ; but there have been but few instances of these for upwards of forty years past.

These spirits used also to form sounds in the air, resembling those of a harp, pipes, crowing of a cock and of the grinding of hand-mills. And sometimes voices have been heard in the air at night, singing Irish songs, the words of which songs some of the author's acquaintances still retain ; one of them resembled the voice of a woman, who died some time before, and the song related to her state in the other world. All these accounts, the author says, he had from persons of as great integrity as any in the world.

So far Mr Martin, whose account is so long that I have given the reader only a short abridgment thereof ; and shall therefore satisfy myself, without relating any further passages, by directing the reader to others also,

learned men, who have written on the same subject.
Laurentius Ananias printed a volume in Latin, at Venice,
anno 1571, about the nature of Demons, where, in
the third book, he writes concerning the second-sight.
The learned Camerarius does the like, and names a
person of his own acquaintance, whom he testifies to
have had that gift.   St Austin himself testifies something (not very different from what we now call the
gift of the second-sight) of one Curina, who lived in
the country of Hippo in Africa.   Bonaysteau tells us
something like it in his "Disc. de Excell. et Dig.
Hominis," concerning the spirit of Hermotimus.   So
do likewise Herodotus and Maximus Tyrius about the
spirit of Aristæus.   Cardan does the same in his "De
rerum variet.," l. 8, c. 84, of his kinsman Baptista
Cardan, a student at Pavia.   Baptista Fulgosus tells
us of what we call the second-sight, in other words,
in his l. 1, "Fact. et dict. memorab.," c. 6.   Among
our own countrymen, the Lord Henry Howard, in
the book he wrote against the supposed prophecies,
in his seventeenth chapter, tells us a wonderful story
of this kind of sight ; and sure that noble lord may be
looked upon as an unexceptionable testimony in a story
he relates of his own knowledge, he having otherwise
little faith in things of this kind.   Mr Cotton Mather,
a minister of New England, in his relation of the
wonders of the invisible world, inserted in his "Eccle-
siastical History" of that country, printed in London,
anno 1702, in folio, has given us several instances of
this kind, as also of many other diabolical operations.
Mr Baxter's book concerning the "Certainty of the
World of Spirits," has the like proofs in it.   Mr Aubrey,
Fellow of the Royal Society, has written largely concerning second-sighted persons ; so has Mr Beaumont,
in his book of genii and familiar spirits, who has
collected almost all the other accounts together, and

many others whose very names it would be tedious to recite. However, as there are a few more passages very curious in themselves, I will venture so far upon the reader's patience as not only to recite the names of the authors, but the accounts themselves, in as succinct and brief a manner as it is possible for any one to do.

Mr Th. May, in his History, lib. 8, writes, that an old man (like an hermit) second-sighted, took his leave of King James I. when he came into England. He took little notice of Prince Henry, but addressing himself to the Duke of York (since King Charles I.), fell a-weeping to think what misfortunes he should undergo, and that he should be one of the most miserable and most unhappy princes that ever was.

A Scotch nobleman sent for one of these second-sighted men out of the Highlands, to give his judgment of the then great George Villiers, Duke of Buckingham. As soon as ever he saw him, "Pish," said he, "he will come to nothing, I see a dagger in his breast;" and he was stabbed in the breast by Captain Felton, as has been at large recounted in some of the foregoing pages.

Sir James Melvil hath several the like passages in his History.

A certain old man, in South Wales, told a great man there, of the fortune of his family, and that there should not be a third male generation. It has fallen out accordingly.

Sir William Dugdale, with his own mouth, informed several gentlemen, that Major-General Middleton (since lord) went into the Highlands of Scotland, to endeavour to make a party for King Charles I. An old gentleman (that was second-sighted) came and told him that his endeavour was good, but he would be unsuccessful; and moreover, that they would put the king to death,

and that several other attempts would be made, but all
in vain; but that his son would come in, but not reign
a long time, but would at last be restored. This Lord
Middleton had a great friendship with the Laird Bocconi, and they made an agreement, that the first of
them that died should appear to the other in extremity.
The Lord Middleton was taken prisoner at Worcester
fight, and was prisoner in the Tower of London, under
three locks. Lying in his bed, pensive, Bocconi appeared to him; my Lord Middleton asked him if he
were dead or alive? He said, dead, and that he was a
ghost; and told him that within three days he should
escape, and he did so, in his wife's clothes. When he
had done his message he gave a frisk, and said—

> "Givanni, Givanni, 'tis very strange
> In the world to see so sudden a change."

And then gathered up and vanished. This account Sir
William Dugdale had from the Bishop of Edinburgh.
And this account he hath written in a book of Mis-
cellanies, which is now deposited (with other books of
his) in the museum at Oxford.

Thus the reader sees what great authorities may be
produced to prove that wonderful and true predictions
have been delivered by many persons gifted with the
second-sight. The most learned men in almost all
nations, who are not in all likelihood deceived themselves; the most celebrated and authentic historians, and
some divines, in England, who, it is not to be thought,
have combined together and made it their business to
obtrude upon us falsehoods; persons of all ranks, from
the highest to the lowest, in Scotland, who it would be
even madness to think, would join in a confederacy to
impose tricks upon us, and to persuade us to the greatest
of impostures as solemn truths delivered from their own
mouths; all these, I say, have unanimously and (as it

were) with one voice asserted, repeated, and confirmed
to us, that there have been at all times, and in many
different nations, and that still there are persons who,
possessed with the gift of a second-sight, predict things
that wonderfully come to pass; and seem to merit very
little less than the name of prophets, for their miraculous
discoveries. Now if any man should come, and without giving the least manner of reason for it (for there
is no reason to be given against such assertions) declare
his disbelief of all these authentic, though strange
accounts; can he with reason imagine that his incredulity shall pass for a token of wisdom? Shall his
obstinacy confute the learned? Shall his want of faith
be thought justly to give the lie to so many persons of
the highest honour and quality, and of the most undoubted integrity? In fine, shall his infidelity, by a
reverse kind of power to that which is attributed to the
philosopher's stone, be able to change the nature of
things, turn and transmute truth into falsehood, and
make a downright plain matter of fact to be more than
a *chimera* or an *ens rationis?* And shall a manifest
experience be so easily exploded?

Taking it therefore for granted that no modest man
whatsoever, though never so hard of belief, which is
certainly as great a weakness as that of too much
credulity, will make bold openly to declare his disbelief
of things so well attested; and taking it much more for
granted still, that it is impossible for any man of common
sense to have the front of declaring his disbelief of them
in such a manner as to urge it for an argument and a
reason why others should disbelieve them too; taking
this, I say, as I think I very well may, for granted, I
think there remains nothing further for me to offer,
before I conclude this chapter, except a few remarks
as to the similitude there is between those actions,
which I have related above to have been performed by

Mr Campbell, and these actions, which so many learned, ingenious, and noble authors, as I have just now quoted, have asserted to have been performed by persons whom they knew to be gifted with the second-sight.

As to what is said (several pages above) concerning Duncan Campbell, when a boy at Edinburgh, that he even told his little companions who would have success at their little matches when they played at marbles ; and that he informed a great gamester there, whose name I have disguised under that of Count Cog, what times he should choose to play if he would win ; as ludicrous as it may have appeared to be, and as much as it may have seemed to my readers to carry with it nothing better than the face of invention and the air of fiction, yet if they will be at the pains of comparing that passage of Duncan Campbell's with the account given in this chapter from the mouth of Sir Norman Macleod, concerning a man who, though he never played at tables in his life, instructed a skilful gamester, when he was at a stand, to place one of his men right, upon which the whole game depended, which the ignorant fellow, when asked how he came to do it, said he was directed to by the spirit Brownie ; whoever, I say, will be at the pains of comparing these passages together, will find they bear a very near resemblance, and that the way we may most reasonably account for Duncan Campbell's prediction, when he was a boy, must be that he was at that time directed by his little genius or familiar spirit, which I described in the precedent pages, as this fellow was by the spirit Brownie, according to Sir Norman Macleod's assertion, which spirit Brownie, as Mr Martin, a very good and credited writer, assures us in his " History of the Western Islands," dedicated to the late Prince George of Denmark, is a spirit usually seen all over that country.

If the reader recollects, he will remember likewise

that in the little discourse which I mentioned to have been held between me and this Duncan Campbell when a boy concerning his little genius, I there say the boy signified to me, that he smelt venison, and was sure that some would come to his mother's house shortly after; accordingly I came thither that morning from the death of a deer, and ordered a part of it to be brought after me to her house. Now Mr Martin's twelfth observation about the second-sight in this chapter clears it plainly up that this knowledge in the boy proceeded from the gift of second-sight. Not to give the reader too often the trouble of looking back in order to judge of the truth of what I say, I will here repeat that observation, which is as follows: things are also foretold by smelling sometimes; for example, fish or flesh is frequently smelt in the fire, when at the same time neither of the two are in the house or in any probability like to be had in it for some weeks or months. This smell several persons have who are endued with the second-sight, and it is always accomplished soon after.

But I will here omit any further remarks by way of accounting how he compassed his predictions when a boy, either by the intervention of his genius or the gift of a second-sight; and examine how nearly those things which I have related to have been done by him in his more advanced years, when he took up the profession of a predictor in London, correspond with the accounts given in this chapter about a second-sight, and how near a resemblance the things done by him bear to those things that are so well attested to have been performed by others, through the efficacious power of this wonderful faculty.

First, then, if we have a mind to make a tolerable guess which way Mr Campbell came acquainted that the death of the beautiful young lady, Mrs W[e]lw[oo]d, was so near at hand, and that, though she was so universally admired, she would die unmarried ; the accounts given of other second-sighted persons in the like cases, will put us in the most probable way of guessing right. This is explained by the seventh observation in this chapter, where it is said from Mr Martin that when a shroud is perceived about one, it is a sure prognostic of death ; the time is judged according to the height of it about the person, for if it be not seen above the middle, death is not to be expected for the space of a year or longer, but as it comes nearer to the head it is expected sooner ; if to the very head, it is concluded to be at hand within a few days, if not hours. Of this we have an example, of which Mr Martin was an eye-witness, concerning the death of his own acquaintance ; but he did not in the least regard it till the death of the person, about the time foretold, confirmed to him the certainty of the prediction.

Secondly, as to the ignominious death that Irwin came to, and which he predicted to his mother so long before when she was in flourishing circumstances, and when there was no appearance that any of her children should be brought to a beggarly condition, and learn among base gangs of company to thieve and be carried to the gallows. The story told in this chapter of some of the inhabitants of Harris sailing round the Isle of Skye, and seeing the apparition of two men hanging by the ropes on the mast of their vessel, and when they came to the opposite mainland finding two criminals just sentenced to death by Sir Donald Macdonald, and seeing their own very masts and ropes made choice of for their execution, clears up the manner how Mr Campbell might predict this of Irwin likewise by the force of the second-sight.

Thirdly, as to Mr Campbell's telling Christallina, the belle and chief toast of the court, and Urbana, the reigning beauty of the city, that they should shortly be married, and who were to be their husbands; it is a thing he has done almost every day in his life to one woman or other that comes to consult him about the man she is to be married to; the manner he probably takes in doing this, may be likewise explained by the foregoing story in this chapter about the servants who said they saw three men standing by the left hand of their master's daughter, and that he that was nearest would marry her first, whom they plainly and exactly described, though they had never seen him but in their vision, as appeared afterwards. For within some months after the very man described did come to the house and did marry her. *Vide* the eighth observation of the second-sight.

Fourthly, as to the predictions delivered by Mr Campbell to the merchant, which are set down at length in the foregoing chapter, I know no better way at guessing the manner how the second-sight operated in him at that time, than by comparing them to these two instances, which I briefly repeat, because they are set down at length before in this chapter. And first it may be asked how did the second-sight operate in Mr Campbell when it gave him to know that the merchant's ships, which repeated intelligences had in appearance confirmed to be lost, were at that time safe, and would return securely home into the harbour designed? The best way of accounting for it that I know, is by the story that Sir Norman Macleod is above affirmed to have told with his own mouth concerning a servant of his who rightly foretold his returning home and landing on the isle of Bernera one night, where his residence was, when there was very little or no likelihood of it, because of the darkness of the night and the danger of coming through the rocks that lie round the isle. When Sir Norman examined him about it, he answered that he knew it by a vision of the spirit Brownie; and hence it may be the most probably conjectured that Mr Campbell's knowledge of the merchant's ships being safe, came from a vision of his particular genius or familiar spirit, which we spoke of before. What I have already instanced in, is, I think, sufficient with regard to the wonderful things which Mr Campbell has performed, either by the intervention of a genius or the power of a second-sight. But as he has frequently done a great many amazing performances, which seem to be of such a nature that they can't be well and clearly explained to have been done either by the intervention of his familiar spirit and genius, or by the power of the second-sighted faculty, we must have recourse to the third means, by which only such predictions and practices can be compassed, before we expound these new mysteries, which appear like incredible riddles and enigmas at the first; and this third means which we must have recourse to for expounding these strange acts of his, is a due consideration of the force and power of natural magic, which, together with a narrative of the acts which he seems magically to bring about, will be the subject of the following chapter.

Chapter viii.

A Dissertation upon Magic.

BUT before we proceed to our disquisitions concerning the power and efficacy of natural magic, and examine what mysterious operations may be brought about and compassed by magical practices, and before we take a further survey of what Mr Campbell has performed in this kind, that relates to his profession and the public part of his life, which concerns other people as well as himself, I shall here relate some singular adventures that he passed through in his private life, and which regard only his own person. In order to this, I must return back to the year 1702, about which time some unaccountable turns of fortune attended him in his own private capacity, which must be very surprising and entertaining to my readers, when they find a man, whose foresight was always so great a help and assistance to others who consulted him in their own future affairs, helpless (as it has been an observation concerning all such men in the account of the second-sight), and blind in his own future affairs, tossed up and down by inevitable and spiteful accidents of fortune, and made the May-game of chance and hazard ; as if that wayward and inconstant goddess was resolved to punish him, when she catched him on the blind side, for having such a quick insight and penetrating faculty in other people's matters, and scrutinising too narrowly into her mysteries, and so sometimes preventing those fatal intentions of hers, into which she would fain lead many mortals hoodwinked, and before they knew where they were. In this light, these mighty and famous seers seem to be born for the benefit and felicity of others, but at the same time to be born to unhappiness themselves. And certainly, inasmuch as we consider them as useful and beneficial, often, but always satisfactory, to persons who are curious in their inquiries about their fortunes, it will be natural to those of us, who have the least share of generosity in our minds, to yield our pity and compassion to them, when they are remarkably unfortunate themselves, especially when that calamity seems more particularly to light upon them for their ability and endeavour to consult the good fortune of other folks.

About the above-mentioned year 1702, Duncan Campbell grew a little tired of his profession. Such a multitude of followers troubled him, several of whom were wild youths and came to banter him, and many more too inquisitive females, to tease him with endless impertinences, and who, the more he told them, had still the more to ask, and whose curiosity was never to be satisfied ; and besides this he was so much envied, and had so many malicious artifices daily practised against him, that he resolved to leave off his profession. He had, I know, followed it pretty closely, from the time I first saw him in London, which was, I think, in the beginning of the year 1698, till the year 1702, with very good success ; and in those few years, he had got together a pretty round sum of money. Our young seer was now at man's estate, and had learned the notion that he was to be his own governor, so far as to be his own counsellor too in what road of life he was to take ; and this consideration, no doubt, worked with deeper impression on his mind than it usually does on others that are in the same blossoming pride of manhood, because it might appear more natural for him to believe that he had a sufficient ability to be his own proper adviser, who had given so many others, and some more aged than himself, counsel with very good success. Now every experienced person knows that when manhood is yet green it is still in the same dangerous condition as a young plant, which is liable to be warped by a thousand cross fortuitous accidents if good measures be not taken to support it against all the contingent shocks it may meet with from the weather or otherwise. Now, it was his misfortune to be made averse to business which he loved before by having too much of it, and to be so soured by meeting with numerous perplexities and malicious rubs laid in his way by invidious people (who are the useless and injurious busybodies, that always repine at the good of others, and rejoice to do harm to the diligent and assiduous, though they reap no profit by it themselves), that he was disgusted and deterred entirely from the prosecution of a profession, by which he got not only a competent but a copious and plentiful subsistence. Nay, indeed, this was another mischief arising to him from his having so much business that he had got money enough to leave it off, when the perplexities of it had made him willing to do so, and to live very comfortably and handsomely like a gentleman without it for a time; and we know the youngest men are not wont to look the furthest before them in matters that concern their own welfare. Now, inasmuch as he had thus taken a disgust to business and application, and was surfeited (as I may say) with the perplexities of it, it must be as natural for him, we know, to search for repose in the contrary extreme, viz., recreation and idleness, as it is for a man to seek rest after toil, to sleep after a day's labour, or to sit down after a long and tiresome walk.

But there are two very distinct sorts of idleness, and two very different kinds of recreations; there is a shameful idleness which is no better than downright sloth; and there is a splendid kind of indolence where a man, having taken an aversion to the wearisomeness of a business which properly belongs to him, neglects not, however, to employ his thoughts, when they are vacant from what they ought more chiefly to be about, in other matters not entirely unprofitable in life, the exercise of which he finds he can follow with more abundant ease and satisfaction. There are some sorts of recreations too that are mean, sordid and base; others that are very innocent, though very diverting, and that will give one the very next most valuable qualifications of a gentleman after those which are obtained by a more serious application of the mind.

The idea which I have already given my readers of our Duncan Campbell will easily make them judge before I tell them, which way, in these two ways, his genius would naturally lead him ; and that when he grew an idle man he would rather indulge himself with applying his mind to the shining trifles of life than be wholly slothful and inactive ; and that when he diverted himself he would not do it after a sordid base manner, as having a better taste and a relish for good company, but that his recreations would still be the recreations of a gentleman. And just accordingly as my readers would naturally judge beforehand in his case, so it really happened. The moment he shook off business, and dismissed the thoughts of it, his genius led him to a very gallant way of life ; in his lodgings, in his entertainments, in paying and receiving visits, in coffee-houses, in taverns, in fencing-schools, in balls, and other public assemblies, in all ways, in fine, both at home and abroad, Duncan Campbell was a well-comported and civil gentleman ; he was a man of pleasure, and nothing of the man of business appeared about him. But a gentleman's life without a gentleman's estate, however shining and pleasant it may be for a time, will certainly end in sorrow, if not in infamy ; and, comparing life, as moralists do, to a day, one may safely pronounce this truth to all the splendid idlers I have mentioned, that if they have sunshiny weather till noon, yet the afternoon of their life will be very stormy, rainy, and uncomfortable ; and perhaps just at the end of their journey, to carry on the metaphor throughout, close in the darkest kind of night. Of this, as I was a man of years, and more experienced in the world than he, I took upon me to forewarn Mr Campbell, as soon as I perceived the first dangerous fit of this elegant idleness had seized him. But when will young men, by so much the more headstrong as they have less of the beard, be guided and brought to learn, and when shall we see that happy age, in which the grey heads of old men shall be clapped upon the shoulders of youth? I told him, that in this one thing he ought to consult me, and acknowledge me to be a true prophet, if I told him the end of the seeming merry steps in life he was now taking would infallibly bring him to a labyrinth of difficulties, out of which, if he extricated himself at all, he would at least find it a laborious piece of work.

His taste had been already vitiated with the sweets which lay at the top of the bitter draught of fortune, and my honest rugged counsel came too late to prevail, when his fancy had decoyed and debauched his judgment, and carried it over into another interest. I remember I writ down to him the moral story, where vicious pleasure and virtue are pictured by the philosopher to appear before Hercules, to court him into two several paths. I told him more particularly, since he had not an estate to go through with the gentlemanly life, as he called it, that if he followed the alluring pleasures, which endeavoured to tempt Hercules, he would involve himself at last in a whole heap of miseries, out of which it would be more than an Herculean labour for him to disentangle himself again. If he had been a man that could have ever heard with either, I would have told the reader, in a very familiar idiom, that he turned the deaf ear to me; for he did not mind one syllable nor tittle of the prescriptions I had set down for him, no more than if he had never read them; but varying the phrase a little, I may say at least, when he should have looked upon my counsel with all the eyes he had, he turned the blind side upon it. I was resolved to make use of the revenge natural to a man of years, and therefore applied that reproachful proverb to him, which we ancients delight much in making use of to youths that follow their own false and hot imaginations, and will not heed the cooler dictates of age, experience, and wisdom. Accordingly I wrote down to him these words, and left him in a seeming passion—"I am very well assured, young man, you think me that am old to be a fool; but I, that am old, absolutely know you who are a young fellow, to be a downright fool; and so I leave you to follow your own ways, till sad and woeful experience teaches you to know it your own self, and makes you come to me to own it of your own accord."

As I was going away after this tart admonition and severe reprimand, I had a mind to observe his countenance, and I saw him smile, which I rightly construed to be done in contempt of the advice of age, and in the gaiety and fulness of conceit which youth entertains of its own fond opinions and hair-brained rash resolves. He was got into the company of a very pretty set of gentlemen, whose fortunes were superior to his; but he followed the same genteel exercises, as fencing, &c., and made one at all their public entertainments; and so being at an equal expense with those who could well afford to spend what they did out of their estates, he went on very pleasantly for a time, still spending and never getting, without ever considering that it must, by inevitable consequence, fall to his lot at last to be entirely reduced to a state of indigence and want. And what commonly heightens the misfortune of such men (and so of all gentlemen's younger brothers), who live upon the ready money that is given them for their portions, is, that the prosperity they live in for a time gains them credit enough just to bring them in debt, and render them more miserable than those very wretches who never had either any money or credit at all. They run themselves into debt out of shame, and to put off the evil day of appearing ruined men as long as they can, and then, when their tempers are soured by adversity, they grow tired of their own lives, and then, in a quarrel, they or some other gentleman, perhaps, is run through, or else, being hunted by bailiffs, they exercise their swords upon those pursuers. Thus, where gentlemen will not consider their circumstances, their very prosperity is a cause of and aggravates their misery; their very pride (which was a decent pride at first), in keeping up and maintaining their credit, subjects them too often to the lowest and the meanest acts, and their courage, which was of a laudable kind, turns into a brutish and savage rage; and all the fine, esteemed, flourishing, and happy gentleman ends and is lost in the contemned poor and miserable desperado, whose portion at last is confinement and a gaol, and sometimes even worse, and what I shall not so much as name here.

Into many of these calamities Mr Campbell had brought himself, before it was long, by his heedlessness, and running, according, to the wild dictates of youth, counter to all sound and wholesome advice. He had, it seems, run himself into debt, and one day, as he was at a coffee-house, the sign of the Three Crowns, in Great Queen Street, in rushed four bailiffs upon him, who, being directed by the creditor's wife, had watched him into that house, and told him they had a warrant against him, and upon his not answering, they being unacquainted with his being deaf and dumb, offered to seize his sword. He started at their offering of violence, and taking them for ruffians (which he had often met with), repelled his assaulters, and drawing his sword, as one man more bold than the rest closed in with him, he shortened his blade, and in the fall, pinned the fellow through the shoulder, and himself through the leg, to the floor. After that he stood at bay with all

the four officers, when the most mischievous assailant
of them all, the creditor's wife, ventured to step into
the fray, and very barbarously took hold of that
nameless part of the man, for which, as she was a
married woman, nature methinks should have taught
her to have a greater tenderness, and almost squeezed
and crushed those vitals to death.   But at last he got
free from them all, and was going away as fast as he
could, not knowing what consequences might ensue.
But the woman, who aimed herself at committing
murder in the most savage and inhuman manner, ran
out after him, crying out, " Murder ! murder ! " as loud
as she could, and alarmed the whole street.   The bailiffs
following the woman, and being bloody from head to
foot, by means of the wound he received, gave credit to
the outcry.   The late Earl Rivers's footmen happening
to be at the door, ran immediately to stop the supposed
murderer, and they indeed did take him at last, but
perceived their mistake, and discovered that, instead of
being assistants in taking a man whom they thought
to be a murderer endeavouring to make his escape from
the hands of justice, they had only been tricked in, by
that false cry, to be adjutants to a bailiff in retaking a
gentleman, who by so gallant a defence, had rescued
himself from the dangers of a prison ; and when they
had discovered this their mistake, they were mighty
sorry for what they had done.   The most active and
busy among the earl's footmen was a Dutchman, and
the earl happening to be in a room next the streets and
hearing the outcry of murder, stepped to the window,
and seeing his own servants in the midst of a bustle,
examined the Dutchman how the matter stood, and
being told it, chid the man for being concerned in
stopping a gentleman that was getting free from such
troublesome companions.   But the Dutchman excused
himself like a Dutchman, by making a very merry

blunder for a reply. "Sacramente," said he, to his lord, "if I had thought they were bailiffs, I would have fought for the poor dumb gentleman, but then why had not he told me they were bailiffs, my lord?"

In short, Duncan Campbell was carried off as their prisoner; but the bailiff that was wounded was led back to the coffee-house, where he pretended the wound was mortal, and that he despaired of living an hour. The proverb, however, was of the fellow's side, and he recovered sooner than other people expected he could. As soon as all danger was over, an action for damages and smart money, as their term is, was brought against Mr Campbell; the damages were exaggerated, and the demand was so extravagant, that Duncan Campbell was neither able, just at that time, nor willing, had he been able, to pay so much, as he thought, in his own wrong; and having no bail, and being ashamed to make his case known to his better sort of friends, who were both able and willing to help him at a dead lift, he was hurried away to gaol by the bailiffs, who showed such a malignant and insolent pleasure as commonly attends powerful revenge, when they put him into the Marshalsea. There he lay in confinement six weeks, till at last four or five of his chief friends came by mere chance to hear of it: immediately they consulted about his deliverance, and unanimously resolved to contribute for his enlargement, and they accordingly went across the water together, and procured it out of hand.

Two of his benefactors were officers, and were just then going over to Flanders. Duncan Campbell, to whom they communicated their design, was resolved to try his fortune in a military way, out of a roving kind of humour, raised in him partly by his having taken a sort of aversion to his own profession in town, and partly by his finding that he could not live, without

"Duncan Campbell was carried off as their prisoner"

following a profession as he had done, any longer.
He, over a bottle, frankly imparted his mind to them
at large; he signified to them that he hoped, since
they had lately done him so great a favour in freeing him from one captivity, they would not think
him too urgent, if he pressed for one favour further,
upon natures so generous as theirs, by whom he took
as great a pleasure in being obliged, as he could receive,
in being capable of obliging others. He wrote to them
that the favour he meant was to redeem him from
another captivity, almost as irksome to him as that
out of which they had lately ransomed him. "This
captivity," continued he, "is, being either forced to
follow my old profession, which I have taken an entire
disgust to, for a maintenance, or being forced to live in a
narrower way than suits with my genius, and the better
taste I have of higher life. Such a state, gentlemen,
you know, is more unpalatable than half-pay; it is
like, either being forced to go upon the forlorn hope,
or else, like a man's being an entirely cashiered and
broken officer, that had no younger brother's fortune,
and no other support but his commission. Thus,
though you have set my body at liberty, my soul is
still under an imprisonment, and will be till I leave
England, and can find means of visiting Flanders,
which I can do no otherwise than by the advantage of
having you for my convoy. I have a mighty longing
to experience some part of a military life, and I fancy,
if you will grant me your interest, and introduce me to
the valiant young Lord Lorne, and be spokesman for a
dumb man, I shall meet with a favourable reception;
and as for you, gentlemen, after having named that
great patron and pattern of courage and conduct in
the field, I cannot doubt but the very name I bear, if
you had not known me, would have made you take me
for a person of a military genius, and that I should do

nothing but what would become a British soldier and a gentleman; nothing, in fine, that should make you repent the recommendation."

These generous and gallant friends of his, it seems, complied with his request, and promised they would make application for him to the Lord Lorne, and Duncan Campbell had nothing to do but to get his bag and baggage ready and provide himself with a pass. His baggage was not very long a getting together, and he had it in tolerable good order, and as for his pass, a brother of the Lord Forbes was so kind as to procure him one, upon the first application Duncan made to him.

Accordingly, in a few days afterwards they went on board, and having a speedy and easy passage, arrived soon at Rotterdam. Duncan met with some of his English acquaintance in that town, and his mind being pretty much bent upon rambling, and seeing all the curiosities, customs, and humours he could in all the foreign places he was to pass through, he went, out of a frolic, with some gentlemen next day, in a boat, to an adjacent village, to make merry over a homely Dutch entertainment, the intended repast being to consist of what the boors there count a great delicacy, brown bread and white beer. He walked out of sight from his company, and they lost one another; and strolling about by himself at an unseasonable hour, as they call it there, after the bell has tolled, Duncan Campbell, who neither knew their laws, nor, if he had, was capable of being guided by the notice which their laws ordain, was taken into custody in the village for that night, and carried away the next day to Willemstad, where he was taken for a spy, and put into a close imprisonment for three or four days.

But some Scotch gentlemen, who had been in company with Mr Campbell at Mr Cloysterman's, a painter in Covent Garden, made their application to the magistrate and got him released. He knew his friends, the officers that carried him over, were gone forward to the camp, and that there was no hope of finding them at Rotterdam, if he should go thither ; and so he resolved, since he had had so many days' punishment in Willemstad, to have three or four days' pleasure there too, by way of amends, before he would set out on his journey after his friends. But on the third night he got very much in drink ; and as he went very boisterously and disorderly along, a sentry challenged him, and the want of the sense of hearing had like to have occasioned the loss of his life. The sentry fired at him and narrowly missed him ; he was taken prisoner, not without some resistance, which was so far innocent as that he knew not any reason why he should be seized, but very troublesome and unwarrantable in so orderly a town ; so the governor's secretary, after the matter was examined into, judging it better for the unhappy gentleman's future safety, advised him to return home to his own country, and accordingly bespoke him a place in a Dutch ship called " Yowfrow Catherine," for his passage to England.

Duncan Campbell had taken up this humour of rambling, first of his own accord, and the troubles which he had run himself into by it, we may reasonably suppose, had pretty well cured him of that extravagant itch ; and there is very little doubt to be made, but that he rejoiced very heartily when he was got on board the ship to return to England ; and that, in his new resolutions, he had reconciled himself to the prosecution of his former profession, and intended to set up for a predictor again as soon as he could arrive at London. But now fortune had not a mind to let him go off so : he had had his own fancy for rambling, and now she was resolved to have hers, and to give

him his bellyful of caprice. Accordingly, when the
Dutch ship called " Yowfrow Catherine" was making
the best of her road for London, and each person in
the vessel was making merry, filled with the hopes of
a quick and prosperous passage, a French privateer
appeared in sight, crowding all the sails she could, and
bearing towards them with all haste and diligence.
The privateer was double-manned, and carried thirty
guns; the Dutch vessel was defenceless in comparison;
and the people on board had scarce time to think,
and to deplore that they should be made a prey of,
before they actually were so, and had reason enough
given them for their sorrow. All the passengers, to a
single man, were stripped, and had French seamen's
jackets in exchange for their clothes. Duncan Campbell had now a taste given him of the fate of war, as
well as of humour of travelling, and wished himself
again, I warrant him, among his greatest crowd of consulters, as tiresome as he thought things to be, instead
of being in the middle of a crew of sea-savages. The
town where the dumb prisoner was at last confined was
Denain. There happened to be some English friars
there, who were told by the others who he was, and to
them he applied himself in writing, and received from
them a great deal of civil treatment. But a certain
man of the Order of Recollects, happening to see him
there, who had known him in England, and what
profession he followed, caused him to be called to
question as a man that made use of ill means to tell
fortunes. When he was questioned by a whole
society of these religious men, he made them such
pertinent and satisfactory answers in writing, that he
convinced them he had done nothing for which he deserved their reprimand; and they unanimously acquitted
him. The heads of his defence, as I have been informed, were these :—

First, he alleged that the second-sight was inborn and inbred in some men; and that every country had had examples of it more or less; but that the country of Scotland, in which he was educated from an infant, abounded the most of any with those sort of people; and from thence, he said, he thought he might very naturally draw this conclusion, that a faculty that was inborn and inbred to men, and grown almost a national faculty among a people, who were remarkably honest, upright, and well-meaning people, could not, without some impiety, be imputed to the possessors of it as a sin; and when one of the fathers rejoined, that it was remarked by several writers, of the second-sight, that it must be therefore sinful, because it remained no longer among the people when the doctrines of Christianity were fully propagated, and the light of the gospel increased among them, and that afterwards it affected none but persons of vicious lives and an ill character, to this objection Mr Campbell replied, that he knew most, even ingenious writers, had made that remark concerning the second-sight, but begged leave to be excused if he ventured to declare that it was no better than a vulgar and common error; and the reasons were these, which he alleged in his own behalf, and to confirm his assertion, he told them that men of undoubted probity, virtue, and learning, both of their own religion, (viz., the Roman Catholic), and also of the reformed religion, and in several nations, had been affected, and continued all their lives to be affected with this second-sighted power, and that there could be, therefore, no room to fix upon it the odious character of being a sinful and vicious (not to say that some called it still worse, a diabolical) talent. He said he would content himself with making but two instances, because he believed those two would be enough to give content to them, his judges too, in that case.

In his first instance he told them that they might find somewhat relating to this in Nicholaus Hemingius, who, in his tracts " De Superstitionibus Magicis," printed at Copenhagen, anno 1575, informs the world that Petrus Palladius, a bishop of Zealand and professor of divinity at Copenhagen, could, from a part of his body affected, foretell from what part of the heavens tempests would come, and was seldom deceived. One of the fathers immediately asked him if he understood Latin? To this Duncan Campbell replied no. " Oh ! " said the friar then, " I do not remember that book was ever translated into English that you mention." " But," rejoined Duncan Campbell, "the passage I mentioned to you I have read in an English book, and word for word, according to the best of my memory, as I have written it down to you." " In what English book ? " said the friar. " I do not remember the name of the book," Duncan Campbell answered, " but very well remember the passages, and that it was in a book of authority, and which bore a credit and good repute in the world ; and you, being scholars, may, if you please, have recourse to the learned original, and I doubt not but you will find what I say to be a truth." For the second instance, he told them that in Spain there are those called Saludadores that have this kind of gift. " There was," continued he in writing, " one of your own religion, venerable fathers, and of a religious order, nay, a friar too, that had this gift ; he was a noted Dominican," said he, " and though I forget his name, you may, by writing a letter to England, learn his name. He was a devout Portuguese, belonging to Queen Catherine Dowager's Chapel, and had the second-sight to a great degree, and was famous and eminent for it." They then asked him what was the full power he had to do by the second-sight. He answered, that as they had intimated

that they had perused some of the skilful writers
concerning the second-sight, he did not doubt but
they found, as well as he could tell them, that as
to the extent of people's knowledge in that secret
way, it reached both present, past, and future events.
"They foresee murders, drownings, weddings, burials,
combats, manslaughters, &c., all of which there are
many instances to be given. They commonly foresee
sad events a little while before they happen; for instance, if a man's fatal end be hanging, they will see
a gibbet, or rope about his neck; if beheading, they
will see a man without a head; if drowning, they will
see water up to his throat; if stabbing, they will see a
dagger in his breast; if unexpected death in his bed,
they will see a winding-sheet about his head; they
foretell, not only marriages, but of good children, what
kind of life men shall lead, and in what condition they
shall die, also riches, honours, preferments, peace,
plenty, and good weather. It is likewise usual with
persons that have lost anything to go to some of
these men, by whom they are directed, how, with
what persons, and in what place they shall find their
goods. It is also to be noted, that these gifts bear
a latitude, so that some have it in a far more eminent
degree than others; and what I have here written
down to you, you need not take as a truth from me,
but as it concerned me so nearly, I remember the
passage by heart, and you will find it very near
word for word in Dr Beaumont's book of Familiar
Spirits."—"Ay," said the friars, "but you have a
genius too that attends you, as we are informed."—
"So," replied Duncan Campbell, "have all persons
that have the second-sight in any eminent degree; and
to prove this I will bring no less a witness than King
James, who, in his 'Demonology,' book the third
and chapter the second, mentions also a spirit called

Brownie, that was wont formerly to haunt divers houses, without doing any evil, but doing, as it were, necessary turns up and down the house; he appeared like a rough man, nay, some believed that their house was all the sonsier, as they called it, that is, the more lucky or fortunate that such spirits resorted there."

With these replies the friars began to own they were very well satisfied, and acquiesced in the account he had given of himself, as a very good, true, and honest account; but they told him they had still a further accusation against him, and that was, that he practised magic arts, and that he used, as they had been informed, unlawful incantations. To this he made answer that there were two kinds of magic, of which he knew they, that were men of learning, could not be ignorant. " The art magic, which is wicked and impious," continued he, " is that which is professed, and has been professed at all times in the world, by witches, magicians, diviners, enchanters, and such-like notorious profligates, who, by having an unnatural commerce with the devil, do many strange, prodigious, and preternatural acts above and beyond all human wisdom; and all the arguments I ever did or ever will deduce," continued he, " from that black art, is a good and a shining argument; it is this, O fathers, I draw a reason from these prodigious practices of wizards, magicians, enchanters, &c., and from all the heathen idolatry and superstition, to prove that there is a deity; for, from these acts of theirs being preternatural and above human wisdom, we may consequently infer that they proceed from a supernatural and immaterial cause, such as demons are. And this is all the knowledge I ever did or ever will draw from that black hellish art. But, fathers, there is another kind of art magic, called natural magic, which is directly opposite to theirs, and the object of which art is to do spiritual good to mankind, as the object of theirs is to torment them and induce them to evil. They afflict people with torments, and my art relieves them from the torments they cause. The public profession of these magical arts has (as you know, fathers, it is a common distinction between black and white magic) been tolerated in some of the most famous universities in Christendom, though afterwards, for a very good reason in politics, making it a public study to such a degree was very wisely retrenched by a prohibition. If this, therefore, be a fault in your own opinions, hear my accusers, but if not, you will not only excuse but commend me."

The friars were extremely well pleased with his defence : but one of them had a mind to frighten him a little if he could, and asked him what he would say, if he could produce some witches, lately seized, that would swear he had been frequently at their unlawful assemblies, where they were making their waxen images and other odd mischievous inventions in black magic to torment folks: " What if I can produce such evidence against you," wrote the father to him by way of strengthening the question ; " will you not own that we have convicted you then ? " And when he had written the note, he gave it Duncan Campbell, with a look that seemed to express his warmth and earnestness in the expostulation. Duncan Campbell took the paper and read it, and far from being startled, returned this answer, with a smile continuing in his face while he wrote it. " No," said he, " fathers, by your leave, they will only prove me a good magician by that oath, and themselves more plainly witches. They will prove their love to torment good folks, and only show their hatred to me, an innocent man, but wise enough to torment them by hindering them from tormenting others." The fathers were well pleased with the shrewdness of the answer : but Duncan Campbell had a mind to exert his genius a little farther with the good friar, who thought likewise he had put him a very shrewd question, so taking up another sheet of paper: "Fathers," said he, "shall I entertain you with a story of what passed, upon this head, between two religious fathers (as you all of you are) and a Prince of Germany, in which you will find that mine ought to be reputed a full answer to the question the last learned father was pleased to propose me? The story is somewhat long, but very much to the purpose, and entertaining: I remember it perfectly by heart, and if you will have patience while I am writing it, I don't doubt but that I shall not only satisfy you, but please you and oblige you with the relation. The author I found it in quotes it from Fromanus (I think the man's name was so, and I am sure my author calls him a very learned man), in his third book of 'Magical Incantation,' and, though I do not understand the language the original is written in, yet, I dare venture to say, upon the credit of my English author, from whom I got the story by heart, that you will find me right, whenever you shall be pleased to search."

The friars were earnest for the story, and expressed a desire that he would write it down for them to read, which he did in the following words.—Note, that I have since compared Mr Duncan Campbell's manuscript with the author's page, out of which he took it, and find it word for word the same; which shows how incomparable a memory this deaf and dumb gentleman has got, besides his other extraordinary qualifications.—The story is this.

"A Prince of Germany invited two religious fathers, of eminent virtue and learning, to a dinner. The prince, at table, said to one of them: 'Father! think you we do right in hanging persons, who are accused by ten or twelve witches to have appeared at their meetings or sabbaths? I somewhat fear we are imposed on by the devil, and that it is not a safe way to truth, that we walk in by these accusations; especially, since many great and learned men everywhere begin to cry out against it, and to charge our consciences with it; tell me therefore your opinion.' To whom the fathers being somewhat of an eager spirit, said, 'What should make us doubtful in this case? or what should touch our consciences, being convicted by so many testimonies? Can we make it a scruple, whether God will permit innocent persons should be so traduced? There is no cause for a judge to stick at such a number of accusations, but he may proceed with safety.' To which, when the prince had replied, and much had been said *pro* and *con* on both sides about it, and the father seemed wholly to carry the point, the prince at length concluded the dispute, saying, 'I am sorry for you, father, that in a capital cause you have condemned yourself, and you cannot complain if I commit you to custody; for no less than fifteen witches have deposed that they have seen you—ay, start not: you, your own self, at their meetings; and to show you that I am not in jest, I will presently cause the public acts to be brought for you to read them.' The father stood in amaze, and with a dejected countenance had nothing here to oppose but confusion and silence for all his learned eloquence."

As soon as Mr Campbell had written down the story, the fathers perused it, and seemed mightily entertained with it. It put an end to all further questions, and the man, whom they had been trying for a conjurer, they joined in desiring, upon distinct pieces of paper, under their several hands, to come frequently and visit them, as being not only a harmless and innocent but an extraordinary well-meaning, good, and diverting companion. They treated him for some time afterwards during his stay, with the friendship due to a countryman, with the civility that is owing to gentlemen, and with the assistance and support which belonged to a person of merit in distress. Money they had none themselves, it seems, to give him, being mendicants by their own profession; but they had interest enough to get him quite free from being prisoner; he participated of their eleemosynary table, had a cell allowed him among them in what they call their dormitory; he had an odd coat and a pair of trousers made out of some of their brown coarse habits, by the poor unfashionable tailor or botcher belonging to the convent; and at last they found means of recommending him to a master of a French vessel, that was ready to set sail, to give him a cast over the Channel to England, and to provide him with the necessaries of life till he got to the port. This French vessel was luckier than the Dutch one had been before to our dumb gentleman; it had a quick and prosperous passage, and arrived at Portsmouth; and as soon as he had landed there, he having experienced the misfortunes and casualties that a man in his condition, wanting both speech and hearing, was liable to, in places where he was an utter stranger to everybody, resolved to make no stay, but to move on as fast as he could towards London. When he came to Hampton Town, considering the indifferent figure he made in those odd kind of clothes which the poor friars had equipped him with, and that his long beard and uncombed wig added much to the disguise, he was resolved to put on the best face he could in those awkward circumstances, and stepped into the first barber's shop he came at, to be trimmed and get his wig combed and powdered.

This proved a very lucky thought to him; for, as soon as he stepped into the first barber's shop, who should prove to be the master of it, but one

Tobit Yeats, who had served him in the same capacity at London, and was but newly set up in the trade of a barber-surgeon at Hampton Town, and followed likewise the profession of schoolmaster. This Tobit Yeats had shaved him quite, before he knew him in that disguise; and Mr Campbell, though he knew him presently, had a mind to try if he should be known himself first. At length, the barber, finding him to be a dumb man, by his ordering everything with motions of the hand and gestures of the body, looked at him very earnestly, remembered him, and in a great surprise called for pen, ink, and paper, and begged to know how he came in that disguise; whether he was under any misfortune and apprehension of being discovered, that made him go in so poor and so clownish a habit, and tendered him any services, as far as his little capacity would reach, and desired him to be free, and command him, if he was able to assist him in anything. These were the most comfortable words that Duncan Campbell had read a great while. He took the pen and paper in his turn; related to him his whole story, gave the poor barber thanks for his good-natured offer, and said he would make so much use of it as to be indebted to him for so much money as would pay the stage-coach, and bear him in his travelling expenses up to London, from whence he would speedily return the favour with interest. The poor honest fellow, out of gratitude to a master whose liberality he had formerly experienced, immediately furnished Mr Duncan Campbell with that little supply, expressing the gladness of his heart that it lay in his power; and the stage-coach being to set out within but a few hours, he ran instantly to the inn to see if he could get him a place. By good luck there was room, and but just room for one more, which pleased Duncan Campbell mightily when he was acquainted with it by his true and trusty servant the barber; for he was as impatient to see London again, it seems, as he had been before to quit it. Well, he had his wish; and when he came to London, he had one wish more for fortune to bestow upon him, which appeared to begin to grow kind again, after her fickle fit of cruelty was over; and this wish was, that he might find his former lodgings empty, and live in the same house as when he followed his profession. This too succeeded according to his desire, and he was happily fixed once more to his heart's content in his old residence, with the same people of the house round about him, who bore him all that respect and affection, and showed all that readiness and willingness to serve him on every occasion, and at every turn, which could be expected from persons that let lodgings in town to a gentleman whom they esteemed the best tenant they ever had in their lives, or ever could have.

Immediately the tidings of the dumb gentleman's being returned home from beyond sea spread throughout all the neighbourhood; and it was noised about from one neighbourhood to another, till it went through all ranks and conditions, and was known as well in a day or two's time all the town over, as if he had been some great man belonging to the state, and his arrival had been notified to the public in the *Gazette* as a person of the last importance. And such a person he appeared indeed to be taken for, especially among the fair sex, who thronged to his doors, crowd after crowd, to consult with him about their future occurrences in life.

These curious tribes of people were as various in their persons, sex, age, quality, profession, art, trade, as they were in the curiosity of their minds, and the questions they had intended to propound to this dumb predictor of strange events, that lay yet as embryos in the womb of time, and were not to come, some of them, to a maturity for birth for very many years after, just as porcelain clay is stored up in the earth by good artificers, which their heirs make china of half a century, and sometimes more than an age afterwards.

These shoals of customers, who were to fee him well for his advice, as we may suppose, now he stood in need of raising a fresh stock, were, unquestionably, as welcome and acceptable to him as they appeared too troublesome to him before, when he was in a state of wealth and plenty.

Fortune, that does nothing moderately, seemed now resolved, as she had been extremely cruel before, to be extremely kind to him. He had nothing to do from early in the morning till late at night, but to read questions, and resolve them as fast as much-frequented doctors write their prescriptions and recipes; and like them also, to receive fees as fast. Fortune was, indeed, mightily indulgent to the wants she had so suddenly reduced him to; and relieved him as suddenly by these knots of curiosos, who brought him a glut of money. But one single fair lady, that was one of his very best consulters after his return, and who had received satisfactory answers from him in other points, before he went abroad, proved (so good fortune would have it) worth all the rest of his customers together, as numerous as they were, and as I have accordingly represented them.

This lady was the relict or widow of a gentleman of a good estate, and of a very good family, whose name was Digby; and a handsome jointure she had out of the estate. This lady, it seems, having been with him in former days, and seen him in a more shining way of life (for he had taken a humour to appear before all his company in that coarse, odd dress, made out of the friar's habit, and would not be per-

suaded by the people of the house to put on a night-
gown till he could provide himself with a new suit),
was so curious, among other questions, as to ask him
whether he had met with any misfortunes, and how
he came to be in so slovenly and wretched a habit?
Here Mr Campbell related the whole story of his
travels to her, and the crosses and disappointments he
had met with abroad. The tears, he observed, would
start every now and then into her eyes when she came
to any doleful passage, and she appeared to have a
mighty compassionate kind of feeling when she read
of any hardship more than ordinarily melancholy that
had befallen him. Mr Campbell, it is certain, had then
a very good presence, and was a handsome and portly
young man; and, as a great many young gentlemen derive the seeming agreeableness of their persons from the
tailor and peruke-maker, the shoemaker and hosier, so
Mr Campbell's person, on the other hand, gave a good
air and a good look to the awkward garb he had on;
and I believe, it was from seeing him in this odd trim
(as they call it) the ladies first took up the humour
of calling him the handsome sloven; add to this, that
he looked his misfortune in the face with a jolly
countenance, and smiled even while he was penning
the relation of his calamities, all which are certainly
circumstances that first soothe a generous mind into a
state of compassion, and afterwards heighten it in the
breast wherein it is conceived. Hence it came that
this pretty and good-natured widow, Mrs Digby, when
she had expressed her commiseration of him by her
looks, began to take the pen and express it in very
tender terms: neither did she think that expression in
words a sufficient testimony of the compassion she bore
to him; the generosity of her mind did lead her to
express it in a more substantial manner still, and that
was, to show it plainly by a very benevolent action.

She laid a purse of twenty guineas before the table, and at the same time smiling, pointed to the table, as signifying her desire that he would accept it; and, running to the door, dropped a curtsey, and scuttled away; and, by the same civil act as she obliged him, she put it out of his power to refuse being so obliged; so that, though the present was very handsome, the manner of giving it was still handsomer.

If being a handsome young man of merit in distress, and bearing his misfortunes with an equal mind, are powerful motives to excite compassion in the mind of a generous lady, so the generosity of a young agreeable widow, expressed in so kind and so benevolent a way to a young gentleman, when he had been tasting nothing but the bitter draughts of fortune before, must stir up an affection in a mind that had any sense of gratitude : and truly, just such was the effect that this lady's civility had upon Mr Duncan Campbell. He conceived from that moment a very great affection for her, and resolved to try whether he could gain her; which he had no small grounds to hope, from the esteem which she appeared to bear towards him already. I remember Mr Dryden makes a very beautiful observation of the near alliance there is between the two passions of pity and love in a a woman's breast, in one of his plays. His words are these : " For pity still foreruns approaching love as lightning does the thunder." Mr Bruyere, a most ingenious member of the French Academy, has made another remark, which comes home to our present purpose. He says, that many women love their money better than their friends ; but yet value their lovers more than their money. According to the two reflections of these fine writers upon the tempers of the pair, Mr Campbell had hopes enough to ground his courtship upon ; and it appeared so in the end by his proving successful. She, from being a

very liberal and friendly client, became at last a most
affectionate wife.   He then began to be a housekeeper,
and accordingly took a little neat one, and very
commodious for his profession, in Monmouth Court.
Here I must take leave to make this observation, that
if Mr Campbell inherited the talents of his second-
sighted mother, he seemed likewise to be an heir to his
father, Mr Archibald Campbell, both in his strange and
accidental sufferings by sea, and likewise in his being
relieved from them, after as accidental and strange a
manner, by an unexpected marriage, just like his
father's.

And here we return again to take a new survey of
him in the course of his public practice as a predictor.
The accounts I shall give of his actions here, will
be very various in their nature from any I have yet
presented to the reader: they are more mysterious
in themselves, and yet I shall endeavour to make the
manner of his operating in this kind as plain as, I
think, I have the following ones; and then, I flatter
myself, they must afford a fresh entertainment for every
reader that has any curiosity and a good taste for things
of so extraordinary a kind; for what I have all along
propounded to myself from the beginning, and in the
progress, and to the end of this history, is, to interweave
entertaining and surprising narratives of what Mr
Campbell has done, with curious and instructive inquiries into the nature of those actions, for which he
has rendered himself so singularly famous.   It was not,
therefore, suitable to my purpose to clog the reader
with numerous adventures, almost all of the same kind;
but out of a vast number of them to single some few of
those that were most remarkable and that were mysteries, but mysteries of very different sorts.   I leave
that method of swelling distorted and commented trifles
into volumes, to the writers of fable and romance: if I

was to tell his adventures with regard, for instance, to women that came to consult him, I might, perhaps, have not only written the stories of eleven thousand virgins that died maids, but have had relations to give of as many married women and widows, and the work would have been endless. All that I shall do, therefore, is to pick out one particular, each of a different kind, that there may be variety in the entertainment.

Upon application to this dumb man, one is told, in the middle of her health, that she shall die at such a time; another, that she shall sicken, and upon the moment of her recovery, have a suitor and a husband; a third, who is a celebrated beauty, with a multitude of admirers round about her, that she shall never become a wife; a fourth, that is married, when she shall get rid of an uneasy husband; a fifth, that hath lost her goods, who stole them, where and when they shall be restored; a sixth, that is a merchant, when he shall be undone, and how and when he shall recover his losses, and be as great on the Exchange as ever; a seventh, that is a gamester, which will be his winning and his losing hour; an eighth, how he shall be involved in a lawsuit, and whether the suit will have a prosperous issue; a ninth, that is a woman with choice of lovers, which she shall be most happy with for life; and so on to many others, where every prediction is perfectly new and surprising, and differs from the other in almost every circumstance. When a man has so extensive a genius as this at foretelling the future occurrences of life, one narrative of a sort is enough in conscience to present the reader with; and several of each kind would not, methinks, be entertaining but tiresome; for he that can do one thing in these kinds by the power of prediction, can do ten thousand; and those who are obstinate in extenuating his talents, and calling his capacity in question, and that will not be convinced by one instance of his judgment, would not own the conviction if ten thousand instances were given them. The best passages I can recommend to their perusal, are those where persons, who came purposely to banter him under the colour of consulting him, and covered over their sly intentions with borrowed disguises, and came in masquerades, found all the jest turned upon themselves in the end, which they meant to our famous predictor; and had the discouragement of seeing their most-concealed and deepest-laid plots discovered, and all their most witty fetches and wily contrivances defeated, till they were compelled universally to acknowledge, that endeavouring to impose upon the judgment of our seer by any hidden artifice and cunning whatsoever was effectually imposing upon their own. His unusual talent in this kind was so openly known and so generally confessed, that his knowledge was celebrated in some of the most witty weekly papers that ever appeared in public. Isaac Bickerstaff, who diverted all the beau-monde for a long space of time with his lucubrations, takes occasion in several of his papers to applaud the speculations of this dumb gentleman, in an admirable vein of pleasantry and humour, peculiar to the writer, and to the subject he wrote upon; and when that bright author, who joined the uttermost facetiousness with the most solid improvements of morality and learning in his works, laid aside the title of a Tatler, and assumed the name of a Spectator and censor of men's actions, he still every now and then thought our Duncan Campbell a subject worthy enough to employ his farther consideration upon. I must take notice of one letter sent concerning him to the *Spectator*, in the year 1712, which was at a time when a lady wanted him, after he had removed from Monmouth Street to Drury Lane.

" MR SPECTATOR,—About two years ago, I was
called upon by the younger part of a country family,
by my mother's side related to me, to visit Mr Campbell, the dumb man; for they told me that was chiefly
what brought them to town, having heard wonders
of him in Essex. I, who always wanted faith in such
matters, was not easily prevailed on to go; but lest
they should take it ill, I went with them, when, to my
own surprise, Mr Campbell related all their past life
(in short, had he not been prevented, such a discovery
would have come out as would have ruined their next
design of coming to town, viz., buying wedding
clothes). Our names, though he never heard of us
before, and endeavoured to conceal, were as familiar
to him as to ourselves. To be sure, Mr Spectator,
he is a very learned and wise man. Being impatient to
know my fortune, having paid my respects in a family
Jacobus, he told me, after his manner, among several
other things, that in a year and nine months I should
fall ill of a new fever, be given over by my physicians,
but should with much difficulty recover; that the first
time I took the air afterwards, I should be addressed
to by a young gentleman of a plentiful fortune, good
sense, and a generous spirit. Mr Spectator, he is the
purest man in the world; for all he said is come to
pass, and I am the happiest woman in Kent. I have
been in quest of Mr Campbell these three months, and
cannot find him out: now, hearing you are a dumb
man too, I thought you might correspond and be able
to tell me something; for I think myself highly
obliged to make his fortune, as he has mine. 'Tis
very possible your worship, who has spies all over this
town, can inform me how to send to him; if you can,
I beseech you be as speedy as possible, and you will
highly oblige your constant reader and admirer,

" DULCIBELLA THANKLEY."

THE "SPECTATOR'S" ANSWER.

"Ordered that the inspector I employ about wonders inquire at the Golden Lion, opposite to the Half Moon Tavern in Drury Lane, into the merit of this silent sage, and report accordingly."—*Vide* the seventh volume of *Spectator*, No. 474; being on Wednesday, September the 3rd, 1712.

But now let us come to those passages of his life the most surprising of all, during the time that he enjoyed this reputation, and when he proved that he deserved the fame he enjoyed. Let us take a survey of him while he is wonderfully curing persons labouring under the misfortune of witchcraft, of which the following story will be an eminent instance, and likewise clear up how he came by his reputation in Essex, as mentioned in the above-mentioned letter to the *Spectator*.

In the year 1709, Susanna Johnson, daughter to one Captain Johnson, who lived at a place adjacent to Romford, in Essex, going one morning to that town to buy butter at the market, was met there by an old miserable-looking woman, just as she had taken some of her change of the market-woman in copper, and this old woman rather demanded than begged the gentlewoman to give her a penny. Mrs Johnson, reputing her to be one of those hateful people that are called sturdy beggars, refused it her, as thinking it to be no act of charity, and that it would be rather gratifying and indulging her impudence than supplying or satisfying her indigence. Upon the refusal, the old hag, with a face more wrinkled still, if possible, by anger than it was by age, took upon her to storm at young Mrs Johnson very loudly, and to threaten and menace her ; but when she found her common threats and menaces of no avail, she swore she would be revenged of the young creature in so signal a manner, that she should repent the denial of that penny from her heart before she got home, and that it should cost her many pounds to get rid of the consequences of that denial and her anger. The poor innocent creature despised these last words likewise, and getting up on horseback, returned homewards; but just as she got about half way her horse stopped, and no means that she could use would make him advance one single step; but she stayed a while, to see if that would humour him to go on. At last the beast began to grow unruly, and snorted and trembled as if he had seen or smelt something that frighted him, and so fell a kicking desperately till he threw the girl from the saddle, not being able to cling to it any longer, though a pretty good horsewoman of her years; so much were the horse's motions and plungings more than ordinarily violent.

As Providence would have it, she got not much harm by the fall, receiving only a little bruise in the right shoulder; but she was dreadfully frighted. This fear added wings to her feet, and brought her home as speedily of herself as she usually came on horseback. She immediately, without any other sign of illness than the pallid colour with which fear had disordered the complexion of her face, alarmed all the family at home with the story, took her bed upon it, complained of inward rackings of the belly, and was never at ease unless she lay doubled up together, her head to her knees, and her heels to her rump, just like a figure of 8. She could not be a single moment out of that posture without shrieking out with the violence of anxious torments and racking pains.

In this condition of misery, amidst this agony of suffering, and in this double posture, was the poor wretched young gentlewoman brought to town. Physicians were consulted about her, but in vain. She was carried to different hospitals for assistance, but their endeavours likewise proved ineffectual. At last she was conducted to the College of Physicians; and even the collective wisdom of the greatest sages and adepts in the science of physic was posed to give her any prescription that would do her service, and relieve her from the inexplicable malady she laboured under. The poor incurable creature was one constant subject of her complaining mother's discourse in every company she came into. It happened at last, and very providentially, truly, that the mother was thus condoling the misfortune of her child among five or six ladies, and telling them, among other things, that by the most skilful persons she was looked upon to be bewitched, and that it was not within the power of physic to compass her recovery. They all having been acquainted with our Mr Duncan Campbell, unanimously advised her to carry her daughter to his house, and consult with him about her. The mother was overjoyed at these tidings, and purposed to let no time slip where her child's health was so deeply concerned. She got the ladies to go with her and her child, to be eye-witnesses of so extraordinary a piece of practice, and so eminent a trial of skill.

As soon as this dismal object was brought into his room Mr Duncan Campbell lifted up her head and looked earnestly in her face, and in less than a minute's time signified to the company that she was not only bewitched, but in as dreadful a condition almost as the man that had a legion of fiends within him.

At the reading of these words, the unhappy creature raised up her head, turned her eyes upwards, and a smile (a thing she had been a stranger to for many months) overspread her whole face, and such a kind of colour as is the flushing of joy and gladness, and with an innocent tone of voice she said she now had a firm belief she should shortly be delivered. The mother and the rest of the company were all in tears, but Mr Campbell wrote to them that they should be of good heart, be easy and quiet for a few moments, and they should be convinced that it was witchcraft, but happily convinced, by seeing her so suddenly well again. This brought the company into pretty good temper; and a little after, Mr Campbell desired she might be led upstairs to his chamber, and left there alone with him for a little while. This occasioned some small female speculation, and as much mirth as their late sorrow, alleviated with the hopes of her cure, would permit.

This, you may be sure, was but a snatch of mirth, just as the nature of the thing would allow of; and all sorts of waggery being laid instantly aside, and removed almost as soon as conceived, the poor young thing was carried in that double posture upstairs. She had not been much above half-an-hour there, when, by the help only of Mr Campbell's arm, she was led downstairs, and descended into that room full of company, as a miracle appearing in a machine from above; she was led backward and forward through the room, while all gazed at her for a while with joyful astonishment, for no arrow was more straight than she. Mr Campbell then prevailed with her to drink a glass of wine, and immediately after she evacuated wind, which she had not done some months before, and found herself still more amended and easy; and then the mother, making Mr Campbell some small acknowledgment at that time, with the promise of more, and her daughter giving thanks, and all the company commending his skill, took their leave and departed with great demonstrations of joy. I shall here, to cut the story short, signify that she came frequently afterwards to make her testimonials of gratitude to him, and continues to enjoy her health to this very day at Greenwich, where she now lives, and will at any time, if called upon, make oath of the truth of this little history, as she told me herself with her own mouth.

The next thing, therefore, it behoves me to do in this chapter is, to give some satisfactory account of magic, by which such seeming mysterious cures and operations are brought about.

This task I would perform in the most perspicuous and most convincing manner I can; for magic, I know, is held to be a very hard and difficult study by those learned, and universally unlawful and diabolical by those unlearned, who believe there is such a science attainable by human genius. On the other hand, by some learned men, who believe there is no such science, it is represented as an inconsistent system of superstitions and chimeras; and again laughed at as such by the unlearned, who are of an incredulous temper. What I would therefore undertake to do in this place is to show the learned men, who believe there is such an art, that the attainment to a tolerable knowledge of the manner how magical practices may be brought about is no such difficult matter as they have represented it to themselves; and by doing this I shall make the system of it so plain, that while the learned approve of it, the unlearned, too, who are not of an unbelieving kind, may understand clearly what I say; and the learned men who have rejected this science as chimerical, may be clearly convinced it is real; and then there is nothing left but obstinate, unbelieving ignorance, which I shall not here pretend by arguments to lead into sense, but leave it to the work of time. In fine, I will endeavour to induce men of sense to say, that what has been accounted mysterious is delivered in a plain, easy, and convincing manner, and to own that they approve; while men of the lower class of understanding shall

confess and acknowledge that they themselves understand it, and that what has hitherto been represented as
arduous and difficult to a great genius is adapted and
rendered not only clear but familiar to persons of
middling talents. In this work, therefore, I shall
follow the strictest order I can (which of all things
renders a discourse upon any subject the most clear);
and that it may be plain to the commonest capacity, I
will first set down what order I intend to follow.

First, I will speak of magic in general.

Secondly, of magic under its several divisions and
subdivisions.

Thirdly, concerning the object of art, as it is good
or bad.

Fourthly, of the persons exercising that art in either
capacity of good or bad, and by what means they become
capacitated to exercise it.

In the fifth place I shall come to the several objections against the art of magic, and the refutation of
those objections.

The first objection shall be against the existence of
good and bad spirits; the refutation of which will
consist in my proving the existences of spirits both
good and bad, by reason, and by experience.

The second objection that will be brought, is to
contain an allegation that there are no such persons as
witches now, and an argument to support that allegation, drawn from the incapacity and impossibility of
anything making (while itself is incarnate) a contract
with a spirit. This objection will be answered by
proving the reality of witches from almost universal
experience, and by explaining rationally the manner
how the devils hold commerce with witches; which
explication is backed and authorised by the opinion of
the most eminent divines and the most learned physicians.

From hence, sixthly and lastly, we shall conclude on the side of the good magic, that as there are witches on the one hand that may afflict and torment persons with demons, so on the other hand there are lawful and good magicians that may cast out demons from people that are possessed with them.

And, first, as to magic in general. Magic consists in the spirit by faith, for faith is that magnet of the magicians by which they draw spirits to them, and by which spirits they do great things, and appear like miracles.

Secondly, magic is divided into three sorts, viz., divine, natural, and diabolical; and natural magic is again subdivided into two kinds, simple and compound; and natural compound magic is again likewise divided into two kinds, viz., natural divine magic and natural diabolical magic. Now, to give the reader a clear and distinct notion of each several species of magic here mentioned, I set down the following definitions :—Divine magic is a celestial science, in which all operations that are wonderfully brought about are performed by the Spirit of God. Natural magic is a science in which all the mysterious acts that are wrought are compassed by natural spirits; but as this natural magic may be exercised about things either in a manner indifferent in themselves, or mere morally good, and then it is mere natural magic, or else about things theologically good and transcendently bad, and then it is not merely and natural magic but mixed and compound. If natural magic be exercised about the most holy operations, it is then mixed with the divine, and may then be called, not improperly, natural divine magic; but if natural magic troubles itself about compassing the wickedest practices, then is it promiscuous with the demoniacal, and may not improperly be called natural diabolical magic.

Thirdly, the object of this art is doing wonders out of the ordinary appearing course of nature, which tend either to great good or bad, by the help and mediation of spirits good and bad.

Fourthly, as to the persons exercising that art in either way, whether good or bad, and by what means they become capacitated to act it, the notion of this may be easily deduced from the notions of the art itself, as considered above in its each different species : for as all magic consists in a spirit, every magician acts by a spirit.

Divine magicians that are of God are spoken of in the sacred book, and therefore I shall not mention the passages here, but pass them over, as I ought to do in a book like this, with a profound and reverential silence, as well as the other passages, which speak of natural and demoniacal magicians; and in all I shall speak of them in this place, I shall only speak of them with regard to human reason and experience, and conclude this head with saying, that natural magicians work all things by the natural spirits of the elements; but that witches and demoniacal magicians, as Jannes and Jambres in Egypt were, work their magical performances by the spirit of demons, and it is by the means of these different spirits that these different magicians perform their different operations.

These things thus distinctly settled and explained, it is now we must come and ground the dispute, between those who believe there are no such things as magicians of any kind, and those who assert there are of all the kinds above specified.

Those who contend there are, have recourse to experience, and relate many well-witnessed narratives, to prove that there have been at all times, and that there are still, magicians of all these kinds; but those who contend that there are no such persons, will give no ear to what

the others call plain experience; they call the stories,
let whatever witnesses appear to justify them, either
fabulous legends invented by the authors, or else tricks
of intellectual legerdemain imposed by the actors upon
the relaters of those actions.   Since, therefore, they say,
though the believers in magic brag of experience never
so much, it may be but a fallible experience; they
reasonably desire to know whether these gentlemen that
stand for magic can answer the objections which they
propose, to prove that the practice of magic, according to the system laid down, is inconsistent with reason,
before they will yield their assent.   Let the stories
be never so numerous, appear never so credible, these
unbelieving gentlemen desire to be tried by reason,
and aver, till that reason is given, they will not be
convinced by the number of stories, because, though
numerous, they are stories still, neither will they believe
them because they appear credible; because seeming so
is not being so, and appearances, though never so fair,
when they contradict reason, are not to be swallowed
down with an implicit faith as so many realities.   And
thus far, no doubt, the gentlemen who are on the unbelieving side, are very much in the right on it.   The
learned gentlemen, on the other hand, who are persuaded of this mighty mysterious power being lodged
in the hands of magicians, answer, that they will take
upon them to refute the most subtle objections brought
by the learned unbelievers, and to reconcile the practicability of magical mysteries, by the capacity of men
who study that art to right rules and laws of reasoning,
and to show that some stories, though never so prodigious, which are told of magicians, demand the belief
of wise men on two accounts; because, as experience
backs reason on the one hand, reason backs experience
on the other, and so the issue of the whole argument
(whether there are magicians or not) is thrown upon

both experience and reason.   These arguments on each side I shall draw up fairly, *pro* and *con*, for I do not pretend to be the inventor of them myself, they belong to other authors many years ago ; be it enough for me to boast of, if I can draw them up in a better and closer form together than they have yet appeared in : in that I take upon myself a very great task ; I erect myself as it were into a kind of a judge ; I will sum up the evidences on both sides, and I shall, wherever I see occasion, intimate which side of the argument bears the most weight with me ; but when I have enforced my opinion as far as I think needful, my readers, like a jury, are still at liberty to bring in their verdict just as they themselves shall see fit ; and this naturally leads me where I promised to come to in the fifth part of this discourse, to the several objections against the power of art magic and refutation of those objections.

The First Objections being against the Existence of Spirits, and the Refutations thereof.

The first objection, which they who reject magic make use of, is, denying that there are any such things as spirits, about which, since those who defend the art say it entirely exerciseth itself, the objectors contend, that if they can make out that there are no such beings as spirits, all pretensions to the art must be entirely groundless, and for the future exploded.

To make this part out, that there are no spirits, the first man they produce on their side is undoubtedly one of very great credit and authority, inasmuch as he has justly borne for many centuries the title of a prince of philosophers.   They say that Aristotle, in his book " De Mundo," reasons thus against the existence of spirits, viz., That since God can do all things of Himself, He doth not stand in need of ministering angels and demons; a multitude of servants showing the weakness of a prince.

The gentlemen who defend the science make this reply: they allow the credit and authority of Aristotle as much as the objectors; but as the objectors themselves deny all the authorities for the spirits, and desire that reason may be the only ground they go upon, so the refuters, on their parts, desire that Aristotle's *ipse dixit* may not be absolutely passed upon them for argument, but that his words may be brought to the same touchstone of reason, and proved if they are standard. If this argument, say they, will hold good, Aristotle should not suppose intelligences moving the celestial spheres, for God sufficeth to move all without ministering spirits; nor would there be need of a sun in the world, for God can enlighten all things by Himself, and so all second causes would be taken away; therefore there are angels and ministering spirits in the world, for the majesty of God, not for His want of them, and for order, not for His omnipotency. And here, if the objectors return and say, Who told you that there are spirits? Is not yours a precarious hypothesis? may not we have leave to recriminate in this place, Pray who told Aristotle that there were intelligences that moved the celestial spheres? Is not this hypothesis as precarious as any man may pretend that of spirits to be? and we believe there are few philosophers at present who agree with Aristotle in that opinion; and we dare pronounce this to be ours, that Aristotle took his intelligences from the Hebrews, who went according to the same whimsical though pretty notion, which first gave rise to the fiction of the nine Muses; but more than all this, it is a very great doubt among learned men, whether this book "De Mundo," be Aristotle's or no.

The next thing the objectors bring against the

existence of spirits, is, that it is nonsense for men to say that there are such beings of which it is impossible for a man to have any notion, and they insist upon it that it is impossible for any man to form an idea of a spiritual substance.   As to this part, the defendants rejoin, that they think our late most judicious Mr Locke, in his elaborate and finished " Essay on Human Understanding," has fairly made out, that men have as clear a notion of a spiritual substance as they have of any corporeal substance, matter, or body ; and that there is as much reason for admitting the existence of the one as of the other ; for that if they admit the latter, it is but humour in them to deny the former.   It is in book the second, chapter 29, where he reasons thus : " If a man will examine himself, concerning his notion of pure substance in general, he will find he has no other idea of it, but only a supposition of he knows not what support of such quality which are capable of producing simple ideas in us, which qualities are commonly called accidents. Thus if we talk or think of any particular sort of corporeal substance, as horse, stone, &c., though the idea we have of either of them be but the complication or collection of those several simple ideas, or sensible qualities, which we use to find united in the thing called horse or stone ; yet because we cannot conceive how they should subsist alone, not one in another, we suppose them to exist in and be supported by some common subject, which support we denote by the name of substance, though it be certain we have no clear or distinct idea of that thing we suppose a support.   The same happens concerning the operations of our mind, viz., thinking, reasoning, and fearing, &c., which we concluding not to subsist of themselves, and not apprehending how they can belong to body, we are apt to think these the actions of some substance which we call spirit.   Whereby it is evident, that having no other notion of matter, but something wherein those many sensible qualities, which affect our senses, do subsist by supposing a substance wherein thinking, knowing, doubting, and a power of moving, &c., do subsist, we have as clear a notion of the nature or substance of spirit, as we have of body; the one being supposed to be, without knowing what is the substratum to those simple ideas which we have, from without, and the other supposed, with a like ignorance of what it is, to be the substratum of the operations which we experiment in ourselves within.   'Tis plain then, that the idea of corporeal substance in matter, is as remote from our conceptions and apprehensions as that of spiritual substance; and therefore from our not having any notion of the substance of spirit we can no more conclude its non-existence, than we can for the same reason deny the existence of body; it being as rational to affirm there is no body, because we cannot know its essence, as it's called, or have the idea of the substance of matter, as to say, there is no spirit, because we know not its essence, or have no idea of a spiritual substance." Mr Locke, also comparing our idea of spirit with our idea of body, thinks there may seem rather less obscurity in the former than the latter.   Our idea of body, he takes to be an extended solid substance, capable of communicating motion by impulse; and our idea of soul is a substance that thinks, and has a power of exciting motion in body by will or thought.   Now, some perhaps will say, they comprehend a thinking thing, which perhaps is true; but, he says, if they consider it well, they can no more comprehend an extended thing; and if they say they know not what it is thinks in them, they mean they know not what the substance is of that thinking thing; no more, says he, do they know what the substance is of that solid thing; and if they say, they know not how they think, he says, neither do they know how they are extended, how the solid parts are united, or where to make extension, &c.

The learned Monsieur Le Clerc, who generally knows how far human reason can bear, argues consonantly to what is before delivered by Mr Locke, in his "Coronis" added to the end of the fourth volume of his philosophical works, in the third edition of them, where he writes as followeth:

"When we contemplate the corporeal nature, we can see nothing in it but extension, divisibility, solidity, mobility, and various determinations of quantity, or figures; which being so, it were a rash thing, and contrary to the laws of right reasoning, to affirm other things of bodies; and consequently from mere body, nothing can be deduced by us, which is not joined in a necessary connection with the said properties. Therefore those, who have thought the properties of perceiving by sense, of understanding, willing, imagining, remembering, and others the like, which have no affinity with corporeal things, to have risen from the body, have greatly transgressed in the method of right reasoning and philosophising, which hath been done by Epicurus, and those who have thought as he did, having affirmed our minds to be composed of corporeal atoms. But whence shall we say they have had their rise? truly, they do not owe their rise to matter, which is wholly destitute of sense and thought, nor are they spontaneously sprung up from nothing, it being an ontological maxim of most evident truth, that nothing springs from nothing."

Having thus given the reader the first ~~objections~~ made against the existence of spirits, and the refutations thereof, I must now frankly own on which side my opinion leans; and for my part, it seems manifest to me that there are two beings we conceive very plainly and distinctly, viz., body and spirit, and that it would be as absurd and ridiculous to deny the existence of the one, as of the other : and really, if the refuters have got the better in their way of reasoning, they have still a much greater advantage over the objectors, when they come to back these reasons with fresh arguments drawn from experience. Of this, there having been many undoubted narratives given in the foregoing pages, concerning the apparitions of spirits, I shall refer the reader back again to them, and only subjoin here one or two instances, which may, if required, be proved upon oath, of spirits seen by two persons of our Duncan Campbell's own acquaintance. In the year 1711, one Mrs Stephens and her daughter were, together with Mr Campbell, at the house of Mr Ramell's, a very great and noted weaver at Haggerstone, where the rainy weather detained them till late at night. Just after the clock struck twelve, they all of them went to the door to see if the rain had ceased, being extremely desirous to get home. As soon as ever they had opened the door and were all got together, there appeared before them a thing all in white ; the face seemed of a dismal pallid hue, but the eyes thereof fiery and flaming like beacons, and of a saucer size. It made its approaches to them, till it came up within the space of about three yards of them ; there it fixed and stood like a figure agaze, for some minutes ; and they all stood likewise stiff like the figure, frozen with fear, motionless, and speechless : when all of a sudden it vanished from their eyes ; and that apparition to the sight was succeeded by a noise, or the appearance of a noise, like that which is occasioned by the fighting of twenty mastiff dogs.

Not long after, Mrs Anne Stephens, who lived in Spitalfields, a woman well known by her great dealings with mercers upon Ludgate Hill, sitting in her house alone, and musing upon business, happened by accident to look behind her, and saw a dead corpse, to her thinking, lie extended upon the floor just as a dead corpse should be, excepting that the foot of one leg was fixed on the ground as it is in a bed, when one lies with one knee up; she looked at it a long while, and by degrees at last stole her eyes from so unpleasing and unexpected an object. However, a strange kind of a curiosity overcame her fears, and she ventured a second time to turn her head that way, and saw it, as before, fixed for a considerable time longer, but durst not stir from her seat; she again withdrew her eyes from the horrible and melancholy spectacle, and resumed the courage, after a little reflection, of viewing it again, and resolving to ascertain herself if the vision was real, by getting up from her seat and going to it, but upon this third retrospection she found it vanished. This relation she writ down to Mr Duncan Campbell, and has told it before Mrs Ramell, her own sister, and many other very creditable persons. Now as to these arguments from experience, I shall also deliver my opinion; I dispute not but that learned men, who have obstinate prepossessions, may produce plausible arguments, why all things should be thought to be done by imposture which seem strange to them, and interfere with their belief; and truly thus far their humour may be indulged, that if only one person relates a very strange and surprising story, a man may be more apt to think it is possible for that person to lie, than that so strange a relation should be true; but if a considerable number of persons of several countries, several religions, several professions, several ages, and those persons looked upon to be of as great sagacity as any the country afford, agree in relations of the same kind, though very strange, and are ready to vouch the truth of them upon oath after having well considered circumstances,

I think it a violation of the law of nature to reject all these relations as fabulous, merely upon a self-presuming conceit, unless a man can fairly show the things to be impossible, or can demonstrate wherein those persons were imposed on; for from hence I form the following conclusive argument: What is possible according to reason grows probable according to belief, where the possibility is attested to have reduced itself into action by persons of known credit and integrity. Now, not only the possibility of the existence of spirits, but the actual existence thereof, is proved above by logical demonstration; therefore are we to believe both by the course of logical reason, and moral faith, that those existences have appeared to men of credit, who have attested the reality thereof upon oath.

Second Objection against the Existence of Witches.

These objections go on to say that, provided they should allow there is an existence of spirits, yet that would be still no argument how magic should subsist, because they deny that it is possible for a man in his body to have a commerce, much less make a contract with spirits; but here again the refuters allege they have both experience and reason on their sides. As a joint argument of reason and experience, they tell you that the numerous witches which have in all countries been arraigned and condemned upon this occasion, are evident testimonies of this commerce and contract being held and made with spirits. They pretend to say that these objectors call not their, the refuters', judgment so much in question, who contend that there is a magic art, as they call in question the judgment of all the wisest legislative powers in Christendom, who have universally agreed in enacting penal laws against such capital offenders.

But here the objectors return and say that it being impossible for us to show the manner how such a contract should be made, we can never, but without reason, believe a thing to be of which we can form no perfect idea.   The refuters, on the other hand, reply with the learned Father le Brune : it's manifest, that we can see but two sorts of beings, spirits and bodies ; and that since we can reason but according to our own ideas, we ought to ascribe to spirits what cannot be produced by bodies.   Indeed, the author of the " Republic of Learning," in the month of August, anno 1686, has given us a rough draft for writing a good tract of witchcraft, which he looks upon as a desideratum, where among other things he writes thus : " Since this age is the true time of systems, one should be contrived concerning the commerce that may be betwixt demons and men."

On this passage, Father le Brune writes thus: "Doubtless here the author complies with the language of a great many persons, who for want of attention and light, would have us put all religion in systems.   Whatever regard I ought to have for many of those persons, I must not be afraid to say that there is no system to be made of those truths, which we ought to learn distinctly by faith, because we must advance nothing here but what we receive from the oracle.   We must make a system to explain the effects of the loadstone, the ebbing and flowing of the sea, the motion of the planets ; for that the cause of these effects is not evidently signified to us, and many may be conceived by us ; and to determine us, we have need of a great number of observations, which by an exact induction, may lead us to a cause that may satisfy all the phenomena.   It's not the same in the truths of religion, we come not at them by groping ; it were to be wished men spoke not of them, but after a decisive and infallible authority.   It's thus we should speak of the power of demons, and of the commerce they have with men; it's of faith that they have power, and that they attack men, and try to seduce them divers ways. It is true indeed, they are sometimes permitted to have it over the just, though they have it not ordinarily but over those that want faith, or fear not to partake of their works; and that to the last particularly, the disordered intelligences try to make exactly succeed what they wish; inspiring them to have recourse to certain practices by which those seducing spirits enter into commerce with men." Thus far Father le Brune. But still these objectors demand to know by what means this commerce may be held between demons and men, and urge us to describe the manner; or pretend that they have still reason to refuse coming into the belief of a thing which we would impose upon them, though wholly ignorant of it ourselves. To that, the refuters answer thus: That both Christian divines, and physicians agree (as to the manner how, which they are so curious in inquiring after), that demons stir up raptures and ecstasies in men, binding or loosing the exterior senses, and that either by stopping the pores of the brain, so that the spirits cannot pass forth (as it's done naturally by sleep), or by recalling the sensitive spirits from the outward senses to the inward organs, which he there retains. So the devil renders women witches ecstatical and magicians, who, while they lie fast asleep in one place, think they have been in divers places and done many things. This the learned objectors say proceeds from no demon, but from the disease called an epilepsy; but, on the other hand, the more learned refuters insist upon it that these ecstasies are not epileptic seizures. This, say they, appears from Bodin, in his " Theatre of Universal Nature," where he says that " those that are wrapt by the devil feel neither stripes nor cuttings, nor no wresting of their limbs, nor burning tortures, nor the application of a red-hot iron ; nay, nor is the beat of the pulse, nor the motion of the heart perceived in them ; but afterwards, returning to themselves, they feel most bitter pains of the wounds received, and tell of things done at 600 miles distance, and affirm themselves to have seen them done." The ingenious Dr Ader makes an admirable physical distinction between this kind of ecstasy and a syncope or stupor caused by narcotic medicines. Sennertus, in his " Institutio Medica," writes of the demoniacal sopor of witches, who think they are carried through the air, dance, feast, and have copulation with the devil, and do other things in their sleep, and afterwards believe the same things waking. Now he says, " Whether they are really so carried in the air, &c., or being in a profound sleep, only dream they are so carried, and persist in that opinion after they are awake, these facts or dreams cannot be natural ; for it cannot be that there should be so great an agreement in dreams, of persons differing in place, temperament, age, sex, and studies, that in one night, and at the same hour, they should, in concert, dream of one and the same such meeting, and should agree as to the place, number, and quality of the persons and the like circumstances. But such dreams are suggested from a preternatural cause ; viz., from the devil to his confederate, by the divine permission of an Almighty power, where punishments are to be permitted to be inflicted upon reprobate sinners."

Whence also, to those witches sincerely converted. and refusing to be any more present at those diabolica₁ meetings, those dreams no longer happen, which is a proof that they proceeded not, before, from a natural cause.

Here begins the great point of the dispute as to that branch of magic which we call natural magic. The objectors may tell us that they will freely own that there may be an existence of spirits, that there may be an existence of witches, that by a divine power men may be influenced so far as to have a communication with good spirits, and that from thence they may become spiritual, divine magicians. They will likewise, perhaps, as freely grant that, by the intervention of a demon, things preternatural may be brought about by persons who have studied the demoniacal magic, but then what they principally insist upon is, that it must be contradictory to all human reason to imagine that there can be such a thing as natural magicians, and thus far they may form their argument. They say that the persons who contend for the magic art own that all that is brought about by magic is by the assistance and help of a spirit, and that consequently what is effected by it must be preternatural. Now they say it is a thing inconsistent by a natural power to bring about a preternatural effect; therefore there can be no such thing as natural magic, which has within itself the efficacy of destroying those acts done by magicians in the diabolical.

To this the refuters take leave to reply, that the foundation upon which the argument is built is wrongly grounded; they have admitted that, in diabolical magic art, there may be a commerce held between men and spirits, by which several preternatural effects may be brought about; and the reason they assign for it there is, because there is a preternatural agent concerned therein, the devil; but then, say they, in natural magic you can pretend to no such agent, and therefore to no such preternatural effect. This argument contains within it two fallacies; first, as to the commerce held between a man and a demon, there is nothing preternatural in getting the acquaintance; the will of the man is entirely natural, either naturally good or naturally corrupted. The black spirit that converseth with him, it is acknowledged is not so, but it is from the will of the man, not from the power vested in the devil that the acquaintance first grows, therefore the acquaintance itself is natural, though it arises from the last corruption and depravations of nature; but being made with a preternatural existence, though the cause of the acquaintance be corruptedly natural, yet the intermediate cause or means after that acquaintance is not so, and therefore the effect of that intermediate cause may be wonderful, and seem to be out of the ordinary course of nature. Now, since it is generally allowed that there are natural spirits of the elements as well as divine and infernal, what we have to prove is only this, that man, by natural magic, may have a commerce with natural spirits of their elements, as witches may have with the spirits or demons. Now, as we said before, the commerce itself depends upon the will of the person, and is therefore natural, and consequently may as well subsist between the one as the other; for the devil cannot force a man to hold a commerce with him whether he will or no. The second fallacy is calling the effect preternatural, no otherwise than as it connotates the agent that brought it about, which is a spiritual agent; for the effect is (in itself considered) natural, and brought about by second causes that are natural, by the devil's penetration, who is subtle enough to make use of them for such and such ends. Now men, by natural spirits, which are of a faculty thoroughly subtle, may as well, with natural second causes, compass the remedy of an evil spirit as the devil is able to infect men with it. From these speculations a farther plain consequence may be deduced, how a man may, by the pure force of natural magic, cure a person that is infested with evils by a demon; for how is it that a demon infests any body with his evil motions? 'Tis

true he is a preternatural agent, but the evil effect
he does is brought about by natural causes.   For
how does a demon stir up raptures or ecstasies in
men?   Why, he does it (as we are told above) by
binding or loosing the exterior senses, by stopping the
pores of the brain, so that the spirits cannot pass forth;
and this the art of physic can compass by its drugs, and
sleep causes the same thing very naturally of itself; therefore as the evil itself is natural, the remedy that is natural
will certainly overcome it.   But then, say you, why
cannot those persons be cured by physicians?   I answer,
not because their remedies are not in themselves sufficient to cure the evils themselves, but because generally
physicians do not administer their drugs as Christians
but as physicians; and when they prescribe them to
the sick they generally prescribe to them only purely
considered as patients, not as Christians, and therein
they come to fail; because the agent, the devil, is a
subtle spirit that brings the evil, and alters its situation
before the remedy, which would master it otherwise,
can take any effect; which agent, the devil, is employed
by the horrible and impious faith of the anti-physician,
viz., the black magician.   But if the physician would
act the Christian at the same time, so far as to have a
faith that things ordained in the course of nature, for the
good of man, would have its effects in spite of a devil,
if taken with a good faith by the patient; that all good
things ordained to be for the natural recovery of
men, if they took it with thankfulness to the sender,
would have due effect; why then the natural spirits of
the elements would resist the farther agency of the
demoniacal spirit, and then nothing but the natural evil
(caused at first by the demon) remaining in the person
without the farther superintendency of the demon,
might demonstratively be taken away by the mere
natural remedy or medicine; and thus good and pious

physicians, making use of such proper remedies as their skill teaches them, and having an honest faith that the goods of nature intended for the use and benefit of man, if received by the patient with the same good faith, is above the power of the devil to frustrate, may not improperly be called natural magicians. These arguments of mine I shall now take leave to back by experience.

Besides what we have urged from reason, concerning the power of natural magic, we shall only subjoin, that divines themselves hold that natural magic, and also natural divinations and prophecies, are proved by quotations from that venerable writ which is their guide; and bring proofs from the same also, that by natural magic demons are also cast forth, but not all kinds of demons, and so many works of efficacy are wrought by natural magic. They tell you such was the Pythonissa that raised the apparition to Saul, which appeared in a body of wind and air. Thus if a person, by natural magic, should cast out demons, it does not follow that this was also from divine magic; and if demons are cast out by natural magic by one that is in the fear of God, it does not follow that he is a true magician of God, but if it exorbitates to demoniacal, then it is condemned; and when natural magic keeps within its bounds, the divines tell us it is not condemned in the venerable book, which is the Christian's sure guide; but, inasmuch as the lawfulness even of natural magic has been called in question by others, I shall, in an Appendix joined to this treatise, examine that matter both according to the reasons of our English laws, and according to the best stated rules of casuistry that I am master of; still submitting my judgment to the superior judgment of those who are professed divines and lawyers; and if my opinions prove erroneous I am willing to retract them. And therefore, in this place, there remains nothing farther for me to do, but only, as I have shown on the one hand, how natural magic and its powerful operations are proved by reason; to show, on the other hand, how far reason in these cases is likewise backed and supported by well-evidenced practice and notorious experience; and to do this, after having mentioned one memorable instance, which I refer the reader to in the body of the book, concerning the performances of Mr Greatrix, to which a Lord Orrery was a witness in Ireland; I shall, to avoid prolixity, bring the other testimonials of practice, from the success which our Duncan Campbell himself has had in this way on other occasions.

In the year 1713, lived in Fenchurch Street one Mr Coates, a tobacco merchant, who had been for many years sorely tormented in his body, and had had recourse for a cure to all the most eminent physicians of the age, even up to the great Dr Radcliffe himself; but all this mighty application for relief was still in vain. Each doctor owned him a wonder and a mystery to physic, and left him as much a wonder as they found him. Neither could the professors of surgery guess at his ailment, or resolve the riddle of his distemper; and after having spent from first to last above a thousand pounds in search of proper remedies, they found the search ineffectual. The learned all agreed that it could proceed from nothing else but witchcraft; they had now, indeed, guessed the source of his illness, but it was an illness of such a kind that, when they had found it out, they thought themselves not the proper persons to prescribe to him any remedies. That task was reserved, it seems, for our Duncan Campbell, who, upon somebody's information or other, was sent for to the bewitched patient, Mr Coates, who found him the wonder that the others had left him, but did wonders in undertaking and compassing his cure. I remember one of the ingredients made use of was boiling his own water, but I cannot tell how it was used ; and, upon turning over the books of some great physicians since, I have found that they themselves have formerly delivered that as one part of the prescriptions for the cure of patients in like cases.   But as there are other things which Mr Campbell performs that seem to require a mixture of the second-sight and of this natural magic before they can be brought about, I will entertain the reader with one or two passages of that sort likewise, and so conclude the history of this so singular a man's life and adventures.

In the year 1710 a gentlewoman lost about six pounds' worth of Flanders lace, and inasmuch as it was a present made to her husband, she was concerned as much as if it had been of twenty times the value ; and a lady of her acquaintance coming to visit her, to whom she unfolded, among other things in discourse, this little disaster ; the lady, smiling, replied with this question, " Did you never hear, madam, of Mr Duncan Campbell ?   It is but making your application to him, things that are lost are immediately found : the power of his knowledge exceeds even the power of laws : they but restrain and frighten, and punish robbers, but he makes thieves expiate their guilt, by the more virtuous way of turning restorers of the goods they have stolen."   " Madam," rejoined the losing gentlewoman, " you smile when you tell me this, but really, as much a trifle as it is, since 'twas a present to my husband, I can't help being sensibly concerned at it ; a moment's disappointment to him in the least thing in nature creates in me a greater uneasiness than the greatest disappointment to my single self could do in things of moment and importance."   " What makes me smile," said the lady, " when I speak of it or think of it, is the oddness and peculiarity of this man's talent in helping one to such things; but without the least jest, I assure you that I know by experience these things come within the compass of his knowledge; and I must seriously tell you, for your farther satisfaction, that he has helped me and several of my friends to the finding again things lost, which were of great value." "And is this, without laughing, true?" said the losing fair, very gravely and demurely, like a person half believing, and desirous to be fully confirmed in such a belief. The lady she advised with did then ascertain her of the truth of the matter, alleging that for a single half-guinea he would inform her of her things, and describe the person that conveyed them away. No sooner was this gentlewoman convinced, but she was eager for the trial, solicited her friend to conduct her to Mr Campbell; and upon the first word of consent, she was hooded and scarfed immediately, and they coached it away in a trice to Mr Campbell's house, whom they luckily found within.

The ladies had not been long seated before he wrote down the name of this new client of his, exactly as it was, viz., Mrs Saxon. Then she was in good hopes, and with much confidence, propounded to him the question about the lace. He paused but a very little while upon the matter before he described the person that took it, and satisfied her that in two or three days she would be mistress of her lace again, and find it in some book or corner of her room. She presented him a half-guinea, and was very contentedly going away; but Mr Campbell very kindly stopped her, and signified to her that if she had no more to offer to him, he had something of more importance to reveal to her. She sat full of expectation while he wrote this new matter; and the paper he delivered to her contained the following account: "As for the loss of a little bit of lace, it is a mere trifle; you have lost a great many

hundreds of pounds, which your aunt (naming her
name) left you, but you are bubbled out of that large
sum.   For while you was artfully required downstairs, about some pretended business or other, one Mr
H—tt—n conveyed your aunt's will out of the desk,
and several other things of value:" and writing down
the names of all the persons concerned, which put Mrs
Saxon in a great consternation, he concluded this paper
with bidding her go home with a contented mind ; she
should find her lace in a few days, and as she found
that prediction prove true, she should afterwards come
and consult about the rest.

When she came home, it seems, big at first with the
thoughts of what she had been told, she rifled and
ransacked every corner, but no lace was to be met
with.   All the next day she hunted in the like manner,
but frightened the whole time, as if she thought the
devil was the only person could bring it, but all to no
purpose ; the third day her curiosity abated, she gave
over the hopes of it, and took the prediction as a vain
delusion, and that what she gave for it was only more
money thrown away after what had been lost before.
That very day, as it commonly happens in such cases,
when she least dreamt of it, she lighted on it by accident
and surprise.   She ran with it in her hand immediately
to her husband, and now she had recovered it again,
told him of the loss of it, and the whole story of her
having been at Mr Campbell's about it ; and then
amplifying the discourse about what he had told her
besides, as to more considerable affairs, she said she
resolved to go and consult him a little farther about
them, and begged her husband to accompany her.   He
would fain have laughed her out of that opinion and
intent, but the end was she persuaded him into it,
and prevailed upon him to seem at least very serious
about the matter, and go with her to the oracle, assur-

ing him there was no room for doubting the same success.

Well, to Mr Campbell's they accordingly came, and after Mr Saxon, in deference to his wife's desire, had paid our predictor a handsome compliment of gold, Mr Duncan Campbell saluted him in as grateful a manner, with the assurance that there was in Kent a little country house with some lands appertaining to it, that was his in right of his wife; that he had the house, as it were, before his eyes, that though he had never substantially seen it, nor been near the place where it stood, he had seen it figuratively, as if in exact painting and sculpture; that particularly it had four green trees before the door, from whence he was positive, that if Mr Saxon went with him in quest of it, he should find it out, and know it as well the moment he came near it, as if he had been an inhabitant in it all his life.

Mr Saxon, though somewhat of an unbeliever, yet must naturally wish to find it true, you may be sure; and yet partly doubting the event, and partly pleased with the visionary promise of a fortune he never expected, laughed very heartily at the oddness of the adventure, and said, he would consider whether it would not savour too much of Quixotism to be at the expense of a journey on such frolics, and on such a chimerical foundation of airy hopes, and that then he would call again and let Mr Campbell know his mind upon that point.

In every company he came into, it served for laughter and diversion; they all, however, agreed 'twas worth his while, since the journey would not be very expensive, to go it by way of frolic. His wife, one morning, saying that she did remember some talk of a house, and such things as Mr Campbell had described, put him forward upon the adventure; and upon Mr Saxon's proposing it to his brother Barnard, Mr Barnard favoured the proposal as a joke, and agreed upon the country ramble. They came on horseback to Mr Campbell's, with a third horse, on which the dumb predictor was mounted, and so on they jogged into Kent towards Sevenoaks, being the place which he described. The first day they set out was on a Saturday morning in June, and about five that afternoon they arrived at the Black Bull at Sevenoaks in Kent. It being a delicate evening, they took an agreeable walk up a fine hill, gracefully adorned with woods, to an old seat of the Earl of Dorset's. Meeting, by the way, with an old servant of the earl's, one Perkin, he offered Mr Barnard, who, it seems, was his old acquaintance, to give them all a sight of that fine ancient seat.

After they had pleased themselves with viewing the antique nobility of that stately structure, this Perkin went back with them to their inn, the Bull at Sevenoaks. They that could talk were very merry in chat; and the dumb gentleman, who saw them laugh, and wear all the signs of alacrity in their countenances, was resolved not to be behind with their tongues, and by dint of pen, ink, and paper, that he made signs should be brought in, was resolved (if one might be said to crack without noise) to crack his jest as well as the best of them; for it may be truly said of him, that he seldom comes into any even diverting company where he is not the most diverting man there, and the head, though we can't call him the mouth, of the cheerful society. After having eyed this Perkin a little, and being grown, by his art, as we may suppose, as familiar with the man's humour, as if he had known him as many years as Mr Barnard—"Pray, Mr Barnard," quoth he, in writing, "how comes it you, that are so staunch and so stiff a Whig, should be so acquainted, and so particularly familiar with such an old Papist, and so violent a Jacobite as I know that Mr Perkin, whom I never saw nor had any notice of in my life, to be?" "And pray," replied Mr Barnard, "what reason have you beyond a pun, to take him for a Jacobite? Must he be so because his name is Perkin? I do assure you in this, you show yourself but little of a conjurer; if you can tell no more of houses than you do of men, we may give over our search after the house you spoke of" (here the reader must understand they discoursed on their fingers, and wrote by turns). Mr Campbell replied, seriously, "Laying a wager is no argument in other things, I own, but in this I know it is, because I am sure, after we have laid the wager, he will fairly confess it among friends, since it will go no farther, and I," said Mr Campbell, "will lay what wager you will apiece with you all round." Hereupon Mr Barnard, who had known him a great many years, was the first that laid, and many more, to the number of five or six followed his example. The decision of the matter was deferred till next day at the return of the old man to the inn; they being about to break up that night, and go to bed.

The next day being Sunday, the landlord carried his guests to see the country, and after a handsome walk, they came through the churchyard. They were poring upon the tombs; no delight can be greater to Mr Campbell than that; and really, by the frequent walks he usually takes in Westminster Abbey, and the churchyards adjacent to this metropolis, one would imagine he takes delight to stalk along by himself on that dumb silent ground, where the characters of the persons are only to be known as his own meaning is, by writings and inscriptions on the marble. When they had sufficiently surveyed the churchyard, it grew near dinner-time, and they went homewards; but before they had got many yards out of the church-yard, Mr Campbell makes a full stop, pointing up to a house; and stopping his friends a little, he pulls out of his pocket a pencil and paper, and notes down the following:—"That, that is the house my vision presented to me, I could swear it to be the same, I know it to be the same, I am certain of it." The gentlemen with him remarked it, but would not take any further notice at that time, intending to inquire into it with secrecy, and so went on to the inn to dinner.

As merry as they had been the night before after supper, they were still more innocently cheerful this day after dinner till the time of service begun. When the duty of the day was performed and over, they returned to divert and unbend their minds with pleasant but harmless conversation. I suppose nobody but a set of very great formalists will be offended with scandal or scruples that, to travellers just ready to depart the town, Mr Perkin came on that good day and decided the wagers by owning to all the company (secrecy being first enjoined) that he was a Roman Catholic, though nobody of the family knew it in so many years as he had lived there, which was before Mr Campbell was born. This and other innocent speeches afforded as much cheerfulness as the Lord's Day would allow of.

On the next day, being Monday, they sent for one Mr Toland Toler, an attorney of the place, to find out to whom that house belonged; but by all the inquiry that could possibly be made with convenient secrecy, nobody could find it out for a long time, but at last it came to light, and appeared to be justly to a tittle as Mr Campbell had predicted.

Being now satisfied, the next day our three travellers returned for London; and the two vocal men were very jocular upon their adventure, and by their outward gesticulations gave the prophetical mute his share of diversion. Mr Barnard, as they passed into a farm-house yard, remarked that all the hogs fell a grunting and squeaking more and more; and as Mr Campbell came nearer (who, poor man! could know nothing of the jest, nor the cause of it, till they alighted and told it him by signs and writing), said to Mr Saxon, laugh-ing, "Now we have found out our house, we shall have only Mr Campbell home again by himself, we have no further need of the devil that accompanied him to the country up to town with us; there are other devils enow to be met with there he knows, and so this, according to the fashion of his predecessor devils, is entered into the herd of swine."

However, the event of this journey, to cut the story short, procured Mr Saxon a great insight, upon inquiry, into several affairs belonging to him, of which he would otherwise have had no knowledge; and he is now engaged in a Chancery suit to do himself justice, and in a fair way of recovering great sums of money, which, without the consultation he had had with this dumb gentleman, he had in all likelihood never dreamt of.

In the year 1711 a gentleman, whose name shall be, in this place, Amandus, famed for his exquisite talents in all arts and sciences, but particularly for his gentle-manlike and entertaining manner of conversation, whose company was affected by all men of wit, who grew his friends, and courted by all ladies of an elegant taste, who grew his admirers;—this accomplished gentleman, I say, came to Mr Campbell, in order to propound a question to him, which was so very intricate, and so difficult to answer, that if he did answer it, it might administer to himself and the ladies he brought with him, the pleasure of admiration in seeing a thing so wonderful in itself performed; or, on the other hand, if he did not make a satisfactory reply to it, then it might afford him and the ladies a very great delight in being the first that puzzled a man who had had the reputation for so many years of being capable of baffling all the wittiest devices and shrewd stratagems that had been, from time to time, invented to baffle his skill, and explode his penetration in the second-sight and the arts which he pretended to. The persons whom Amandus brought with him were the illustrious Lady Delphina, distinguished for her great quality, but still more celebrated for her beauty; his own lady, the admired Amabella; and a young, blooming, pretty virgin, whom we will call by the name of Adeodata, about which last lady the question was to be put to Mr Campbell. Adeodata, it seems, was the natural daughter of this very fine gentleman, who had never let her into the knowledge of her own birth, but had bred her up from her infancy, under a borrowed name, in the notion that she was a relation's daughter, and recommended to his care in her infancy. Now the man that had the second-sight was to be tried. It was now to be put to the proof whether he could tell names or no. Amandus was so much an unbeliever as to be willing to hazard the discovery. Amabella and Delphina were strangers to her real name, and asked Duncan Campbell, not doubting but he would set down that which she ordinarily went by. Amabella had indeed been told by Amandus that Adeodata was the natural daughter of a near friend of his; but who this near friend was remained a secret. That was the point which lay upon our Duncan Campbell to discover. When the question was proposed to him what her name was, he looked at her very steadfastly and shook his head, and after some time he wrote down that it would be a very difficult name for him to fix upon; and truly so it proved: he toiled for every letter till he sweated; and the ladies laughed incontinently, imagining that he was in an agony of shame and confusion at finding himself posed. He desired Amandus to withdraw a little, for that he could not so well take a full and proper survey of ladies' faces when a gentleman was by. This disturbance and perplexity of his afforded them still more subject of mirth; and that excuse was taken as a pretence and a put-off to cover his shame the better, and hide from one at least, that he was but a downright bungler in what he pretended to be so wonderful an artist. However, after two hours' hard sweat and labour, and viewing the face in different shades and lights (for I must observe to the reader that there is a vast deal of difference; some he can tell in a minute or two, with ease, some not in less than four or five hours, and that with great trouble), he undeceived them with regard to his capacity. He wrote down that Adeodata's real name was Amanda, as being the natural daughter of Amandus. Delphina and Amabella were surprised at the discovery; and Amandus, when he was called in, owning it a truth, his wife Amabella applauded the curious way of her coming by such a discovery, when Adeodata was just marriageable; took a liking to her as if her own daughter; and everything ended with profit, mirth, and cheerfulness.

I could add a thousand more adventures of Mr Campbell's life, but that would prove tedious; and as the town has made a great demand for the book it was thought more proper to conclude it here. The most diverting of all are to be found best to the life in original letters that passed between Mr Campbell and his correspondents, some select ones of which will be shortly published in a little pocket volume for the further entertainment of such readers as shall relish this treatise; in which the author hopes he shall be esteemed to have endeavoured at the intermingling of some curious disquisitions of learning, with entertaining passages, and to have ended all the merriest passages with a sober, instructive, and edifying moral, which even to those who are not willing to believe the stories, is reckoned sufficient to recommend even fables themselves.

APPENDIX

IT is not that Mr Duncan Campbell stands in need of my arguments to prove that he is in no respect liable to the Acts of Parliament made against fortune-tellers, &c., that I undertake the writing of this appendix, the true reason thereof being the more completely to finish this undertaking. For having in the body of the book itself fully proved a second-sight, and that the same frequently happens to persons, some of them eminently remarkable for piety and learning, and have from thence accounted for the manner of Mr Campbell's performing those things he professes, to the great surprise, and no less satisfaction of all the curious who are pleased to consult him ; and at the same time proved the lawfulness of such his performances from the opinions of some of the most learned in holy science ; I thought it not improper to add the following short appendix (being a summary of several Acts of Parliament made against fortune-tellers, conjurers, Egyptians, sorcerers, pretenders to prophesy, &c., with some proper remarks, suited to our present purpose), as well to satisfy them who are fantastically wise, and obstinately shut their eyes against the most refulgent reason, and are wilfully deaf to the most convincing and persuasive arguments, and thereupon cry out that Mr Campbell is either an impostor and a cheat, or at least a person who acts by the assistance of unlawful powers; as also to put to silence the no less waspish curs, who are always snarling at such, whom Providence has distinguished by more excellent talents than their neighbours. True merit is always the mark against which traducers level their keenest darts; and wit and invention oftentimes join hands with ignorance and malice to foil those who excel. Art has no greater enemy than ignorance, and were there no such thing as vice, virtue would not shine with half its lustre. Did Mr Campbell perform those wonderful things he is so deservedly famous for, as these cavillers say, by holding intelligence with infernal powers, or by any unjustifiable means, I am of opinion he would find very few in this atheistical age who would open their mouths against him, since none love to act counter to the interest of that master they industriously serve. And did he, on the other hand, put the cheat upon the world, as they maliciously assert, I fancy he would then be more generally admired, especially in a country where the game is so universally, artfully, and no less profitably played, and that with applause, since those pretenders to wisdom merrily divide the whole species of mankind into the two classes of knaves and fools, fixing the appellation of folly only upon those whom they think not wise, that is, wicked enough to have a share with them in the profitable guilt.

Our laws are as well intended by their wise makers to screen the innocent as to punish the guilty; and where their penalties are remarkably severe, the guilt they punish is of a proportionable size. Art, which is a man's property when acquired, claims a protection from those very laws which false pretenders thereto are to be tried and punished by, or else all science would soon have an end; for no man would dare make use of any talent Providence had lent him, and his own industrious application had improved, should he be immediately tried and condemned by those statutes which are made to suppress villains by every conceited and half-learned pedant.

'Tis true, indeed, those excellent statutes which are made against a sort of people who pretend to fortune-telling, and the like, are such as are well warranted, as being built upon the best foundation, viz., religion and policy; and were Mr Campbell guilty of any such practice as those are made to punish, I openly declare that I should be so far from endeavouring to defend his cause that I would be one of the first that should aggravate his crime, thereby to enforce the speedier execution of those laws upon him which are made against such offenders. But when he is so far from acting that he doth not even pretend to any such practice, or for countenancing the same in others, as is manifest from the many detections he has made of that sort of villainy which the book furnishes us with, I think myself sufficiently justified for thus pleading in his defence.

I cannot but take notice, in reading the statutes made against such offenders, our wise legislature hath not in any part of them seemed so much as to imply that there are in reality any such wicked persons as they are made against, to wit, conjurers, &c., but that they are only pretenders to those infernal arts, as may reasonably be inferred from the nature of the penalties they inflict; for our first laws of that sort only inflicted a penalty which affected the goods and liberty of the guilty, and not their lives, though indeed they were afterwards forced to heighten the punishment with a halter; not that they were better convinced, as I humbly conceive, but because the criminals were most commonly persons who had no goods to forfeit, and to whom their liberty was no otherwise valuable, but as it gave them the opportunity of doing mischief. Indeed, our law books do furnish us with many instances of persons who have been tried and executed for witchcraft and sorcery, but then the wiser part of mankind have taken the liberty to condemn the magistrate at that time of day of too much inconsideration, and the juries of an equal share of credulity. And those who have suffered for such crimes have been commonly persons of the lowest rank, whose poverty might occasion a dislike of them in their fellow creatures, and their too artless defence subject them to their mistaken justice; so that upon the whole I take the liberty to conclude, and I hope not without good grounds, that those laws were made to deter men from an idle pretence to mysterious and unjustifiable arts, which, if too closely pursued, commonly lead them into the darkest villainy, not only that of deceiving others, but, as far as in them lie, making themselves slaves to the devil; and not to prevent and hinder men from useful inquiries, and from the practice of such arts which, though they are in themselves mysterious, yet are and may be lawful.

I would not, however, be thought in contradiction to my former arguments, to assert that there never were, or that there now are, no persons such as wizards, sorcerers, &c.; for by so doing I should be as liable to be censured for my incredulity as those who defame Mr Campbell on that account are, for their want of reason and common honesty. Holy and profane writ, I confess, furnishes us with many instances of such persons; but we must not from thence hastily infer, that all those men are such, who are spitefully branded with the odious guilt; for were it in the devil's power to make every wicked man a wizard, and woman a witch, he soon would have agents enough to shake this lower

world to atoms; but the Almighty, who restrains him,
likewise restrains those.

Having premised thus much, I shall now proceed to
consider some of the Acts of Parliament themselves, the
persons against whom they were made, and the necessity
of making the same; and some of the first Acts we
meet with were those which were made against a sort
of people called Egyptians; persons who, if in reality
such, might, if any, be suspected of practising what we
call the black art, the same having been for many ages
encouraged in their country; nay, so much has it been
by them favoured, that it was introduced into their
superstitious religion (if I may, without an absurdity,
call it so), and made an essential part thereof; and, I
believe, Mahometanism has not much mended the matter
since it has imperiously reigned there, or in any respect
reformed that idolatrous nation.   Now the mischief
these persons might do (being so much in the devil's
power), among the unwary, was thought too considerable not to be provided against; and therefore our wise
legislature, the more effectually to prevent the same by
striking at the very foundation, made an Act in the 22
Hen. VIII., 8, that if any, calling themselves Egyptians, do come into this realm, they shall forfeit all their
goods; and being demanded, shall depart the realm
within fifteen days, upon pain of imprisonment; and the
importers of them, by another Act, were made liable to
heavy penalty.   This Act was continued by the 1 Phil.
and Mary; conjuration, witchcraft, enchantment and
sorcery, to get money, or consume any person in his
body, members, or goods, or to provoke any person to
unlawful love, was by the 33 Hen. VIII., 14, the 5
Eliz., 16, and the 1 Jac. I., 12, made felony; and by
the same 33 Hen. VIII., 14, it was made felony to
declare to another any false prophecies upon arms, &c.;
but this Act was repealed by the 1 Edw. VI., 12; but

by another Act of the 3 & 4 Edw. VI., 15, it was again enacted, that all such persons who should pretend to prophecies, &c., should, upon conviction, for the first offence forfeit ten pounds, and one year's imprisonment; and for the second offence all his goods, and imprisonment for life. And by the 7 Edw. VI., 11, the same was made to continue but till the then next session of Parliament. And by the 5 Eliz., 15, the same Act was again renewed against fantastical prophesiers, &c.; but both those Acts were repealed by the 1 Jac. I., 12.

Thus far we find, that for reasons of state, and for the punishment of particular persons, those Acts were made and repealed, as occasion required, and not kept on foot, or indeed were they ever made use of, as I can remember in my reading, against any persons whose studies led them into a useful inquiry into the nature of things, or a lawful search into the workings of nature itself, by which means many things are foretold long before they come to pass, as eclipses, and the like; which astrologers successfully do, whose art has been in all ages held in so great esteem, that the first monarchs of the east made it their peculiar study, by which means they deservedly acquired to themselves the name of Magi, or wise men; but, on the contrary, were provided against persons profligate and loose, who, under a pretence and mask of science, commit vile and roguish cheats. And this will the more plainly appear, if we consider the letter and express meaning of the following Acts, wherein the persons I am speaking of are described by such characters, which sufficiently prove the assertion; for in the 39 of Eliz., 4, it was enacted, "That all persons calling themselves scholars, going about begging, seafaring men, pretending losses of their ships and goods at sea, and going about the country begging, or using any subtile craft, feigning themselves to have knowledge in physiognomy, palmistry, or any other the like crafty science, or pretending that they can tell destinies, fortunes, or such like fantastical imaginations, shall be taken and deemed rogues, vagabonds, and sturdy beggars; and shall be stripped naked from the middle upwards, and whipped till his or her body be bloody." And by the 1 Jac. I., 12, for the better restraining of the said offences, and for the further punishing the same, it was further enacted, "That any person or persons using witchcraft, sorcery, &c., and all their aiders, abettors, and counsellors, being convicted, and attainted of the same offences, shall suffer pain of death, as felons, without the benefit of clergy; or to tell and declare in what place any treasure of gold and silver should or might be found in the earth, or other secret places; or where goods or things lost or stolen should be found or become; or to provoke any person to unlawful love; such offender to suffer imprisonment for one whole year, without bail or mainprize, and once in every quarter of the said year, shall in some market town, or upon the market day, or at any such time as any fair shall be kept there, stand openly in the pillory by the space of six hours, and there shall openly confess his or their offence; and for the second offence shall suffer death as felons without the benefit of clergy."

That these laws were made against a set of villains, whose natural antipathy to honesty and labour furnished them with pretensions to an uncommon skill, thereby the more easily to gull and cheat the superstitiously credulous, and by that means discover from them some such secrets that might further them in perpetrating the more consummate villainy, is plain, from the very words and expressions of the very Acts themselves, and the description of the persons they are made against; and not, as I before observed, to prevent and hinder men from the lawful inquiry after useful, delightful, and profitable knowledge.

Mr Campbell, who has been long a settled and reputable inhabitant in many eminent parts of the city of London, cannot, I am sure, be looked upon as one of those these Acts of Parliament were made against, unless we first strip the Acts themselves of their own natural, express, and plain meaning, and clothe them with that which is more obscure, unnatural, forced, and constrained; a practice which, if allowed, would make them wound the innocent and clear the guilty, and render them not our defence, but our greatest evil. They would, by that means, become a perfect enigma, and be so far from being admired for their plainness, that they would be even exploded, like the oracles of the heathen, for their double meaning.

If Mr Campbell has the second-sight, as is unquestionable from the allowed maxim, that what has been may be again, and by that means can take a view of contingencies and future events; so long as he confines these notices of approaching occurrences to a good purpose, and makes use of them only innocently and charitably to warn persons from doing such things that, according to his conceptions, would lead them into misfortune, or else in putting them upon such arts that may be of use and benefit to themselves and posterity, always having a strict regard to morality and religion, to which he truly adheres: certainly, I think he ought so much the more to be admired for the same, by how much the more this his excellent knowledge is surpassing that of other men, and not be therefore unjustly upbraided with the injurious character of a cheat, or an ill man. However, this I will presume to affirm, and I doubt not but to have my opinion confirmed by the learned sages of the law, that this his innocent practice, and I venture to add honest one too, doth by

no means entitle him to the penalties of the before-
mentioned laws made against fortune-tellers, and such
sort of profligate wretches ; which it is as great an
absurdity to decry as it would be to call him, who is a
settled and reputable inhabitant, a stroller, or wandering
beggar.

Again, it is true that Mr Campbell has relieved
many that have been supposed to have been bewitched,
as is related and well attested in the book of his life ;
but will any one from thence argue that he himself is a
real conjurer or wizard, because he breaks the chains
by which those unhappy wretches were bound ? No,
surely, for if that were the case, we might then as well
indict the physician who drives away a malignant
distemper, and roots out its latent cause by his
mysterious skill in plants and drugs ; or conclude that
the judge who condemns a criminal is, for the same
reason, guilty of the self-same crime for which the
offender is so by him condemned. Persons who
delight in such unnatural conclusions must certainly be
in love with the greatest absurdities, and must entirely
abandon their natural reason, before they can be brought
to conclude that the prince of darkness would assist men
in destroying his own power.

The best answer I can afford those men is silence ;
for if they will not argue upon the principles of reason,
or be guided by her dictates, I think them no more fit
to be contended with in a rational and decent manner
than bedlamites, and such who are bereft of all understanding. A rod is the best argument for the back of
a fool, and contempt the best usage that ought to be
shown to every headstrong and ignorant opponent.

In a word, I know of no branch of Mr Campbell's
practice that bears the least resemblance to those crimes
mentioned in the foregoing Acts. That he can and
doth tell people's names at first sight, though perfect

strangers to him, is confessed by all who have made the curious inquiry at his hands ; but what part of the Acts, I would fain know, is that against ? Knowledge, and a clear sight into things not common, is not only an allowable, but a commendable qualification ; and whether this knowledge in him be inherent, accidental, or the result of a long study, the case is still the same, since we are assured he doth it by no unlawful intelligence, or makes use of the same to any ill purpose, and therefore is undoubtedly as lawful as to draw natural conclusions from right premises. Hard is the fate of any man to be ignorant, but much harder would his lot be, if he were to be punished for being wise, and, like Mr Campbell, excelling others in this kind of knowledge.

Much more might be said in defence of Mr Campbell and the art he professeth, but as the arguments which are brought against him by his enemies, on the one hand, are trivial and ill-grounded, I therefore think they deserve no farther refutation ; so, on the other, his innocency is too clear to require it.

After having thus taken a survey of Mr Campbell's acts, with regard to their legality according to the statutes and the laws of the nation wherein he lives, we will consider next, whether, according to the stated rules of casuistry among the great divines eminent for their authority, it may be lawful for Mr Campbell to predict, or for good Christian persons to visit his house, and consult him about his predictions. I have, upon this head, examined all the learnedest casuists I could meet with in ancient times ; for I cannot meet, in my reading, with any moderns that treat thoroughly upon this case, or I should rather have chosen them, because, perhaps, the second-sight was less known in those ancient days than it has been since, and so might escape their notice.

My design is first to give the reader a distinct summary of all that has been said of this matter, and to do it as succinctly and briefly as possible, and then to argue myself, from what they agree upon, as to this man's particular case.

That the reader may have recourse to the authors themselves, if they have a curiosity, and find that I don't go about to impose upon their judgments, I will here tell the reader where he may find the whole contents of the following little abstract of divinity and casuistry, because it would be a tedious piece of work to set down the words of each of them distinctly, and quote them every one round at the end of their several different sentences, which tend to the same meaning, but I will strictly keep to the sense of them all; and I here give the reader their names, and the places, that he may consult them himself if his inclination leads him to be so curious : Thomas Aquinas, 4, Distin. 34, quæstio. 1, art. 3, Bona, 2, Dist. 7, art. 2, quæst. 1 ; Joannes Major, 4, Dist. 34, quæst. 2 ; Sylvester, "Verbo Malefic.," quæst. 8 ; Rosella, "Verb. Impedimentum," 15, cap. 18 ; Tabiena, "Verb. Imped." 12 vers. ; Cajetan, tom. 2, opusc. 12, "De Malefic.;" Alphonsus, a Cast. lib. 10, "De Justâ Hæreticorum punitione," cap. 15 ; Cosmus Philiarchus, "De Offic. Sacerdot.," p. 2, l. 3, cap. ii. ; Toletus, in "Summa," lib. 4, cap. 16 ; Spineus, in "Tract. de Strigibus;" Petrus Binsfield, in "Tract. de Confessionibus Maleficorum."

These divines have generally written upon impious arts of magic, which they call by the name of divination ; and this divination (as they term it) they divide into two kinds, the one in which the devil is expressly invoked to teach hidden and occult things, the other, in which he is tacitly called upon to do the same. An express invocation is by word or deed, by which a real pact is actually made with the devil; and that is a sin that affects the death of the soul, according to the laws of theology, and ought to affect the death of the body, according to civil and political laws. The tacit invocation of demons is then only, when a man busies himself so far with such persons, that it is meet and just that the devil should be permitted to have to do with him, though it was opposite to the intention of the man.

But then this express invocation again is subdivided into several species, according to the diverse manners by which the devil instructs these men.

The first is enchantment, which I need not describe, and of which I will speak no more, because it is what everybody knows to be detestable, and nobody ought to know the art thereof.

The second is divination by dreams, when any instructions are expected from the devil by way of dream, which is a capital crime.

The third is called necromancy, which is, when by the use of blood and writing, or speaking certain verses, the dead seem to rise again, and speak and teach future things. For though the devil cannot recall a soul departed, yet he can (as some have thought) take the shape of the dead corpse, himself actuate it by his subtlety, as if it was informed with a soul. And some affirm, that by the divine permission the devil can do this, and spake so in the case of Samuel and Saul. But divines of a more solid genius attribute that power only to the Deity, and say, with reason, that it is beyond the devil's capacity. But it is certain this was a divination done in dead animals by the use of their blood, and therefore the word is derived from the Greek νεκρὸν, which signifies dead, and Μαντήα, which signifies divination.

The fourth species is called divination by the

Pythians, which was taken from Apollo, the first diviner, as Thomas Aquinas says in his "Secundâ secundæ," qu. 95, artic. 3.

The fifth is called geomancy, which is when the devil teaches anything by certain signs appearing in the earthly bodies, as in wood, iron, or polished stones, beryls, or glass.

The sixth is named hydromancy, as when a demon teaches anything by appearances in the water.

The seventh is styled aeromancy; and it is when he informs people of such things by figures in the air.

The eighth is intituled pyromancy; that is, when it instructs people by forms appearing in the fire.

The ninth is termed aruspicy; which is, when by signs appearing in the bowels of sacrificed animals the demon predicts at altars.

Thus far as to express divination or invocation of the devil, which is detestable, and the very consulting of persons that use such unlawful means, is, according to the judgment of all casuists, the high road to eternal damnation.

Now as to tacit divination or invocation of the devil, that is divided into two subaltern kinds. The first kind is, when, for the sake of knowing hidden things, they make use of a vain and superstitious disposition existing in things to judge from; which disposition is not of a sufficient virtue to lead them to any real judgment. The second kind of tacit divination is, when that knowledge is sought by the disposition of those things, which men effect on purpose and of their own accord, in order to come by and acquire that knowledge.

Both these kinds of tacit divination are again subdivided into several species, as are particularly mentioned by St Thomas, "Secundâ secundæ," quæst. 95, artic. 3; Gregory de Valentine, tom. 3, disput. 6, quæst. 12, puncto 2 ; Toletus, in " Summâ," lib. 4, cap. 15, and Michael Medina, lib. 2, " De rectâ in Deum fide : post sanctum Augustinum," lib. 2, "De Doct. Christ.," cap. 19, et sequen.

The first of these kinds of tacit divination contains under it the following several species.

The first species is called genethliacal, which is when, from the movement or situation of the stars, men's nativities are calculated and inquired into so far, as that from such a search, they pretend to deduce the knowledge of human effects, and the contingent events that are to attend them. This Thomas Aquinas and Sixtus Quintus condemns ; but I shall, with humility and submission to greater judgments, inquire hereafter into their reasons, and give my opinion why I think this no evil art ; but I submit my opinion, if, after it is given, it is thought erroneous.

The second is augury, when anything is predicted from the chattering of birds, or the voice of animals, and this may be either lawful or unlawful. If it comes from natural instinct (for brutes, having only a sensitive soul, have their organs subject to the disposition of the greater bodies in which they are contained, and principally of all to the celestial bodies) his augury is not amiss. For if when crows are remarked to caw (as the vulgar phrase is) more than ordinary, it is, judging according to the instinct of their nature, if we expect rain, and we may reasonably depend upon it we shall be right if we foretell rain to be at hand. But sometimes the devils actuate those brute animals to excite vain ideas in men, contrary to what the instinct of their nature compels them to. This is superstitious and unlawful, and forbid in holy writ.

The third is aruspicy, when, from the flight of birds or any other motion of any animals whatsoever, persons pretend to have an insight and a penetrative knowledge into occult and hidden matters.

The fourth consists in omens, when, for example, a man, from any words which others may have spoken on purpose or by accident, pretends to gather a way of looking into and knowing anything of futurity.

The fifth is chiromancy, which consists in making a pretence to the knowledge of future things by the figures and the lines of the hands: and if it be by consulting the shoulder-bones of any beast, it goes by the name of spatulamancy.

As the first kind of divination, by a tacit invocation of the devil, is divided into five species above mentioned; so also is the second kind of tacit divination, or invocation of the devil, divided into two species by St Thomas of Aquin, " Secundâ secundæ, quæstione nonagesimâ quintâ articulo tertio," and too tedious to insert here.

Now all these ways are by these divines counted wicked, and I set them down that people may avoid them. For how many gipsies and pretenders to chiromancy have we in London and in the country? How many that are for hydromancy, that pretend in water to show men mighty mysteries? And how many in geomancy, with their beryls and their glasses, that, if they are not under the instigation of the devil, propagate the scandal at least by being cheats, and who ought to be punished to the utmost severity, as our English laws enact? Mr Campbell, who hates, contemns, and abhors these ways, ought, methinks, to be encouraged by their being restrained; and people of curious tempers, who always receive from him moral and good instructions, which make them happy in the conduct of life, should be animated in a public manner to consult him, in order to divert the curious itch of their humours from consulting such wicked impostors or diabolical practisers, as too frequently abound in this nation, by reason of the inquisitive vulgar, who are more numerous in our climate than any I ever read of.

But now to argue the case of conscience with regard to his particular practice by way of the second-sight, whether, *in foro conscientiæ*, it is lawful for him to follow it, or others to consult him? The divines above-mentioned having never had any notice of that faculty, in all likelihood, or if they had, never mentioning it, makes it a point more difficult for me to discuss; but I think they have stated some cases, by the making of which my premises, I can deduce from all the learned men I have above quoted a conclusion in favour of our Mr Duncan Campbell, and of those who consult him; but my opinion shall be always corrected by those who are wiser than myself, and to whom I owe entire submission. I take leave to fix these premises from them first, and to form my argument from them afterwards in the following manner.

First, it is allowed by all these divines, that a knowledge which one may have of future things within the order of nature is, and may be lawful.

Secondly, they imply that where justice is not violated, it is lawful both to predict and to consult.

Thirdly, many of them, but particularly Aureolus, puts this question:—"Is it lawful to go to one that deals in the black art, to persuade them to cure any innocent body that another necromancer or dealer in the black art may have maliciously afflicted and tormented with pains?" And some of these casuists, particularly Aureolus, say, it is lawful on such occasion to go to such a conjurer, because the end is not conjuration, but freeing a person from it.

But I take leave to dissent from these great men, and think they are in a double mistake; first, in stating the question, and then in making such an answer, provided the question had been stated right.

The question is founded upon this supposition (which is passed by as granted), viz., that one necromancer could release a person bewitched by another, which is absolutely false; for it is against the nature of the devil to be made an instrument to undo his own works of impiety. But admitting and not granting this to be possible, and the question to be rightly stated, why, still these casuists are out in their answer. "It is lawful," reply they, "because the end of going to the conjurers is not conjuration, but freeing a good person from it." But the end is not the point here to be considered, it is the medium which is bad that is to be considered. It is by conjuration (according to their hypothesis) the other conjuration is to be dissolved; and does not the common rule, that a man must not do evil that good may come of it, forbid this practice? And to speak my opinion plainly in that case, the friend that should consult a conjurer for that end would be only so kind to put his own soul in danger of being guilty of hell-torments to relieve his afflicted friend from some bodily pains, which 'twould be a virtue in him to suffer with patience and resignation.

Others, almost all divines indeed, agree, that it is and may be lawful to go to a conjurer that torments another, and give him money not to afflict the patient any longer; because that's only feeing him to desist from acting after his conjuring manner.

These premises thus settled, if we allow the second-sight to be inborn and inbred, and natural and common to some families, which is proved in the book; and if all that Mr Campbell has predicted in that second-sighted way terminates with moral advice, and the profit of the consulter, and without the violation of justice to others, as the book shows all throughout; if he can relieve from witchcraft, as it seems oath is to be had he can, which no one that deals in black art can do, why then I need not draw the conclusion; every reader will do it naturally; they will avow all the stricter laws of casuistry and morality to be in favour of Mr Campbell and his consulters.

A REMARKABLE PASSAGE OF
AN APPARITION

A REMARKABLE PASSAGE OF
AN APPARITION,

RELATED BY THE REV. DR RUDDLE, OF LAUN-
CESTON IN CORNWALL, IN THE YEAR 1665.

I N the beginning of this year, a disease happened in
this town of Launceston, and some of my scholars
died of it. Among others who fell under the malignity then triumphing, was John Elliot, the eldest son of
Edward Elliot of Treherse, Esq., a stripling of about
sixteen years of age, but of more than common parts
and ingenuity. At his own particular request, I
preached at the funeral, which happened on the 20th
day of June 1665. In my discourse (ut mos reique
locique postulabat), I spoke some words in commendation of the young gentleman ; such as might endear his
memory to those that knew him, and, withal, tended to
preserve his example to the fry which went to school
with him, and were to continue there after him. An
ancient gentleman, who was then in the church, was
much affected with the discourse, and was often heard
to repeat, the same evening, an expression I then used
out of Virgil :—

> " Et puer ipse fuit cantari dignus."

The reason why this grave gentleman was so concerned at the character, was a reflection he made upon a son of his own, who being about the same age, and, but a few months before, not unworthy of the like character I gave of the young Mr Elliot, was now, by a strange accident, quite lost as to his parent's hopes and all expectation of any further comfort by him.

The funeral rites being over, I was no sooner come out of the church, but I found myself most courteously accosted by this old gentleman; and with an unusual importunity, almost forced against my humour to see his house that night; nor could I have rescued myself from his kindness, had not Mr Elliot interposed and pleaded title to me for the whole of the day, which, as he said, he would resign to no man. Hereupon I got loose for that time, but was constrained to leave a promise behind me to wait upon him at his own house the Monday following. This then seemed to satisfy, but before Monday came I had a new message to request me that, if it were possible, I would be there on the Sunday. The second attempt I resisted, by answering that it was against my convenience, and the duty which mine own people expected from me. Yet was not the gentleman at rest, for he sent me another letter on the Sunday, by no means to fail on the Monday, and so to order my business as to spend with him two or three days at least. I was indeed startled at so much eagerness, and so many dunnings for a visit, without any business; and began to suspect that there must needs be some design in the bottom of all this excess of courtesy. For I had no familiarity, scarce common acquaintance with the gentleman or his family; nor could I imagine whence should arise such a flush of friendship on the sudden.

On the Monday I went, and paid my promised devoir, and met with entertainment as free and plentiful as the invitation was importunate. There also I found a neighbouring minister who pretended to call in accidentally, but by the sequel I suppose it otherwise. After dinner this brother of the coat undertook to show me the gardens, where, as we were walking, he gave me the first discovery of what was mainly intended in all this treat and compliment.

First he began to tell the infortunity of the family in general, and then gave an instance in the youngest son. He related what a hopeful, sprightly lad he lately was, and how melancholic and sottish he was now grown. Then did he with much passion lament, that his ill-humour should so incredibly subdue his reason; for, says he, the poor boy believes himself to be haunted with ghosts, and is confident that he meets with an evil spirit in a certain field about half a mile from this place, as often as he goes that way to school.

In the midst of our twaddle, the old gentleman and his lady (as observing their cue exactly) came up to us. Upon their approach, and pointing me to the arbour, the parson renews the relation to me; and they (the parents of the youth) confirmed what he said, and added many minute circumstances, in a long narrative of the whole. In fine, they all three desired my thoughts and advice in the affair.

I was not able to collect thoughts enough on the sudden to frame a judgment upon what they had said, only I answered, that the thing which the youth reported to them was strange, yet not incredible, and that I knew not then what to think or say of it; but if the lad would be free to me in talk, and trust me with his counsels, I had hopes to give them a better account of my opinion the next day.

I had no sooner spoken so much, but I perceived myself in the springe their courtship had laid for me; for the old lady was not able to hide her impatience, but her son must be called immediately. This I was forced to comply with and consent to, so that drawing off from the company to an orchard near by, she went herself and brought him to me, and left him with me.

It was the main drift of all these three to persuade me that either the boy was lazy, and glad of any excuse to keep from the school, or that he was in love with some wench and ashamed to confess it; or that he had a fetch upon his father to get money and new clothes, that he might range to London after a brother he had there; and therefore they begged of me to discover the root of the matter, and accordingly to dissuade, advise, or reprove him, but chiefly, by all means, to undeceive him as to the fancy of ghosts and spirits.

I soon entered into a close conference with the youth, and at first was very cautious not to displease him, but by smooth words to ingratiate myself and get within him, for I doubted he would be too distrustful or too reserved. But we had scarcely passed the first situation, and begun to speak to the business, before I found that there needed no policy to screw myself into his breast; for he most openly, and with all obliging candour did aver, that he loved his book, and desired nothing more than to be bred a scholar; that he had not the least respect for any of womankind, as his mother gave out; and that the only request he would make to his parents was, that they would but believe his constant assertions concerning the woman he was disturbed with, in the field called the Higher-Broom Quartils. He told me with all naked freedom, and a flood of tears, that his friends were unkind and unjust to him, neither to believe nor pity him; and that if any man (making a bow to me) would but go with him to the place, he might be convinced that the thing was real, &c.

By this time he found me apt to compassionate his

condition, and to be attentive to his relation of it, and therefore he went on in this way :—

"This woman which appears to me," saith he, "lived a neighbour here to my father, and died about eight years since; her name, Dorothy Dingley, of such a stature, such age, and such complexion. She never speaks to me, but passeth by hastily, and always leaves the footpath to me, and she commonly meets me twice or three times in the breadth of the field.

"It was about two months before I took any notice of it, and though the shape of the face was in my memory, yet I did not recall the name of the person, but without more thoughtfulness, I did suppose it was some woman who lived thereabout, and had frequent occasion that way. Nor did I imagine anything to the contrary before she began to meet me constantly, morning and evening, and always in the same field, and sometimes twice or thrice in the breadth of it.

"The first time I took notice of her was about a year since, and when I first began to suspect and believe it to be a ghost, I had courage enough not to be afraid, but kept it to myself a good while, and only wondered very much about it. I did often speak to it, but never had a word in answer. Then I changed my way, and went to school the Under Horse Road, and then she always met me in the narrow lane, between the Quarry Park and the Nursery, which was worse.

"At length I began to be terrified at it, and prayed continually that God would either free me from it or let me know the meaning of it. Night and day, sleeping and waking, the shape was ever running in my mind, and I often did repeat these places of Scripture (with that he takes a small Bible out of his pocket), Job vii. 14: 'Thou scarest me with dreams, and terrifiest me through visions.' And Deuteronomy xxviii. 67: 'In the morning, thou shalt say, Would

God it were even; and at even thou shalt say, Would God it were morning; for the fear of thine heart, wherewith thou shalt fear, and for the sight of thine eyes, which thou shalt see.' "

I was very much pleased with the lad's ingenuity in the application of these pertinent Scriptures to his condition, and desired him to proceed.

"When," says he, "by degrees, I grew very pensive, inasmuch that it was taken notice of by all our family; whereupon, being urged to it, I told my brother William of it, and he privately acquainted my father and mother, and they kept it to themselves for some time.

"The success of this discovery was only this; they did sometimes laugh at me, sometimes chide me, but still commanded me to keep to my school, and put such fopperies out of my head. I did accordingly go to school often, but always met the woman in the way."

This, and much more to the same purpose, yea, as much as held a dialogue of near two hours, was our conference in the orchard, which ended with my proffer to him, that, without making any privy to our intents, I would next morning walk with him to the place, about six o'clock. He was even transported with joy at the mention of it, and replied—"But will you, sure, sir? Will you, sure, sir? Thank God! Now I hope I shall be relieved." From this conclusion we retired into the house.

The gentleman, his wife, and Mr Sam were impatient to know the event, insomuch that they came out of the parlour into the hall to meet us; and seeing the lad look cheerfully, the first compliment from the old man was, "Come, Mr Ruddle, you have talked with him; I hope now he will have more wit. An idle boy! an idle boy!" At these words, the lad ran up the stairs to his own chamber, without replying, and I soon

stopped the curiosity of the three expectants by telling
them I had promised silence, and was resolved to be
as good as my word ; but when things were riper they
might know all. At present, I desired them to rest
in my faithful promise, that I would do my utmost in
their service, and for the good of their son. With
this they were silenced ; I cannot say satisfied.

The next morning before five o'clock, the lad was
in my chamber, and very brisk. I arose and went
with him. The field he led me to I guessed to be
twenty acres, in an open country, and about three
furlongs from any house. We went into the field,
and had not gone above a third part, before the spectrum, in the shape of a woman, with all the circumstances he had described her to me in the orchard the
day before (as much as the suddenness of its appearance
and evanition would permit me to discover), met us
and passed by. I was a little surprised at it, and
though I had taken up a firm resolution to speak to it,
yet I had not the power, nor indeed durst I look back;
yet I took care not to show any fear to my pupil and
guide, and therefore only telling him that I was satisfied in the truth of his complaint, we walked to the
end of the field and returned, nor did the ghost meet
us that time above once. I perceived in the young
man a kind of boldness, mixed with astonishment ; the
first caused by my presence, and the proof he had
given of his own relation, and the other by the sight
of his persecutor.

In short, we went home : I somewhat puzzled, he
much animated. At our return, the gentlewoman,
whose inquisitiveness had missed us, watched to speak
with me. I gave her a convenience, and told her that
my opinion was that her son's complaint was not to
be slighted, nor altogether discredited ; yet, that my
judgment in his case was not settled. I gave her

caution, moreover, that the thing might not take wind, lest the whole country should ring with what we had yet no assurance of.

In this juncture of time I had business which would admit no delay ; wherefore I went for Launceston that evening, but promised to see them again next week. Yet I was prevented by an occasion which pleaded a sufficient excuse ; for my wife was that week brought home from a neighbour's house very ill. However, my mind was upon the adventure. I studied the case, and about three weeks after went again, resolving, by the help of God, to see the utmost.

The next morning being the 27th day of July 1665, I went to the haunted field by myself, and walked the breadth of the field without any encounter. I returned and took the other walk, and then the spectrum appeared to me, much about the same place where I saw it before, when the young gentleman was with me. In my thoughts, it moved swifter than the time before, and about ten feet distance from me on my right hand, insomuch that I had not time to speak, as I had determined with myself beforehand.

The evening of this day, the parents, the son, and myself, being in the chamber where I lay, I propounded to them our going all together to the place next morning, and after some asseveration that there was no danger in it, we all resolved upon it. The morning being come, lest we should alarm the family of servants, they went under the pretence of seeing a field of wheat, and I took my horse and fetched a compass another way, and so met at the stile we had appointed.

Thence we all four walked leisurely into the Quartils, and had passed above half the field before the ghost made appearance. It then came over the stile just before us, and moved with that swiftness that by the time we had gone six or seven steps it passed by. I immediately turned head and ran after it, with the young man by my side ; we saw it pass over the stile by which we entered, but no farther. I stepped upon the hedge at one place, he at another, but could discern nothing ; whereas, I dare aver, that the swiftest horse in England could not have conveyed himself out of sight in that short space of time. Two things I observed in this day's appearance. 1. That a spaniel dog, who followed the company unregarded, did bark and run away, as the spectrum passed by ; whence it is easy to conclude that it was not our fear or fancy which made the apparition. 2. That the motion of the spectrum was not gradation, or by steps, and moving of the feet, but a kind of gliding, as children upon the ice, or a boat down a swift river, which punctually answers the descriptions the ancients gave of their *Lemures*, which was Κατὰ ῥύμτω ἀ ἑριον καὶ ὁρμὴν ἄπζαποδισον (Heliodorus).

But to proceed. This ocular evidence clearly convinced, but, withal, strangely frightened the old gentleman and his wife, who knew this Dorothy Dingley in her lifetime, were at her burial, and now plainly saw her features in this present apparition. I encouraged them as well as I could, but after this they went no more. However, I was resolved to proceed, and use such lawful means as God hath discovered, and learned men have successfully practised in these irregular cases.

The next morning being Thursday, I went out very early by myself, and walked for about an hour's space in meditation and prayer in the field next adjoining to the Quartils. Soon after five I stepped over the stile into the disturbed field, and had not gone above thirty or forty paces before the ghost appeared at the farther stile. I spoke to it with a loud voice, in some such sentences as the way of these dealings directed me ;

whereupon it approached, but slowly, and when I came near, it moved not. I spake again, and it answered, in a voice neither very audible nor intelligible. I was not in the least terrified, and therefore persisted until it spake again, and gave me satisfaction. But the work could not be finished at this time; wherefore the same evening, an hour after sunset, it met me again near the same place, and after a few words on each side, it quietly vanished, and neither doth appear since, nor ever will more to any man's disturbance. The discourse in the morning lasted about a quarter of an hour.

These things are true, and I know them to be so, with as much certainty as eyes and ears can give me; and until I can be persuaded that my senses do deceive me about their proper object, and by that persuasion deprive myself of the strongest inducement to believe the Christian religion, I must and will assert that these things in this paper are true.

As for the manner of my proceeding, I find no reason to be ashamed of it, for I can justify it to men of good principles, discretion, and recondite learning, though in this case I choose to content myself in the assurance of the thing, rather than be at the unprofitable trouble to persuade others to believe it; for I know full well with what difficulty relations of so uncommon a nature and practice obtain belief. He that tells such a story may expect to be dealt withal as a traveller in Poland by the robbers, viz., first murdered and then searched,—first condemned for a liar, or superstitious, and then, when it is too late, have his reasons and proofs examined. This incredulity may be attributed—

1. To the infinite abuses of the people, and impositions upon their faith by the cunning monks and friars, &c., in the days of darkness and popery; for they made apparitions as often as they pleased, and got

both money and credit by quieting the *terriculamenta vulgi*, which their own artifice had raised.

2. To the prevailing of Somatism and the Hobbean principle in these times, which is a revival of the doctrine of the Sadducees; and as it denies the nature, so it cannot consist with the apparition of spirits; of which, see "Leviathan," p. 1, c. 12.

3. To the ignorance of men in our age, in this peculiar and mysterious part of philosophy and of religion, namely, the communication between spirits and men. Not one scholar in ten thousand (though otherwise of excellent learning) knows anything of it or the way how to manage it. This ignorance breeds fear and abhorrence of that which otherwise might be of incomparable benefit to mankind.

But I being a clergyman and young, and a stranger in these parts, do apprehend silence and secrecy to be my best security.

"In rebus abstrusissimis abundans cautela non nocet."

Sept. 4, 1665.

POSTSCRIPT.

It is possible that the unacquaintedness of some men with Church history and the writings of the ancient fathers may be one cause of their prejudice against things and narratives of this nature. I could cite out of them hundreds of passages in confirmation (*a pari*) of what I have now done and written. But a single testimony shall serve to fill up this page.

St Cyprian was a father of the third century, contemporary with Origen, Tertullian, Lactantius, Clemens of Alexandria, and other learned men. Observe his words (S. Cypriani Epist. ad Demetrium Ethnicum, p. 328) :—

"Si audire velles et videre quando spiritus mali a nobis adjurantur et torquentur spiritualibus flagris ; quando dæmones ejulantes et gementes humanâ voce venturum judicium confitentur ; videbis nos rogari ab iis quos tu rogas, et tamen ab iis quos tu adoras ; videbis sub manu nostrâ stare vinctos et tremere captivos, quos tu veneraris ut dominos.   Certè vel sic in erroribus tuis confundi poteris, cum conspexeris et audieris deos tuos quid sint, nostrâ interregatione, statim prodere," &c.*

See Pamelius, " Notes on Tertullian," n. 64.

* "If you would hear and see when evil spirits are by us adjured and put to spiritual torture ; when the very devils, groaning and lamenting with a human voice, confess a future judgment ; you shall hear us intreated by those whom you intreat, and by those whom you adore : you shall see those stand fettered, as it were, under our hands, and tremble like captive slaves, whom you worship as deities.   Certainly you must be thus confounded in your errors when you shall see and hear your gods, upon questions we put to them, immediately betray what they are."

THE FRIENDLY DEMON

OR

THE GENEROUS APPARITION

THE FRIENDLY DEMON

OR

THE GENEROUS APPARITION

To my anonymous worthy Friend, Physician, and Philo-
*   sopher, whose name, for certain reasons, I forbear*
*   to mention.*

SIR,—I cannot, without great ingratitude, forget
the friendly visits, and kind advice, I frequently
received from you, during not only a dangerous
but tedious indisposition, which surprisingly seized me
in the year 1717, and, notwithstanding your extraordinary care, as well as unquestionable judgment,
continued on me till the latter end of the year 1725;
in which long interval of time, the attendance you
gave, and the trouble you gave yourself, abstracted
from all interest, made you truly sensible of my unhappy condition, and myself equally apprehensive of
the great obligations I shall ever be under to so sincere
a friend.

The first occasion of my illness, as I have good
reason to imagine, was a very shocking surprise, given
me by certain persons, who pretended to be my friends

in a considerable affair then depending, wherein their treachery threatened me with succeeding ruin, had not Providence interposed, and delivered the oppressed from the cruel hands of such deceitful enemies. Upon whose hard usage, and the news of my disappointment, I was struck, at first, with a kind of epilepsy, and deprived of all my senses in an instant, dropped down in the public coffee-house, under violent agitations, which, it seems, are generally concomitant with this miserable distemper; but being luckily assisted, and kindly supported by some gentlemen present, I happened to escape those ill consequences that might, otherwise, have attended me, during the extremity of my convulsions, which were reported, by those that held me, to be so strong, as to be almost insupportable, till the paroxysm declined, which terminated in a cold sweat, trembling, and weeping, and this was the first attack that ever this terrible assailant made upon me; though afterwards he forced himself into a further familiarity with me (much against my will). Nor could your kind endeavours, by the art of physic, backed with my own strength of constitution, fright away this evil companion from me, till my good genius, by the direction of Providence, communicated a particular secret to me, which, with God's blessing, has lately proved my deliverance, in what manner, before I conclude, I shall very freely acquaint you, in hopes you will favour me with your candid opinion in answer thereunto.

Near eight years was a long time to continue under the frequent returns, and uncomfortable dread of such a shocking affliction, which, upon every little disorder of mind, or disappointment in business, never failed to visit me; till, by convulsive, or other involuntary motions in my head, and other parts of my body, my eyes were buried in their sockets; my other features contracted; my bowels sometimes racked with intolerable pains, and all the faculties of my mind so greatly weakened and impaired, that I, who, for many years before, had been esteemed as an oracle by the most polite and curious part of both sexes, was now, for want of strength of mind, and ability of body to employ my talent, and exercise my art, as usual, treated like an old soldier, who had lost his limbs in the service of his country, and thought only worthy, by way of requital, to be made a hobbling pensioner in some starving hospital.   But, I thank my stars, it proved not quite so bad with me, for though some ladies were too hasty and importunate to bear with the least disappointment, or admit of any delay, without showing their resentment, or refusing to trust their money till my convulsions afforded me a rational interval, wherein I might be able to give them ample satisfaction ; yet others, of a more considerate, easy, and compassionate temper, were so highly concerned for my too apparent indisposition, that, in order to drive out this tormenting demon that possessed me, they brought me all the old recipes they could muster up among their crazy aunts and grandmothers, practised upon all occasions in their several families, perhaps ever since the time of Galen and Hippocrates.   But, having been long under the care and friendship of so able a physician as yourself, though to little or no purpose, I could not put faith enough in old women's medicines to receive benefit thereby ; so, under a kind of despondency of everything but Providence, I suffered my distemper to take its own course, till my fits increased upon me to at least twenty in a day, and by their frequent reiterations, brought, at length, such a dimness upon my sight, such a weakness in my joints, and tremor upon my nerves, that rendered me incapable of all manner of business, especially that which I had so long professed, and successfully performed, to the full satisfaction and great

astonishment of thousands ; but being now unable to
write, and, for want of speech, having no other way
of communicating my answers to the demands of the
ladies and gentlemen that applied themselves to me,
except by digitation, which they understood not, I was
forced, sometimes, when much disordered by my convulsions, to send them away dissatisfied, which, if it
were any mortification to them, proved a much greater
to myself, because, upon my ready performances in the
mystery I am master of, depends the welfare of my
whole family.

Under these unhappy circumstances I laboured till
the month of October, in the year 1724, confined, by
my distemper, to my own habitation, not daring to go
abroad for fear of falling in the streets, having been
surprised by my fits in St James's Park, and several
other places.   But, about this time, being possessed with
a strong inclination to the Cold Bath, near Sir John
Oldcastle's, and the great desire I had to experience
the same being highly encouraged by your advice and
approbation, I summoned all the strength I had to my
assistance, and, pursuant to the dictates of my own
restless mind, had recourse thither accordingly, attended
by a proper person to take due care of me, for fear of
the worst.

I had not repeated this cold expedient above twice
or thrice, but I was sensible of the benefits I received
thereby, for my distemper began to treat me with less
severity than usual, and my fits were succeeded with a
greater defluxion of tears than what was common
before I applied myself to the bath ; so that, after my
weeping was over, I found myself much refreshed, and
all my faculties abundantly more alert, than at any time
they had been since my first illness, insomuch, that,
from a timely continuance of this external application,
I entertained great hopes of a perfect recovery ; but,

notwithstanding my diligent prosecution of this sharp
and shivering method, I was, to my great sorrow,
unhappily disappointed; for my convulsions were as
frequent, though not so violent, as formerly, and I was
now again divested of all hopes of relief, except by
the hand of Providence, having nothing to trust to, but
that infallible Physician who can cure all things in an
instant.

The despondency I was now under of any assistance
from human art, and the slender opinion you seemed
to entertain of my recovery, made my intervals as
melancholy as my fits were troublesome.   Oppressed
with these hard circumstances, I supported a burthensome life, and dragged on the tedious hours till the
latter end of the year 1725, about which time, as I
was slumbering one morning in my bed, after a restless
night, my good genius, or guardian angel, clothed in a
white surplice, like a singing boy, appeared before me,
holding a scroll, or label, in his right hand, whereon
the following words were wrote in large capitals :—

READ, BELIEVE, AND PRACTISE; THE LOAD-
STONE SHALL BE YOUR CURE, WITH AN ADDI-
TION OF THE POWDER HERE PRESCRIBED YOU;
BUT KEEP THE LAST AS A SECRET, FOR WITH
THAT AND THE MAGNET YOU SHALL RELIEVE
NUMBERS IN DISTRESS, AND LIVE TO DO
GREATER WONDERS THAN YOU HAVE HITHER-
TO PERFORMED; THEREFORE BE OF GOOD
CHEER, FOR YOU HAVE A FRIEND UNKNOWN,
WHO, IN THE TIME OF TROUBLE, WILL NEVER
FAIL YOU.

This comfortable news, though delivered to me after
so surprising a manner, yet was it very welcome to a
languishing person, under a complication of misfortunes.
Notwithstanding, I had a great struggle with my natural
reason, before I could convince myself of what I was

yet confident my very eyes had seen, or, at least, had been represented to me after an extraordinary manner, for betwixt really seeing a vision, or verily believing we do see it, there is but a slender difference. However, the entire confidence I had put in Providence, and the great desire I had to be relieved, were to me convincing arguments, beyond all objection, that my guardian angel had actually appeared, and communicated to my eyes the very scroll that I had read, the words of which, lest my memory should have proved treacherous, I entered in my pocket-book, as they are before recited, the recipe only excepted.

Having thus subjected my reason to my senses, or, at least, my faith (for I either saw, or believed I saw, what I have here reported), I had nothing else to do, but to put in practice the recipe which my good genius had imparted to me, though how to come at a loadstone, seemed to me as difficult as to find out the Philosopher's Stone, having but a slender knowledge of the thing itself, and much less of its virtues. However, upon inquiry, I soon found out a certain virtuoso, near Moorfields, who is an eminent dealer in such sort of curiosities, and, by his assistance, I presently furnished myself with what I wanted, and sending for some fat amber, and a certain preparation of steel, which I privately dispensed in a very particular manner, according to the recipe communicated by my genius; then applying both as directed, was miraculously delivered, in a great measure, from those racking convulsions which had so long afflicted me, and, in less than a month's time, my whole microcosm was restored to such a happy state of health, strength, and vivacity, that, heaven be praised, I could do anything as usual. But, if I leave off my loadstone for two or three days, which I have sometimes done, merely out of curiosity, my fits, as yet, will remind me of my foolish presumption, and force me to have recourse to my wonderful preservative, which has not only proved so great a friend to myself, but has relieved others in the like distress, and, as I have found by three or four late experiments, is as effectual in suppressing vapours, and removing or preventing hysteric fits in women, as it is in epilepsies and convulsions in our own sex, either men or children.

Now, doctor, since I have happily conquered so stubborn an enemy, by such miraculous means as do not fail to assist others as well as myself, I desire you will vouchsafe me your real sentiments of this uncommon way of cure, your notions of the genii, and the wonderful manner of communicating the recipe; your thoughts of the loadstone and the virtues thereof; your opinion of sympathy, and the cures performed thereby, for I know you are a philosopher sufficient, as well as physician, to give a very good light into all these mysteries, in which I own I am to seek; therefore hope you will condescend so far as to spend a leisure hour upon the foregoing particulars, and you will infinitely oblige, sir, your assured friend, and humble servant,

DUNCAN CAMPBELL.

—❦—

To my deaf and dumb Friend, MR DUNCAN CAMPBELL, *in answer to his letter to an anonymous worthy Friend, Physician, and Philosopher.*

SIR,—I received your letter, and read the same with no less surprise than satisfaction; for, as I am greatly pleased at your miraculous recovery, so I am equally astonished at the wonderful means by which it was obtained. I confess, I have been too

great a student in physic and natural philosophy, to
entertain any extraordinary opinion of miracles, no
ways accountable to human reason, except those that
concern religion, which are brought down to our
knowledge well attested, and recommended to our
faith by unexceptionable authorities; not but that I
am ready to admit, that the power of healing is in the
hand of Providence, and that some patients, when their
distempers, through the frailty of human judgment,
derive their essence from so obscure an original that
even puzzles the physician—then, I say, I am so free
to acknowledge, when the blessing of God accompanies
the administration, that the most trifling application in
the eyes of art, may recover such persons from the
most dangerous infirmities. This I look upon to be
your extraordinary case, and therefore think not the
means to which you ascribe your cure, or the manner
of the recipe's being communicated to you, a proper
subject for a physical inquiry, unless you had sent me
the prescription of your genius, which I understand
by your letter you are obliged to conceal, and then,
perhaps, I should have been able to have judged, in
some measure, which of the applications are most
essential, the powder or the loadstone, also, how far
your guardian angel is a regular proficient in the modern
practice of physic.

However, as you desire my opinion of the genii, the
loadstone, the powder of sympathy, and the like, I
shall not be only willing to give you my own thoughts,
but the sentiments of others, before I take my leave,
who have made the foregoing particulars their principal
studies, and are therefore better acquainted with the
nature of spirits, than I pretend to be.

As for the genii or familiar spirits, good and bad,
believed and reported, by the most wise and learned
of the ancients, to attend mankind, and the various

operations they have had upon human minds as well as
bodies, I cannot but confess, seem very wonderful to
my defective understanding ; yet, when we observe
what innumerable instances have been handed to us by
the most reputable authors, both ancient and modern,
attested from time to time by unquestionable authorities,
who, that, before he dived into these mysteries, looked
upon the same to be whimsy, can forbear staggering in
his opinion ?

The most celebrated instance of a genius among the
ancients, is that of Socrates, one of the wisest of the
philosophers in the age he lived in ; and that he had
such a familiar spirit to attend him, which the Greeks
called Dæmon, and the Latins, Genius, is sufficiently
testified by three of his cotemporaries, viz., Plato,
Xenophon, and Antisthenes ; also further confirmed
by Laertius, Plutarch, Maximus Tyrius, Dion, Chrysostomus, Cicero, Apuleius, and Facinas ; besides others
more modern, as Tertullian, Origen, Clemens Alexandrinus, &c.   But that which is of greater authority
than all the vouchers aforementioned, is what Socrates
says of himself in Plato's Theage, viz., "By some divine
lot, I have a certain demon, which has followed me
from my childhood, as an oracle ; and this voice," says
he, for so he terms it, "whenever it speaks to me,
dissuades me from engaging in what I am about to put
in action, but never prompts me to attempt anything."
This, I presume, might be the chief reason why
Socrates pursued not his own inclinations, which were
naturally vicious, as himself confessed to the physiog-
nomist, but was always accompanied with a divine
spirit that restrained him from it ; for, in speaking
to Alcibiades, a vicious nobleman of Athens, but re-
claimed by Socrates, says he, "My tutor" (meaning the
spirit that attended him) "is wiser and better than you."
And to show further, that what he called his demon

was something more than a secret impulse of the mind, or dictates of a good conscience, Theocritus affirms in Plutarch, that a vision attended Socrates from his childhood, going before him, and guiding him in all the actions of his life, being a constant light to him in such affairs as lay not within the reach of human understanding, and that the spirit often spoke to him, divinely governing and inspiring his intentions. A thousand instances of the like nature I could collect from the ancients, to prove that what you have reported to me, in your letter, may be no delusion, but real fact, with all its surprising circumstances, could the task be comprised within the compass of a letter ; but, a treatise of this nature being much fitter for a volume, I shall only proceed to a few familiar instances of a more modern date, that your wonderful cure may gain credit with the public, because I know your sincerity.

Froissart reports, that in the time of Edward III. there was a certain knight in France, called Corasse, who could tell everything transacted throughout the whole world, in a day or two at the most, were the distance never so remote ; and this he did by an invisible intelligencer or familiar spirit, which he called Orthone, who was always at his command, and brought him news continually for many years, till at last he lost the benefit of so useful a companion, through a vain desire of gratifying his curiosity after the following manner, viz. : the knight, having hitherto only heard the voice of his spiritual emissary, was now infatuated with an earnest inclination to behold his shape, which favour he requested of Orthone ; accordingly, whose answer was, that the first thing he should see on the morrow morning, after he was risen from his bed, should be the object he desired, or words to that effect. The knight, the next morning, pursuant

to the direction of the spirit, arose from his bed, looked
about him, but could not discover anything worthy of
remark; upon which disappointment, he upbraided
Orthone with being worse than his word; who replied, he had kept his promise, desiring the knight to
remind himself of what he had first observed after his
rising. The knight, upon recollection, replied, that he
saw nothing uncommon, but a couple of straws tumb-
ling upon the ground, and sporting one with another,
as if agitated by the wind. "That was I," saith the
spirit, "and therefore I kept my word." Then the
knight desired to see him once more, in such a shape
as might induce him, the next time, to take more
notice of him, to which the spirit consented, saying,
"The first thing you see on the morrow morning, after
your uprising, shall be me again." Accordingly, when
the time appointed was come, and the knight risen
from his bed, looking out of his chamber-window, the
first object he espied, was a lean, ill-favoured sow, so
deformed and ugly, that he was not able to abide the
sight of her; and not expecting Orthone to appear to
him in so homely a manner, he set his dogs upon the
sow to drive her away, who being highly affronted
at such an unfriendly usage, immediately vanished, to
the knight's great surprise; and his old acquaintance
Orthone never came near him after. This relation
Froissart asserts he had from the knight's own mouth,
with whom he was very intimate.

From hence I conclude, that the same sort of spirit
that attended Corasse, has been always a friend to you,
not only of late, in your miraculous recovery, but has
at all times assisted you in writing the name of
strangers, discovering the most secret intrigues, and
foretelling future events, for which you have been
famous. As for a further proof of the existence of
spirits, and that, at some other times, as well as in

your case, they have prescribed physic to their living friends, I shall quote an instance out of Mr Glanvil's Reports, attested by the Lord Orrery, the famous Mr Greatrix, and many others, living in the reign of King Charles the Second.

A gentleman in Ireland, near to the Earl of Orrery's house, sending his butler one afternoon to a neighbouring village to buy cards, as he passed a field, espied a company in the middle thereof, sitting round a table, with several dishes of good cheer before them, and moving towards them, they all rose and saluted him, desiring him to sit down and take part with them. But one of them whispered these words in his ear, viz., "Do nothing this company invites you to;" whereupon, he refusing to accept of their kindness, the table, and all the dainties it was furnished with, immediately vanished, but the company fell to dancing and playing upon divers musical instruments. The butler was a second time solicited to partake of their diversions, but would not be prevailed upon to engage himself with them; upon which, they left off their merrymaking and fell to work, still pressing the butler to make one among them, but to no purpose; so that, upon his third refusal, they all vanished and left the butler alone, who, in a great consternation, returned home without the cards, fell into a fit as he entered the house, but soon recovering his senses, related to his master all that had passed.

The following night, one of the ghostly company came to his bedside, and told him, that if he offered to stir out the next day, he would be carried away; upon whose advice, he kept within till towards the evening, and having occasion to make water, ventured to set one foot over the threshold of the door, in order to ease himself, which he had no sooner done, but a rope was cast about his middle, in the sight of several standers-by, and the poor man was hurried from the porch with unaccountable swiftness, followed by many persons ; but they were not nimble enough to overtake him, till a horseman, well mounted, happening to meet him upon the road, and seeing many followers in pursuit of a man hurried along in a rope, without anybody to force him, catched hold of the cord and stopped him in his career, but received, for his pains, such a strap upon his back with one end of the rope, as almost felled him from his horse. However, being a good Christian, he was too strong for the devil, and recovered the butler out of the spirits' clutches, and brought him back to his friends.

The Lord Orrery, hearing of these strange passages, for his further satisfaction of the truth thereof, sent for the butler, with leave of his master, to come and continue some days and nights at his house, which, in obedience to his lordship, the servant did accordingly ; who, after his first night's bedding there, reported to the earl in the morning, that his spectre had again been with him, and assured him, that on that very day he should be spirited away, in spite of all the measures that could possibly be taken to prevent it. Upon which he was conducted into a large room, with a considerable number of holy persons to defend him from the assaults of Satan ; among whom was the famous stroker of bewitched persons, Mr Greatrix, who lived in the neighbourhood, and knew, as may be presumed, how to deal with the devil as well as anybody ; besides several eminent quality were present in the house, among the rest, two bishops, all waiting the wonderful event of this unaccountable prodigy.

Till part of the afternoon was spent, the time slid away in nothing but peace and quietness, but, at length, the enchanted patient was perceived to rise from the floor without any visible assistance, whereupon Mr

R

Greatrix, and another lusty man, clapt their arms over his shoulders, and endeavoured to weigh him down with their utmost strength, but to no purpose, for the devil proved too powerful, and, after a hard struggle on both sides, made them quit their hold, and snatching the butler from them, carried him over their heads and tossed him in the air, to and fro, like a dog in a blanket, several of the company running under the poor wretch to save him from the ground; by which means, when the spirits' frolic was over, they could not find that in all this hurry-scurry, the frighted butler had received the least damage, but was left in *statu quo*, upon the same premises, to prove the devil a liar.

The goblins, for this bout, having given over their pastime, and left their May-game to take a little repose, that he might in some measure be refreshed against their next sally, my lord ordered, the same night, two of his servants to lie with him, for fear some devil or other should come and catch him napping; notwithstanding which, the butler told his lordship the next morning, that the spirit had again been with him in the likeness of a quack doctor, and held in his right hand a wooden dish full of grey liquor, like a mess of porridge, at the sight of which he endeavoured to awake his bedfellows; but the spectre told him, his attempts were fruitless, for that his companions were enchanted into a deep sleep, advising him not to be frighted, for he came as a friend, and was the same spirit that cautioned him in the field against complying with the company he there met, when he was going for the cards; adding, that if he had not refused to come into their measures, he had been for ever miserable; also wondered he had escaped the day before, because he knew there was so powerful a combination against him; that for the future there would be no

more attempts of the like nature; further telling the
poor trembling butler, that he knew he was sadly
troubled with two sorts of fits, and, therefore, as a
friend, he had brought him a medicine that would cure
him of both, beseeching him to take it.   But the poor
patient, who had been scurvily used by these sort of
doctors, and fearing the devil might be at the bottom
of the cup, would not be prevailed upon to swallow
the dose, which made the spirit angry; who told him,
however, he had a kindness for him, and that if he
would bruise the roots of plantain without the leaves,
and drink the juice thereof, it should certainly cure
him of one sort of his fits, but as a punishment for his
obstinacy in refusing the liquor, he should carry the
other with him to his grave.   Then the spiritual doctor
asked his patient if he knew him; the butler answered
no.   "I am," says he, "the wandering ghost of your
old acquaintance John Hobby, who has been dead and
buried these seven years; and ever since, for the
wickedness of my life, have been lifted into the company of those evil spirits you beheld in the fields, am
hurried up and down in this restless condition, and
doomed to continue in the same wretched state till the
day of judgment;" adding, that "had you served your
Creator in the days of your youth, and offered up your
prayers that morning before you were sent for the cards,
you had not been treated by the spirits that tormented
you, with so much rigour and severity."

After the butler had reported these marvellous
passages to my lord and his family, the two bishops,
that were present, among other quality, were thereupon
consulted, whether or no it was proper for the butler
to follow the spirit's advice, in taking the plantain
juice for the cure of his fits, and whether he had done
well or ill, in refusing the liquid dose which the spectre
would have given him.   The question, at first, seemed

to be a kind of moot point, but, after some struggle in the debate, their resolution was, that the butler had acted, through the whole affair, like a good Christian, for that it was highly sinful to follow the devil's advice in anything, and that no man should do evil that good might come of it; so that, in short, the poor butler, after his fatigue, had no amends for his trouble, but was denied, by the bishops, the seeming benefit that the spirit intended him.

I do not introduce this old surprising story to amuse you, but to let you know, that it is no new thing for spectres to turn doctors to ailing persons as they retain a respect for, and that your genius was not the first spirit that ever practised physic. Therefore, if this narrative, reported by Glanvil, Beaumont, and others, may obtain credit, upon the authorities of my Lord Orrery, Mr Greatrix, and divers persons, who were in a great measure eye-witnesses of the matter, I see no reason I have to doubt the truth of your letter, since I know your integrity; besides, it has always been allowed by such demonologers as have published their thoughts upon the visibility of spirits, that Scotland is never without such a sort of people as they call second-sighted, who have not only the power of discerning apparitions, but, by their frequent conversation with spirits, foretell future events, to the great astonishment of all persons that consult them. That there are such a sort of diviners in the world, especially in Scotland, I am thoroughly convinced; of which number I take yourself to be one. But how to account for your mysterious performances, I readily confess I know not, and therefore shall submit that task to such as are qualified with a more subtle penetration.

I doubt I have tired your patience with too much prolixity upon familiar spirits, therefore, to make you amends, I will be but short in my dissertation upon the loadstone, which, in the first place, is a very ponderous fossil, found in different climates, and seems in its nature and qualities to be nearly related to iron ore, from whence it is endowed with a peculiar property of drawing to itself by the power of sympathy, or the natural disposition it has to embrace that particular metal. In Egypt there are large mines of it; some few magnets have been found in Æthiopia, which have attracted iron very forcibly. But two sorts are dug up at the foot of the Sardinian mountains, of such different natures, that as one draws iron, the other will repel it; as you will find it reported by Johannes Jonstonus, in his "History of Nature;" also by Pliny, in his Second Book, who, for the aforesaid reason, calls this stone Theamedes. As to the singular virtues hitherto discovered in the common loadstone, the most admirable of all are the strict correspondence it maintains with the two poles, and the wonderful property it communicates by a touch to the needle, for the benefit of mariners. The power of its attraction is thought by some virtuosos to be owing to a clammy bituminous substance, by which the contexture of the more solid parts are closely cemented and confirmed; to prove this, work a loadstone in the fire and it shall cast forth a bluish flame, like that of lighted brimstone, and so continue till it spends its life, and loses the power of attraction. There is a great deal of sulphur in iron as well as in the loadstone, which is the principal cause of their sympathising with each other, and if you destroy the first in either, the last will fail in course, which is the reason why the loadstone will not attract the rust of iron, though it will the filings, because in the former the bituminous matter is quite spent, and nothing left but a kind of *caput mortuum*. The loadstone hath also two poles, which answer those in the heavens; if you touch the needle with the north pole of the stone, it will point to the Arctic, if with the south part thereof, as it stood posited in the mine, it will point to the Antarctic, but not with the utmost exactness, except it stands in the meridian. But to be further satisfied in these mysteries, have recourse to Libavius, Cardanus, Pliny, Bodin, Porta, our own "Philosophical Transactions," and such authors as have treated more largely upon this subject, for, I suppose, all that you want to know of me is, if ever I have heard from others, or discovered by my own experience, any such physical virtue in the loadstone, as may tend to the cure of any chronical or other disease incident to human bodies, that may strengthen the opinion you seem to entertain of it in such cases, from the benefit yourself has lately received in so extraordinary a manner.

In answer to this, I confess, I have heard affirmed (but not by a physician), that the loadstone hath withdrawn the inflammation, and given ease in the gout, and by changing the application of it from one side to the other, has at length chased it away, to the perfect recovery of the patient; but in any other case, excepting your own, I never heard of a cure so much as facilitated or attempted to be performed thereby ; therefore, as the use of it in any disease is quite foreign to the common practice of physic, if others, as well as yourself, have received benefit by this new discovery, I think not myself obliged to account for it, till it becomes practical among my own fraternity, and then it will be time enough for any physician to give his thoughts thereon. Besides, I am a stranger to the preparation prescribed to you by your genius, and without the knowledge of that material secret, it is impossible for any physician, in your case, to make a clear judgment, or to know which of the two your cure is chiefly owing to, the powder or the loadstone ;

for how far the latter may operate upon a body prepared by *pulvis martis* or other chalybeates, I shall not pretend to determine, though, for aught I know, wonderful cures may be performed in that way; but upon what reason in nature such a new system can be founded, seems very remote from my present understanding. But, since you are become sole master of so wonderful a secret, my advice is, that you keep the recipe to yourself, in obedience to your genius, and though you assist others, never do it without fee or reward, for all useful discoveries ought to be rendered profitable.

In answer to the last article of your request, I shall now proceed to say something of sympathy, and the cures reported to have been done thereby. The sympathetic powder, so highly esteemed about a hundred years since, by men of art in this kingdom, was first brought into Europe by a religious Carmelite, who, in his travels through India, Persia, and China, had made himself master of this secret, and from some of those eastern countries, came over into Tuscany, where he performed many considerable cures by this occult method, to the great astonishment of the most eminent physicians and surgeons in those parts; insomuch that the Duke of Tuscany himself was very desirous of becoming master of this surprising arcanum, but the honest friar, by many handsome excuses, brought himself off, and would not be prevailed upon to communicate his nostrum to his highness.

Some few months after this, our famous English virtuoso, Sir Kenelm Digby, happening, in his travels, to be at the Grand Duke's Court, an opportunity fell accidentally in the knight's way to do the friar a service, which the good old man took so kindly at his hands, that he recompensed the courtesy with a discovery of his secret; and soon after returning into

Persia, left no man in Europe master of the same but Sir Kenelm, who was the first person that brought the recipe into England, and that here wrought cures by it himself, and recommended it to the practice of others ; so that, in a little time, every mother-midwife and country flaybeard became topping surgeons, especially for the cure of green wounds ; for it is not to be trusted to in other cases.

This sympathetic powder, by which many miracles have been performed at great distances, is nothing more than the simple powder of Roman vitriol, either chemically prepared, or imperfectly calcined in the beams of the sun ; from whence, 'tis said, it derives a very balsamic virtue. A little of this applied to any instrument that has done mischief, or to a rag dipped into, or stained with the blood of a wound, never fails of curing the patient at the widest distance, provided the wound be curable.

Sir Kenelm Digby, to advance the credit of this surprising medicine, speaks very largely in commendation thereof, in a little treatise of his, written first in French, upon the same subject ; wherein he boasts of a remarkable cure performed by himself, in a most wonderful manner, with only the use of this astonishing powder ; and therefore, as in religious cases example goes beyond precept, so, to convince you of the miracles performed by sympathy, instances, perhaps, may prove more effectual than arguments : for which reason, I shall proceed to furnish you with a notable experiment of this magical powder, and so conclude.

Mr James Howell, a trusty servant to King James I., famous in those days for compiling a treatise, entitled " Dendrologia," and afterwards for his legacy to the world, called " Epistolæ Ho-Elianæ," happened, when he was a young gentleman, to accidentally come by, when two of his dearest friends were fiercely engaged in a very dangerous duel, and to prevent further mischief, very likely to ensue, too rashly catched hold, with his naked hand, of his sword, whose passion prompted him to be the most desperate ; in which attempt, the weapon being drawn through Mr Howell's palm, cut the nerves and muscles thereof to the very bone, and, as they were thus scuffling, holding up the same hand to defend one of his friends from a blow upon his head, received another cut upon the back of his hand, cross all the veins and tendons, more terrible than the former ; which, his friends perceiving, put a sudden stop to their inebrious fury, ran both to embrace him, and express their sorrow for the unhappy accident, lending him their assistance to bind up his wounds with his own garters, and so conducted him to his lodgings, where they sent directly for a surgeon, who found the case desperate, for he bled abundantly.

Mr Howell being a gentleman much respected by the quality, the news of his misfortune soon reached the court ; and his Majesty having a great regard for him, sent one of his own surgeons to attend him, who found the case to be so very bad that he seemed doubtful of a cure, without cutting off his hand ; which occasioned Mr Howell, about five days after the hurt was received, to apply himself to his good friend and neighbour, Sir Kenelm Digby, who at that time was famous for the sympathetic powder, begging his assistance in that painful extremity, telling him, that his surgeons were apprehensive of a gangrene.

Sir Kenelm, opening the wounds, found a terrible case of it, and a dangerous inflammation upon the part, which, Mr Howell acknowledged, gave him such intolerable pain as was scarce supportable. The knight asked him if he had any bandage with the blood upon it. Mr Howell answered, yes ; accordingly sent his servant for the bloody garter which had first bound up his wounds, and delivered it to Sir Kenelm, who, calling for a basin of water, went into his closet for a handful of his powder, which he infused therein, and then soaked the garter in the same liquor, whilst Mr Howell was talking with another gentleman, at the further end of the room, not knowing in the least what Sir Kenelm was doing; who, after he had bathed the garter in the basin about a minute, called to his patient, and asked him how he found himself, who answered, " So wonderful easy that the inflammation seems to be totally extinguished, the pain quite gone off, and my hand I find as cool and as much refreshed as if it was wrapped up in a wet napkin." "Then," replied the knight, " fling off your dressings, meddle no more with plaisters, only keep your wounds clean and from the air, and I doubt not, but in a few days' time, I shall effectually cure you, without putting you to any further trouble." Much comforted with this assurance, Mr Howell took a thankful leave of Sir Kenelm, and so departed.

Mr Howell had not been gone above a quarter of an hour, before the knight took the garter out of the liquor, to dry it before the fire, and carelessly hanging it a little too near, the extraordinary heat, by the concatenation of effluvias, had such an effect upon the patient, that he made as many wry faces as a cook that had burnt his fingers ; upon which he despatched his servant, with all imaginable expedition, to let his doctor know what a condition he was relapsed into.

Sir Kenelm, who presently conjectured the cause of this disaster, smiling at the message the servant had delivered, and snatching the garter from the fire, told him that his master should be very easy by the time he could return to him, which the footman, by the acknowledgment of his master, found to be true accordingly, Sir Kenelm doing nothing more to work this change, than cooling the reeking garter by a speedy repetition of his former application; so that, without any further accident interposing, the patient was thoroughly cured, in five or six days' time, by this extraordinary method, to the inexpressible admiration of all his Majesty's surgeons.

Sir, this is all, at present, I am at leisure to say in answer to your letter, and, I doubt, you will think it enough too, except more to the purpose. What extraordinary cures you happen to perform by your new method, I desire you will communicate to me as soon as you can conveniently, for to hear of your success will be no little satisfaction to, sir, your assured friend, and humble servant.

THE END.

Printed by BALLANTYNE, HANSON & CO.
Edinburgh and London.